FOOD LOVERS'
GUIDE TO
MEMPHIS

FOOD LOVERS' SERIES

FOOD LOVERS'
GUIDE TO
MEMPHIS

The Best Restaurants, Markets & Local Culinary Offerings

First Edition

Pamela Denney

gPP

Guilford, Connecticut

Editor: Kevin Sirois
Project Editor: Julie Marsh
Layout Artist: Mary Ballachino
Text Design: Sheryl Kober
Illustrations by Jill Butler with additional art by Carleen Moira Powell and MaryAnn Dubé
Maps: Alena Pearce © Morris Book Publishing, LLC

ISBN 978-0-7627-8261-1

Printed in the United States of America
10 9 8 7 6 5 4 3 2 1

All the information in this guidebook is subject to change. We recommend that you call ahead to obtain current information before traveling.

Contents

Recipes, 263

Appendices, 291

About the Author

Pamela Denney has worked as a writer and editor for newspapers and magazines for more than 30 years. After graduating from Syracuse University, she worked as a reporter for the *Danville Register* in Danville, Virginia, and then relocated to Los Angeles, joining Copley Los Angeles Newspapers as a wire editor, copy editor, and city editor. She is now a journalism professor at the University of Memphis and the food editor for *Memphis* magazine, where she reviews restaurants and writes the magazine's food blog, a celebration of the city's community table called *Memphis Stew*. For many years a reluctant cook, Pam embraced her own kitchen when she rediscovered local food thanks to a CSA and her own vegetable garden.

Acknowledgments

A heartfelt thank you to my upbeat and loving cheerleaders: my daughter, Anna, whose artistic focus inspired me, and my husband, Tony, who fed me with encouragement and an ever-changing menu from his backyard grill.

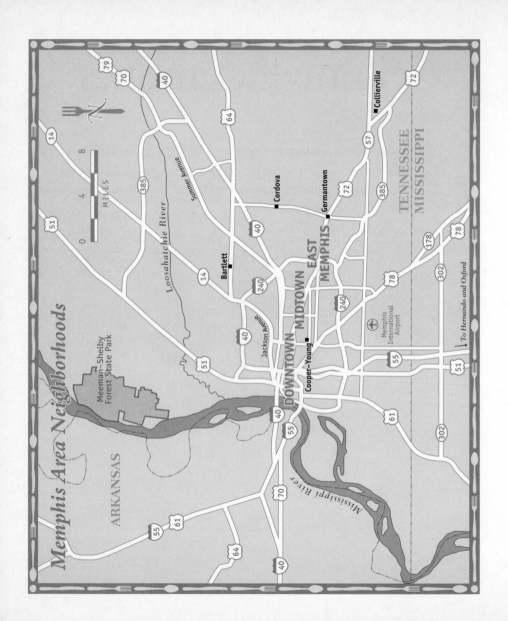

Memphis Area Neighborhoods

Introduction

Quick! Answer this question: What do people in Memphis eat?

More than likely, your answer starts with a B and ends with a Q, an association as irrevocably linked with Memphis as the King of Rock 'n' Roll. Here in the Bluff City, we have a ubiquitous love affair with slow-cooked pork. Seasoned chefs and backyard grillers talk barbecue with spirited expertise, uniting residents and visitors alike with the sacrosanct belief that few things taste better than a pulled pork sandwich.

While barbecue and Elvis bookend the city's culinary and cultural personalities, Memphis these days has moved beyond smokers and home cooking. Demographic shifts, economic development, and energetic young chefs are reinventing Southern cooking in fun and sophisticated ways. (How about osso bucco with shiitake grits, collard greens, and mushroom jus, or sweet corn griddle cakes with crabmeat ravigote?) Simply put, the culinary scene in Memphis is exploding thanks to talent, timing, and the availability of local food. From fine dining to vegan cafes, there is an intuitive understanding of farm-to-table in Memphis,

1

where people have always grown their own okra and tomatoes. Add in the city's temperate climate, and no wonder Memphis boasts more than a dozen farmers' markets, with several operating year-round.

Food politics matter, too. Church and community volunteers are tackling the city's food deserts with aggressive programs to build and plant vegetable gardens in underserved neighborhoods. Fresh-food advocate Tony Geraci is the new director of nutrition for Memphis City Schools. The subject of the documentary *Cafeteria Man,* Geraci is a charismatic missionary intent on buying food from local farmers to transform processed school lunches into more healthy choices.

The entrepreneurial spirit in Memphis also is invigorating the citywide menu. At L'École Culinaire, chefs in training experiment with recipes for the school's restaurant, The Presentation Room. At small commercial kitchens spread across town, artisan producers turn out red velvet cupcakes, strawberry champagne truffles, and vegetarian casseroles to go. And, yes, Memphis has food trucks (finally!) along with small ethnic eateries like La Michoacano, where dozens of fruit and cream *paletas* change flavors every day.

Exploring food in Memphis has never been more diverse or exciting. From barbecue nachos to global cuisine, chefs and pur-veyors are marrying invention with regional charm. In fact, four of the city's most successful independent chefs graduated from the same local high school in 1998, confirming that many food lovers in Memphis are both prodigious and homegrown.

How to Use This Book

Is there a right way to organize a *Food Lovers' Guide to Memphis?* Probably not, but we've done our best to be sensible. The chapters in this guide are categorized geographically, and within each chapter are these features:

Foodie Faves

So what's a foodie fave? Anything we deem worth a visit, from established favorites to new upstarts that many locals have yet to discover.

Landmarks

Many of the restaurants in this category grew up with us. (Or was it vice versa?) Some have been family run for generations, and all continue to thrive thanks to excellent service, customer loyalty, and culinary aplomb.

Barbecue & Blue Plates

It's no surprise to us that *U.S. News & World Report* named Memphis the best barbecue city in America. More than 80 businesses offer barbecue in the Bluff City, and dozens more serve home-cooking and soul food such as biscuits, greens, meat loaf, and grits.

Specialty Stores, Markets & Producers

A city's collective palate depends, not only on its chefs, home cooks, and restaurant patrons, but on its unique collection of local butchers, artisan purveyors, and specialty markets. Find our favorites here.

Price Code

Price information for restaurants uses the following scale for a single entree:

$	Less than $10
$$	$10 to $20
$$$	More than $20

Getting Around

Since its early history as a waterway to the American West, Memphis has been an important center for moving cargo and people. Today about 1 million passengers a year make their way through Memphis International Airport, a hub for Delta Airlines and a route for Air Tran, which is slated to become part of the Southwest fleet. The airport's unusual terminal building, designed in the early 1960s by renowned architect Roy Harrover, was built to accommodate two-story jet ways. A midcentury salute to the promise of jet travel, the building is especially appealing at night, when soft white lights accentuate its martini-glass structure. During the holidays, the lights alternate from red to green.

The terminal's interior has been recently renovated with streamlined security and a themed decor honoring Memphis barbecue and music. Airport concessions play along: Check out Corky's BBQ in

Terminal A and Interstate Bar-B-Que, Sun Studio Cafe, and Memphis City Blues Wine Bar in Terminal B. Although the airport is centrally located to most of Memphis, visitors need to grab a car, cab, or pickup by a friend to travel downtown or into the city's sprawling suburbs. Unfortunately, public transportation is limited except within the city's central business district. There are no local trains or subways, and the municipal bus company—Memphis Area Transit Authority, or MATA—can be unpredictable.

Once downtown, Memphis becomes more user friendly. The Beale Street entertainment district, along with some of the city's finest restaurants, is walking distance from most hotels. A charming Main Street Trolley with restored vintage cars and ADA-accessible stops also winds its way near a seasonal Saturday farmers' market and downtown landmarks like The Peabody hotel. The trolley's 2.5-mile Riverfront Loop includes views of the Mississippi River, and the Madison Avenue line connects downtown with the city's medical district. A daily pass for all routes is $3.25, with discounted rates for seniors and riders with disabilities.

For explorations beyond downtown, driving isn't complicated because Memphis developed on an east–west and north–south grid. The city's main east–west thoroughfare, Poplar Avenue, connects downtown with Memphis's lovely tree-filled neighborhoods. While there are certainly faster routes, sticking with Poplar ensures visitors won't get lost. Throw in Mapquest directions or a smartphone GPS, and even obscure foodie favorites should be easy to find.

Keeping Up with Food News

Expanded food coverage by both traditional and electronic media reflects the growing culinary scene in Memphis. Find a food writer or blogger who shares your taste from the list below.

Best Memphis Burger, bestmemphisburger.com. Memphis loves a newsy post on burgers, which explains the popularity of the *Best Memphis Burger* blog. Not long ago, a laudatory post on burgers stuffed with cheese found its way to me. Since then, I've been drawn repeatedly back to the blog to see how many ways one guy can describe a burger. He's already eaten burgers from more than 40 restaurants, along with chips, fries, and onion rings. (He likes his sides crispy.) Burgers are rated with one to five stars, and readers can make suggestions for reviews with an easy-to-find link. Up next for the burger man: chicken wings, the spicier the better.

Chubby Vegetarian, chubbyvegetarian.blogspot.com. Justin Fox Burks, the Chubby Vegetarian, isn't chubby anymore since he started running marathons. He's also part of a team with spouse Amy Lawrence. Together they turn vegetarian cooking into a fun-filled romp of recipes and eye candy, thanks to Burks's gorgeous photography. The couple can do some fancy cooking, too, whipping together inventions like triple-ginger apple crisp and vegetarian Frogmore stew. Lawrence handles the baking, or as Burks explains, "I'm savory; she's sweet." Fans of the blog are cooking, too—testing recipes for the team's book, *The Southern Vegetarian Cookbook*.

The Commercial Appeal, commercialappeal .com; **and Whining & Dining,** whiningdining .com. The *Commercial Appeal* is the city's daily newspaper and, like most dailies, publishes a food section on Wednesday. In addition to local food features, the section includes a Whining & Dining column by food writer Jennifer Biggs, a chatty and informative roundup of food news and Biggs's adventures eating out and cooking at home. Biggs also writes a blog by the same name for the paper's online edition, where her connection with readers is friendly and personal. In the paper's Friday *Go Memphis* tabloid section, look for a weekly restaurant review, a Best Bet feature on a favorite dish, and a Q&A spotlight on a local chef.

Cork It, memphiscorkit.com. A glossy newcomer from publisher Allison Jacob and sommelier Chris Thorn, *Cork It* is a quarterly magazine targeted to the full range of wine lovers, from novice to collector. The magazine includes columns from local wine experts, features on national and regional wineries, tasting notes on wines to watch, and advertorials from local independent restaurants. With its oversize, color format, *Cork It* is a fast and accessible way to get a feel for the dining scene in Memphis. The magazine is distributed free of charge at restaurants, liquor stores, and online, where an excellent click-thru calendar of dinner and wine pairings also is available.

Dining with Monkeys, diningwithmonkeys.blogspot.com. Stacey Greenberg loves to eat out, but "dining with monkeys" (her two sons, Satchel and Jiro) was rough when they were toddlers. So Greenberg started blogging in 2005 about the challenges of eating out with kids, establishing an enthusiastic cache of readers who like watching her sons grow up one meal at a time. (She's trained them not to touch their food until she snaps a photo!) A repeat winner for the *Memphis Flyer*'s best blogger award, *Dining with Monkeys* is a worthwhile read, whether you have kids or not, because Greenberg has a knack for finding off-the-radar restaurants well worth investigating.

Eat Local Memphis, eatlocalmemphis.org. A tireless supporter of small, local food businesses, Thomas Robinson jumped into blogging about local food early on, so he's on the deep inside, sharing tweets and posts from other bloggers with a nice one-for-all-and-all-for-one style. He likes to mix sports and pop culture references into his blog. They are catchy even if they don't quite make sense—for example, linking **Stone Soup Cafe** (p. 95) to Van Morrison's "And It Stoned Me." The motto for Robinson's blog is "Break the chain, eat local," a slogan prominently circulated around Memphis on T-shirts and stickers.

Edible Memphis, ediblecommunities.com/memphis. Part of the Edible Communities publications popular in many cities, *Edible Memphis* and editor Melissa Petersen are at the heart of the city's local food effort, pulling together people and businesses with a colorful quarterly publication trumpeting local and seasonal food. Distributed free of charge at restaurants and specialty markets, the magazine includes recipes and cookbook reviews, along with stories on farmers, food producers, and nonprofits that are using local food to impact education and policy.

From the Southern Table, paulandangela.net. Memphians Paul and Angela Knipple like to travel—a lot. Their blog is a family diary of sorts, chronicling their road trips and cooking adventures in the kitchen. Over the past few years, they traveled from Virginia to Alabama to study how ethnic traditions shape Southern food. The resulting book, *The World in a Skillet: A Food Lover's Tour of the New American South,* was published in early 2012. Now they are back on the road again, hunting down local products like country ham and sorghum molasses for an upcoming book on agribusiness in Tennessee.

Fuzzy Brew, fuzzybrew.com. *Fuzzy Brew* is a joint venture between three beer-loving buddies who enthusiastically brew beer, drink beer, and share beer. They admit in their blog introduction that they've done more of the first two. The blog is about craft beers, beer-related events in Memphis and the Mid-South, and the trio's homebrewing. This is a great blog for readers new to craft beers because the posts are well reported and written with an easy, self-effacing style.

Memphis, memphismagazine.com; and **Memphis Stew**, memphis magazine.com/Blogs/Memphis-Stew. The city's monthly magazine, *Memphis* focuses on trends, people, and entertainment, and devotes a considerable number of pages to an in-depth guide to area restaurants. In addition to alphabetical listings with description, address, and price, the guide also separates restaurants by category (sports bar, deli, etc.). The magazine's monthly restaurant reviews give an inside look at the city's independent restaurants in a part-feature/part-critique format, and an annual Readers' Restaurant Poll includes favorite restaurants in more than 40 different categories. *Memphis Stew*, the magazine's food blog on restaurant news and local food, is written by the author of this book.

Memphis Flyer, memphisflyer.com; and **Hungry Memphis**, memphisflyer.com/blogs/HungryMemphis. Since 1989, the *Memphis Flyer* has been the alternative voice for Memphis politics and entertainment. In addition to an engaging Food News column every week by Hannah Sayle, the *Flyer* runs restaurant listings and a recommended dish, featuring both sophisticated and arcane picks. Every September, the *Flyer's Best of Memphis* issue also offers reader favorites for an entertaining list of food categories. Dining and food coverage continues online, where the blog *Hungry Memphis*, written by managing editor Susan Ellis, covers all aspects of eating in the Bluff City, from you-read-it-here-first news to must-try dishes and random culinary quirks. *Hungry Memphis* is the *Flyer's* most popular blog, thanks to Ellis, who is funny, irreverent, and informed.

Vegan Crunk, vegancrunk.blogspot.com. By day, Biana Phillips is an associate editor for the *Memphis Flyer*. At mealtime, she's the soulful creator of *Vegan Crunk,* a blog started in 2007 about how an inventive vegan can thrive in the Mid-South. Even for a pork lover like me, *Vegan Crunk* is an accessible blog about meals at home, meals eaten out, new cookbooks, and the most comprehensive listing of vegan and vegan-friendly restaurants in Memphis. There's nothing sanctimonious about Phillips's blogging, just an upbeat message about having fun with food. Her forte, after all, is veganizing Southern favorites like country-fried steak. Phillips also posts plenty of recipes on her blog, including many from her new book, *Cooking Crunk: Eating Vegan in the Dirty South.*

Food events in Memphis range from neighborhood get-togethers like the Cooper-Young Chili Cook Off to citywide blowouts like the World Championship Barbecue Contest held every May on the banks of the Mississippi River. Most food events fall somewhere in between with a two-prong purpose: raise money for local nonprofits and celebrate regional food. But as Memphis continues to move into the national spotlight, unexpected culinary events are popping up too. In 2012, the Cochon 555 tour, a prestigious snout-to-tail cook-off, held one of its 10 regional events in downtown Memphis. So be sure to check local media and bloggers for events not included on this annual calendar.

January

Farm-to-Fork Tour, memphisfarmersmarket.org/dinnertour. Is anything better than a unique menu of local ingredients created by independent chefs? Not for food lovers in Memphis, who buy tickets early for the Farm-to-Fork dinners held about every six weeks starting in late January. Dinner proceeds benefit the **Memphis Farmers Market** (p. 67), and that's a good thing, but the real thrill is discovering how delicious locally sourced menus can be. Chefs go all out with seasonal ingredients, offering simple dishes like sweet-potato bread pudding or something more adventurous like rabbit-stuffed crepe with beer mustard sauce. Participating restaurants are located from downtown to East Memphis and include such award-winning favorites as **Restaurant Iris** (p. 92), **Felicia Suzanne's** (p. 39), **Interim** (p. 138), and **The Elegant Farmer** (p. 134).

February

Farm to Table Conference for Mid-South Producers, grow memphis.org. A gathering of farmers, consumers, and food-policy advocates, the Farm to Table Conference puts wintertime to good use. Participants are a hard-working and passionate group who believe a thriving local food system builds neighborhoods, stimulates the economy, and promotes healthy eating. (Amen!) Sessions at the conference focus on farming, marketing, and consumer interests, and reflect practical and entrepreneurial concerns: new farmer start-ups, cooperative distribution, collective branding, urban agriculture, and school lunch programs. Overall, the conference is equal parts cheerleading, networking, and brainstorming for the people in the Mid-South who want the farm-to-table mantra to reshape the way Southerners think about food.

Youth Villages Soup Sunday, youthvillages.org. How full can you get on soup served in small paper cups? Plenty full, if you make it around the entire FedEx Forum, where Memphis restaurants set up a soup kitchen of sorts to benefit Youth Villages, an advocacy center for emotionally troubled children. Since its start in 1990,

Soup Sunday has raised almost $1 million, providing families with an affordable and fun event to chase away the cold weather blues. In addition to dozens of soups, breads, and desserts, Soup Sunday features events for kids, such as the Oreo stacking contest (biggest stack to date: 30 cookies). Be forewarned: Pacing is important at the all-you-can-eat event, so here's a good strategy: Skip breakfast, avoid second helpings, and work the soup stations in reverse to beat the lines.

March

Memphis Wine & Food Series at the Brooks Museum, memphis wineandfoodseries.org. Formerly called the Art of Good Taste, the Memphis Brooks Museum of Art's Memphis Wine & Food Series is the museum's premiere annual fund-raiser, bringing together hundreds of wine and food lovers for a series of events that run from late March to mid-May. Some events are more moderately priced, like the Uncorked wine tasting in April, while others are high-ticket extravaganzas. The patron dinner includes a live auction for trips, fine art, and world-class wines in 50-plus lots. The food is always excellent because it is prepared under the direction of chefs Wally Joe and Andrew Adams, who also operate **Acre** (p. 127), a popular restaurant in East Memphis serving new American cuisine.

River City's Brewers Festival, rivercitybrewersfestival.com. If you don't know your pilsner from your stout, grab a ticket to the daylong River City's Brewers Festival and start tasting 100 different crafts beers from across the county. The outdoor tasting, held in downtown Beale Street's Handy Park, includes music, samplings of signature dishes from local chefs, and beers ranging from Abita Beer Turbo Dog to locally brewed **Ghost River** (p. 205). My personal favorite is Lazy Magnolia's Southern Pecan Nut Brown Ale: Produced by Mississippi's first microbrewery, the dark mahogany ale is reportedly the world's only beer made from whole roasted pecans.

Waffle Shop at Calvary Episcopal Church, calvarymemphis .org/waffles. About the time the Lenten roses bloom in Memphis, the volunteers at downtown's Calvary Episcopal Church are readying waffle irons and recipes for the annual Waffle Shop, a lunch-only serving of fellowship and home cooking. Held annually since 1928, the Waffle Shop serves midday meals Monday through Friday throughout Lent. The menu is a charming mix of waffles, daily specials like corned beef and cabbage, and traditional Southern fare made from recipes passed down from one generation to the next. For a step back in time, try the Calvary salad plate: shrimp mousse, tomato aspic (yes, it wiggles), and cottage cheese topped with half a pear and a dollop of homemade mayonnaise. Lunches are priced under $10 and are also available to go, which is a good option for visitors interested in the Lenten Preaching Series that begins promptly at 12:05 p.m.

SMELL THE SMOKE: WORLD CHAMPIONSHIP BARBECUE AND A LITTLE BIT OF ELVIS

For three days every spring, more than 100,000 people swamp the banks of the Mississippi in downtown Memphis for the World Championship Barbecue Cooking Contest, a signature event of the city's month-long celebration called Memphis in May.

Many teams return regularly for recognition and prize money, but newcomers also compete. In 2011, a first-time team of renowned chefs called Fatback Collective used hickory wood to cook a mangalitsa, a heritage-breed pig prized for its flavor and thick cap of fat. The team won third place in the coveted whole hog category, an impressive victory for both the chefs and the emerging cachet of family farmers in the South raising sustainable breeds.

Overall, about 250 cooking teams from Europe, Canada, and across the United States compete every year, making the Memphis in May contest the most-recognized barbecue cook-off in the world. The competition is also popular with local and out-of-town visitors who can't resist the aromatic veil that drapes the event's mile-long stretch of tents, rigs, and smokers.

Getting a taste of barbecue, however, isn't always easy because local health regulations prohibit teams from selling food directly to the public.

"People sometimes forget that this is a cooking competition," says Diane Hampton, executive vice president of Memphis in May. "But we recognize visitors want to sample."

To make the contest friendlier for visitors, organizers have added new entertainment, barbecue sampling, cooking team meet-ups, and

100 high-ticket VIP Pit passes. The passes offer a cornucopia of extras, including a private tent with snacks, wine, and beer, and 6 eating extravaganzas with championship barbecue teams.

"For $395, people are treated like barbecue royalty," Hampton says. "Last year, we sold out."

Most folks opt for the contest's more affordable $9 entry fee. The ticket covers "Cooker Caravan" tours with cooking-team members who share tips on equipment, technique, and recipes. Tour leaders, who are longtime Memphis in May volunteers, also explain judging criteria and the competition's history. Tours are offered every 30 minutes between 11:30 a.m. and 3:30 p.m. on Thursday and Friday.

Nightly entertainment also kicks off on Thursday with the Ms. Piggie Idol Contest, a perennial favorite (seeing is believing) and performances by R&B and country music artists on a large outdoor stage.

On Saturday, the Ultimate Elvis Tribute Artist Contest joins the entertainment lineup, an event added in 2012 as a qualifying competition for Elvis Week in August.

"We're pretty sure Elvis loved barbecue," Hampton says. "So it makes sense to combine the city's two biggest attractions."

So how can visitors who aren't Elvis taste the 'cue? For $5 on Thursday and Friday, visitors can take a Tour of Champions, sampling 5 barbecues from 20 different teams and voting for their favorite. On Saturday, only judges get to taste, picking winners in championship barbecue categories and auxiliary divisions, such as best sauce, best coleslaw, and best baked beans.

Beale Street Great Wine Race, bealestreetmerchants.com.
Historic Beale Street is the kind of place that can turn a
ho-hum night out into party blowout of music, cold beer,
and soul food. Just ask the entertainment district's restaurant workers, or better yet, watch them strut their
stuff in an annual relay run to see which team can dash
down Beale, balance filled wine glasses on a tray, and
not spill a drop. Did I mention that participants are scantily
clad? Risqué attire is one of many eccentric spins to this
drink-fueled folly that also includes a Queen of the Vine
contest and a spirited parade down Beale. Started as an
insider kickoff to the start of Beale Street's busy tourist
season, the wine race today attracts several thousand onlookers
who cheer enthusiastically for relay contestants.

Memphis Brewfest, memphisbrewfest.com. Crave a craft beer?
Try one of more than 100 varieties from around the world at the
Memphis Brewfest, a beer tasting to benefit baseball in the inner
city and to promote a better understanding of muscular dystrophy.
Held at downtown's Autozone Park, home of the city's Triple-A
team, the Memphis Redbirds, the Memphis Brewfest features
American craft beers as well as exotics with an international focus.
This festival is new to the annual calendar of food events, but it
is well timed to ride the wave of interest in craft beers and home-
brews. Tickets cover the tasting, and food is available for purchase.

The Rajun Cajun Crawfish Festival, porterleath.org. For the uninitiated, eating crawfish is a messy proposition that poses a bit of a quandary. What is a crawfish anyway? Is it a shrimp? What's with that weird head? Do you eat it or throw it away? And why are people so worked up about crawfish anyway? To understand, jump into the Rajun Cajun Crawfish Festival held in April when crawfish—also called mudbugs and crawdads—are plentiful from the Gulf of Mexico. Crawfish season is short, about three months, which amps up the fervor even more. Along with a gumbo cook-off, there's Cajun and zydeco music, ridiculous contests like crawfish bobbing and a daylong frenzy where participants power through more than 15,000 pounds of crawfish.

Southern Hot Wing Contest and Festival, southernhotwing festival.com. About 10 years ago, some Memphis hometowners got fed up with pork and beef barbecue getting all the attention. What about the chicken wing, they asked? So they decided to give hot wings their rightful place with a cook-off and festival to benefit the Ronald McDonald House of Memphis. Apparently, plenty of other folks have a soft spot for wings, too. These days teams from across the region head to downtown Memphis for a street fair and competition to decide the best hot wings in the South. Even if wings aren't your thing, stop by for music and a gander at the names of competing teams. After all, who can say Winga Linga Ding Dong without smiling?

May

Memphis Italian Festival, memphisitalianfestival.com. Twenty years ago, Holy Rosary Parish School in East Memphis threw up a few tents in nearby Marquette Park to start a friendly Italian cook-off. Today, the Memphis Italian Festival attracts thousands to a festival that includes competitions in a dozen divisions, including best homemade wine. Held the last weekend in May, the festival is a feel-good start to summer, offering contests (grape stomping, pizza throwing, and bocce), cooking demonstrations (the secret to Sunday gravy), and a surprisingly good assortment of vendor food (cannoli, toasted ravioli, Peroni beer). The Italian fest also stages better-than-average entertainment, presenting locals who've made it like singer-songwriter Keith Sykes, classic rocker Larry Raspberry, and blues standouts like the legendary Robert Cray. Parking can be tricky, so give festival shuttles a try.

July

Lauderdale County Tomato Festival, lauderdalecountytn.org/living_tomato.html. Many parts of the country take immense regional pride in their homegrown tomatoes, but the folks in Lauderdale County aren't swayed. They've built a thriving local industry with the rich red color and taste of Ripley tomatoes, named after the county seat and grown in mineral-rich river soil from the nearby Mississippi. Since 1984, the festival has trumpeted the fruit's peak season with a two-day event in Ripley, Tennessee, that includes vendors, entertainment, and the crowning of a tomato queen. Even more fun is a contest where participants dice, slice, fry, squeeze, and sauté tomatoes in unimaginable ways. (Think tomato ice cream.) Don't miss the scrumptious "Saturday (Tomato) Salads" and be sure to bring a salt shaker for the car because you'll be eating warm tomatoes on the ride back home.

September

Zoo Rendezvous, memphiszoo.org/zoorendezvous. Let's get the price of a ticket to Zoo Rendezvous out of the way first: Tickets to the major fund-raiser for the Memphis Zoo cost $200 each. If that blows your entertainment budget, we understand. If you are still intrigued, here's the short story: Eating and drinking with exotic animals in the zoo's lush and congenial setting is one hell of a party. More than 75 local restaurants and liquor distributors set up stations throughout the zoo, staging a culinary backdrop (we're talking elegant food, people!) for such animals as the zoo's giant pandas named Ya Ya and Le Le and the grizzlies and trumpeter swans in Teton Trek. I never understood the appeal of Zoo Rendezvous until I scored a ticket. Now I'm disappointed anytime I can't go.

Memphis Farmers Market Harvest Celebration and Holiday Market, memphisfarmersmarket.org. About the time shoppers are starting to miss their favorite local growers, the **Memphis Farmers Market** (p. 67) holds its annual love fest in downtown's historic Central Station to thank volunteers, vendors, and customers for supporting the most popular open-air market in the city. For 3 hours on a Sunday afternoon, hundreds of hungry market fans taste a smorgasbord of dishes prepared by Memphis chefs. There's entertainment by local musicians, beer, and wine—included with the price of a ticket—and a rollicking auction for everything from compost bins to cosmetics, all locally sourced. A month or so later, the market swings back into the station's outdoor pavilion for a final flourish before winter. Growers and artisans set up a Santa's workshop for cooking, decorating, and DIY gifts. At the holiday market expect such wares as juniper and holly wreaths, lard soap in the shape of a pig, and winter greens and root vegetables sold by the bag or bushel.

Food Trucks

Food trucks are a guiltless way to enjoy decadent and delicious calories. It's just a taco, right? So goes the thinking in Memphis, where food truck fervor is revved up after an agonizingly long wait for an ordinance in 2011 to be approved by the city council.

A year later, the parade of food trucks at a downtown rodeo and the hundreds of city workers willing to wait for a stand-up lunch confirm what other cities already know: Meals on wheels are fun, affordable, and gourmet, offering delectable choices like bison chili, crispy pig ear with creamed collards, and vegetarian tacos with roasted garlic aioli.

While only a dozen or so trucks are routinely spotted around town, many more are forthcoming, according to Taylor Berger, cofounder of **YoLo Frozen Yogurt & Gelato** (pp. 29 and 130) and the organizer behind the Memphis Food Truckers alliance. By mid-2012, about 45 vendors held operating permits, and another 30 to 40 permits were pending, Berger said at the group's first meeting. "With almost 100 trucks trying to operate, that means there's a big appetite in the city for mobile food."

In Memphis, some trucks stay focused on special events, but others are more visible thanks to Facebook and Twitter. One of the first tasks of the Memphis Food Truckers Alliance is to compile a map with truck locations in real time for the group's Facebook page. In the meantime, here are some of our best picks, as of mid-June 2012.

Central BBQ, cbqmemphis.com; Barbecue; $. Central BBQ is an award-winning brick-and-mortar restaurant well known for its ribs, barbecue nachos, and homemade potato chips. The restaurant recently took to the streets in a colorful tie-dyed truck that's hard to miss. Typically, it is parked every Saturday at the downtown **Memphis Farmers Market** (p. 67), where the truck's chefs recognize local providers by using heritage Berkshire pork from **Newman Farm** (p. 254) for their chopped pork sandwiches.

Crumpy's on Wheels, crumpys.com; @crumpsonwheels; Grill; $. Crumpy's Wings & More operates two restaurant locations along with its mobile trunk. Look for Crumpy's during the week near Winchester and Riverdale Roads and order a foot-long Crumpy dog, a catfish and wing combo, or a basket of fries loaded with chili, cheese, and jalapeños. The truck's fried green tomatoes are also excellent.

Fuel Food Truck, fuelcafememphis.com; @fuelfoodtruck; American/Vegetarian; $. Is there any cuter name for a food truck than Fuel? Probably not, especially when the truck is an extension of Midtown's **Fuel Cafe** (p. 84). Classically trained chef Erik Proveaux, who also owns the brick-and-mortar Fuel, is committed to fresh, locally sourced ingredients for both menus. Try his bison chili made with a little chocolate, or grilled cheese with arugula and tomatoes. Fuel was one of the first trucks on the street and likes to move around, but it might show up at the downtown dog park at the corner of Main Street and Jefferson.

Healthylicious, @karenfebles; Smoothies & Juices; $. Healthylicious is a bright yellow truck with a personality as sunny as its operator. Karen Febles farms with her husband in nearby Ripley, Tennessee, so her fruits and vegetables couldn't be any fresher. Her smoothies are cold and frothy with a Mexican twist. She mixes smoothies to order using yogurt, soy milk, or coconut milk and a choice of sweeteners, including agave and raw sugar.

Kona Ice of Memphis, (901) 794-5662; Shaved Ice & Snow Cones; $. Husband-and-wife team David Maxey and Cheryl Sessions did a midlife career change to bring the first Kona Ice franchise to Memphis. Their shaved-ice truck has 45 flavors, including several that are kosher and diet. Ten spouts with the most popular flavors let kids of all ages customize their own cups, while inside the truck are combos like tangerine, mango, and pineapple. Look for Kona Ice at special events and at the children's playground in Shelby Farms Park on Thursday and Friday.

Mark's Grill Food Truck, marksgrill.com; @Marksgrill; Grill; $. Mark Hamilton's food truck could be one of the most extravagant food trucks in the country. No wonder he stores it in a covered commercial garage. Hamilton spent 14 months and over six figures customizing this big red beauty with more bells and whistles than a commercial kitchen. When he's rolling, Hamilton serves standard grill favorites: chili cheese dogs, stuffed bacon blue cheese burgers, "real deal" Philly cheesesteaks, and tacos filled with fish, chicken, or steak.

Memphis Dawgs, @memphisdawgs and @dawgertom; Hot Dogs; $. Don't look for a Memphis Dawgs food truck. There isn't one. Instead brothers Todd and Tommy Bourne keep things simple: quarter-pound, all-beef Nathan's hot dogs with a dozen toppings sold from carts. Todd is usually at the Wolfchase Galleria mall (he likes the air-conditioning), while Tommy tends to work Amro music in Midtown or the Kirby Gate Kroger on Quince. The brothers' signature Memphis Dawg is topped with coleslaw, celery salt, and a secret barbecue sauce.

Memphis Munchies, missbirdsongsweetooth.com; @memphis munchies; Grill/Candy Apples; $. Tabitha Birdsong started her business with handmade Granny Smith candy apples in novelty flavors such as saltwater taffy, orange Creamsicle, and pink lemonade. Special order customers can select from 40 different flavors, and favorites show up on Birdsong's truck called Memphis Munchies. In addition to candy apples, Birdsong, who has been trucking since 2009, serves deep-fried hot dogs, smoked-sausage slaw dogs, hot wings, and fried fruit pies.

Revival: Southern Food Company, revivalsouthernfood.com; @ revival_food; Upscale Southern; $. Revival typically splits its time between the University of Tennessee Medical Center and downtown's Court Street. Chef Crash Hethcox brings tasty regional whims and family recipes to his gourmet Southern menu of sliders, tacos, and veggie sides like stewed tomatoes, squash, and zucchini. Save room for dirty shoestring fries covered with andouille gravy, mushrooms, onions, and shredded cheese, or Krispy Kreme bread pudding, a classic dessert reinvented with the South's favorite glazed donut.

Rock 'n Dough Pizza Co., (901) 674-8545; Pizza; $. Jeremy Denno is a cook and kitchen manager at **Trolley Stop Market** (p. 50), but he still found time to start his own company with his wife, Amanda. The couple use custom-built trailers to haul wood-fired ovens, delighting customers with handmade pizzas sold by the slice or as individual pies. The couple uses all local ingredients for their products, which in addition to pizzas include fritters, hoagies, and wraps with ham, cheese, roast beef, or turkey, with basil-garlic mayo and drinks, including house-made strawberry lemonade. Look for Rock 'n Dough Pizza at the **Memphis Farmers Market** (p. 67), special events, and behind Trolley Stop, where the couple plans to open a permanent pop-up restaurant from 9 p.m. until after midnight.

Scooter's Bar-B-Que, (901) 412-3885; Barbecue; $. Scooter Moore has been smoking baby back ribs, turkey legs, rib tips, and pork shoulder over charcoal and hickory since 1992, mostly at special events like the Memphis in May Beale Street Music Festival. More recently, he's parked his truck at Winchester and Riverdale Roads, turning out ribs and sandwiches. Don't miss his barbecue bologna, which peaks out of its roll for a tasty round of nibbling before you start on the bread.

A Square Meal on Wheels, (901) 573-9264; Grill; $. Before Iraq vet Derrick Clark graduated from L'École Culinaire in Cordova, Tennessee, his truck was already rolling. Clark converted a Cintas van into his meal on wheels with finds from Craigslist. He's proud of his thriftiness and his food, serving Southern favorites like fried pickles, green-fried tomatoes, fish tacos, chicken salad wraps, and 100 percent Angus beef burgers.

Tacos Los Jarochos Food Truck, (901) 314-5735; Tacos & Tamales; $. Tacos Los Jarochos is the real deal: 7 types of corn tacos, 2 different *alambres,* and the sweet Mexican soft drink Jarritos in 2 flavors. Two good choices: the 4-meat *discada jarocha* taco and *barbacoa,* or beef barbecue. The food at Los Jarochos is affordable and ready to go in minutes. Plus there's a carnival-like feel to the truck at night, which is typically parked at the southwest corner of Perkins Road and Summer Avenue from about 3 to 10 p.m.

Tamale Trolley, @tamaletrolley; Tacos & Tamales; $. Why take sides in the taco versus tamale debate? Ken Hooper sells excellent versions of both thanks to his singular focus. For his New Mexican–style red chile sauce, he uses both ancho and morita chiles because the smoky flavor complements the masa. "Tamales are about corn," he says, "and that is where the focus needs to stay." Amen. The Tamale Trolley's Ensenada-style tacos are also delicious, especially when stuffed with fish, grilled cabbage, onions, and lime-cilantro sour cream. Hooper typically moves between downtown and the **Agricenter Farmer's Market** (p. 189) and also shows up for special events like the Overton Park concerts at the Levitt Shell.

YoLo Frozen Yogurt & Gelato, yolofroyo.com; @yolofroyo; Frozen Yogurt/Gelato; $. YoLo sells frozen yogurt from a vintage Airstream painted pastel blue, so it's easy to gravitate toward artisan frozen flavors like sea-salt caramel pretzel or dreamy dark chocolate. The YoLo truck extends the local chain's reach, showing up for special events such as family concerts at Shelby Farms Park. The only hard part of YoLo is deciding between dozens of locally sourced toppings. Here are two good suggestions: crumbled **Makeda's Homemade Butter Cookies** (p. 115) and **Dinstuhl's** candies (p. 163).

Let's Talk Barbecue: Words You Need to Know

Memphis barbecue is a delicious but complex culinary club that includes secret recipes, regional pride, and a kitschy vernacular that can't even decide how to spell the word. In Memphis, look for spellings such as barbecue, barbeque, BBQ, Bar-B-Q, and Bar-B-Que, just to name few.

For newbies, plowing through a barbecue menu can be equally confusing. Walk into a Memphis restaurant and say, "I'd like barbecue, please," and the server is likely to give you an odd, blank stare before launching into a litany of questions along these lines: "Pork or chicken? Wings or ribs? Wet or dry? Pulled or chopped? Sandwich or plate?"

To better navigate, here's a glossary of barbecue terms to help you order (and eat) like a Memphis native. If you can't remember the list, go with Memphis's favorite happy meal: a pulled pork sandwich with slaw, beans, and sweet tea.

Barbecue plate: a spin-off of the South's much-loved "meat-and-three" that includes barbecue, slaw, beans baked with sauce, and white bread or rolls.

Barbecue spaghetti: spaghetti served with chopped barbecue and sauce.

Chopped barbecue: beef or pork chopped by hand with a heavy cleaver.

'Cue: a popular abbreviation for barbecue of any kind.

Dry ribs: ribs rubbed with a dry marinade made from a mix of spices and herbs such as garlic powder, paprika, chili powder, kosher salt, and whole seeds like allspice, mustard, coriander, or celery.

Full rack: between 14 and 16 baby pork ribs; a half rack is 7 or 8.

Pulled pork: meat hand pulled from a cooked pork shoulder.

Pulled pork sandwich: pulled pork, coleslaw, and a dash of sauce on a bun.

Rib tips: the short, meaty sections of rib that are attached to one end of the spare rib.

Vous: nickname for **Charlie Vergos' Rendezvous** (p. 52) in downtown Memphis, the most popular barbecue restaurant in the world.

Wet ribs: ribs made with tomato-based barbecue sauce seasoned with vinegar and spices.

Downtown Memphis

From its bluff-top perch above the Mississippi River, downtown Memphis has been the city's heartbeat for government and commerce for almost 200 years. Retail and entertainment, on the other hand, have swung in and out, following economic and residential shifts. Nothing in the 20th century hit Downtown harder than the 1968 assassination of Martin Luther King Jr. at the Lorraine Motel, located several blocks south of the city's core. Turbulent social times pushed residents east, and businesses followed.

Fortunately, many of the city's historic brick buildings were locked but not torn down. In the early 1980s, urban pioneers moved back in, renovating storefronts and factories into apartments, lofts, and boutique businesses. The historic Peabody hotel reopened in 1981, restored to its earlier grandeur. City officials also partnered with business leaders to develop Mud Island into a river museum and amphitheater and to resurrect Beale Street as the home of the blues.

A small group of activists raised money a decade later to save the Lorraine Motel from demolition, and its rebirth as the National Civil Rights Museum accelerated the appeal of downtown Memphis for residents and visitors alike.

These days, downtown Memphis is roughly defined by Front Street along the river bluff, Danny Thomas Boulevard to the east, Jackson Boulevard to the north, and Lamar Avenue to the south. Within those confines, three neighborhoods offer a vibrant mix of restaurants, music clubs, bars, and lounges.

With its restored Central Station, the South Main Street Historic Arts District is home to the Memphis Farmers Market, and cafe and landmark favorites like the Arcade, well known to many from the film *Mystery Train*. World-famous Beale Street edges central downtown, mixing music and home cooking into a soulful Memphis stew. A pedestrian-friendly Main Street mall also links Beale Street entertainment to casual and fine dining restaurants serving Asian, new American, and upscale Southern cuisines. There's plenty of libation action, too, from cold drafts at Bardog Tavern to seasonal martinis at Felicia Suzanne's.

Visitors to downtown Memphis might find the one-way streets and pedestrian mall a little confusing. If so, jump on the Main Street Trolley. There will be something good to eat or drink at almost any stop.

Automatic Slim's, 83 S. 2nd St., Memphis, TN 38103; (901) 525-7548; automaticslimsmemphis.com; American/Brunch/Cocktails; $$–$$$. In the early 1990s, before the revitalization of downtown Memphis, Karen Carrier extended the globally inspired food of her catering company, Another Roadside Attraction, to Automatic Slim's, located across the street from The Peabody hotel. Named after a legendary bluesman, the restaurant quickly established itself as a go-to destination for drinks, music, and eclectic food with a Caribbean spin. In 2008 Carrier sold the restaurant, and for a year or two it struggled with building a new identity. These days, the restaurant has settled into a nice groove with a new American menu focused on seasonal ingredients and excellent cocktails with a nod to its fun-loving past. Slim's bartenders say they have the largest martini menu in Memphis, which is a good reason to stop by any day of the week from 11 a.m. to 7 p.m. for $5 martinis. Try Creamsicle (360 Vanilla vodka, Triple Sec, orange juice, and cream) or the Tennessee martini (tea-infused vodka, simple syrup, and a lemon twist). In addition to daily lunch and dinner, the restaurant serves a weekend brunch from 9 a.m. to 3 p.m. on Saturday and Sunday. Try a New York strip or seared Diver scallops with pistachio cream and herb risotto for dinner or sunnyside-up eggs with chorizo potato hash for brunch.

Bleu Restaurant and Lounge, 221 S. 3rd, Memphis, TN 38103; (901) 334-5950; downtownbleu.com; Global/Fusion; $–$$$. Located across the street from the FedEx Forum where the Memphis Grizzlies play, Bleu is the on-site restaurant for the Westin Hotel, serving breakfast, lunch, dinner, and cocktails. The ambience is upscale but comfortable, and Chef Robert Nam Cirillo brings a cacophony of flavors to the table. His dad is first-generation Italian, and his mom is first-generation Irish. The couple adopted Cirillo and his brother from Korea, immersing the boys in a culinary melting pot. Lucky for us, those influences shape a delightfully expressive menu at Bleu. For lunch, build your own sandwich from a tempting selection of proteins, cheeses, sauces, and toppings. For dinner, try striped bass with a light citrus curry rub or grilled pork chops with creamy spinach and shiitake grits. Stop by the Blue Lounge where songstress Lee Taylor performs Friday and Saturday nights, and a bar menu includes small plates like ahi tuna wontons, steamed bun sliders, and smoked Gouda mac and cheese. Don't miss the restaurant's outdoor patio where the Bleu Steel martini tastes particularly good. The restaurant's signature cocktail mixes vodka, simple syrup, lemon juice, and muddled blueberries and is garnished with a sprig of fresh thyme.

Bluefin Sushi Lounge, 135 S. Main, Memphis, TN 38103; (901) 528-1010; bluefinmemphis.com; Japanese/Sushi & Sashimi; $–$$.

Don't be put off by the big-as-a-bed lounges scattered around Bluefin Sushi. There is nothing else early '90s about this downtown favorite that is open until 1 a.m. on the weekends, cranking out nigiri, sashimi, and more than three dozen specialty rolls, including the THC (it begins with shrimp tempura) and the Memphis Seoul: grilled beef tenderloin, scallions, cucumbers, carrots, and daikon topped with house-made kimchee. For those who think sushi is, well, yuk, Bluefin also has built an impressive non-sushi menu with such dishes as osso bucco, crab fondue, and flash-seared mussels with spicy dashi broth. Meat eaters take note: A changing Chef's Trio pulls out the stops, offering choices like veal hanger steak and short ribs with truffle potato puree. Bluefin also shakes up a diverse selection of libations, including a dozen different martinis and 18 kinds of sake ranging from sparkling to unfiltered.

Capriccio Grill, 149 Union Ave, Memphis, TN 38103; (901) 529-4199; peabodymemphis.com/dining; Italian/Steak House; $$–$$$. The full-service restaurant at the historic Peabody hotel, Capriccio Grill wears many hats. Astute readers may know that a capriccio is an improvisational musical composition that breaks the rules, a fitting name for this Italian steak house. For dinner, US prime steaks and chops, including Wagyu Kobe strip steak, join a full component of market seafood, mussels, and lobster. Also on the menu: pastas and popular Italian entrees, such as veal or chicken piccata with preserved-lemon caper sauce, parmigiana with marinara and mozza-rella, and scaloppine with Marsala sauce and mushrooms. At lunch, the Capriccio Grill offers soups, salads, entrees, sandwiches, and pizzas. The spicy buffalo burger with apple-wood-smoked bacon is a pleaser, as is the *salsiccia* pizza with imported pepperoni, piquillo peppers, and Italian sausage. For a sweet and satisfying comple-ment to any meal at the Grill, try Capriccio's signature milk shake or a selection of Peabody desserts served in shooter glasses.

Dyer's Burgers, 205 Beale St., Memphis, TN 38103; (901) 527-3937; dyersonbeale.com; Burgers; $. Dyer's Burgers may be more story than substance, but the restaurant's location on Beale Street across from W. C. Handy Park makes it a convenient stopover for a quick and affordable meal. Plus, the story behind Dyer's is a good one. Elmer "Doc" Dyer started the restaurant in 1912, developing a trademark burger that is deep-fried in a skillet instead of grilled. The frying oil is strained every day and reused, making a cherished oil starter, sort of like sourdough. In fact, the oil is so valuable that when Dyer's changes locations, as it has over the years, its cooking grease is transported with armed police escorts. (I swear this is the truth.) The menu is streamlined at Dyer's: hand-cut fries, chicken tenders, a fried bologna sandwich, and burgers with cheese in single, double, and triple stacks. Go with whatever size burger you can handle and top it with mustard, pickle, and onions. And don't worry about that grease because a Dyer's burger is one of *Esquire* magazine's "60 Things Worth Shortening Your Life For."

Eighty3, 83 Madison Ave., Memphis, TN 38103; (901) 333-1224; eighty3memphis.com; New American; $$–$$$. Let me out Eighty3 up front. The restaurant and bar adjoin the Madison Hotel, but Eighty3 (named after its street address) is no predictable hotel sidekick. Instead, the restaurant complements the Madison's boutique genre with excellent food and a fun and lively setting. Retooled by consultant Rodelio Aglibot, better known on the Food Channel as the Food Buddha, Eighty3's catchphrase of "nosh, drink, dine" hits the mark. Combining Midwestern sensibilities with innovations from West Coast kitchens, Executive Chef Connor O'Neill creates bar snacks like candied bacon with maple vinegar, as well as full-plate entrees like honey-soy-glazed sea bass with braised grapefruit, endive, and fennel. Small plates also are thoughtful and delicious. Try elk carpaccio with fried capers and arugula, and the restaurant's signature corn bread, served piping hot in a small cast-iron skillet. Before or after dinner, take the Madison's lobby elevator to the rooftop deck for the city's best view of the Mississippi River. Better yet, carry up a cocktail and settle in for as long as you like. See Chef O'Neill's recipe for **Shrimp Mole with Apple Kohlrabi Slaw & Johnny Cakes** on p. 271.

Evelyn & Olive Restaurant, 630 Madison Ave., Memphis, TN 38103; (901) 748-5422; evelynandolive.com; Jamaican/Vegetarian; $. Be prepared for a fork fight at Evelyn & Olive over the last bite on your plate. The food is that good. The new restaurant's namesakes are the mothers of owners Tony Hall and Vicki Newsum, and the feel-good vibe of the place is a lovely tribute. An upstart on a transitional block of Madison Avenue, the restaurant's menu blends Jamaican flavors (Hall is from Kingston) with a touch of the South (Newsum is a Memphis native). Start off with shrimp, crispy and lightly breaded (the pink shrimp shows through) and served with garlic-pepper Boom Boom sauce, so you control the dip and the kick. The menu's pan-seared Kingston Stew Fish is deservingly popular, but don't overlook the restaurant's specials for such delectable surprises as curry chicken and dumplings over rice and peas or a lovely molten chocolate cake with kiwi sauce and strawberry compote. Chef Zena Lovelady's menu is also packed with veggie-centric food, and she is happy to adapt dishes for vegans and vegetarians. Toss in Red Stripe and sensible prices, and Evelyn & Olive feels already like a neighborhood favorite.

Felicia Suzanne's, 80 Monroe Ave., Memphis, TN 38103; (901) 523-0977; feliciasuzanne.com; Upscale Southern; $$–$$$. Long before local was part of the foodie lexicon, Chef/Owner Felicia Willett was hauling in oysters from the Gulf Coast and tracking down local growers for her updated interpretation of Southern food with low-country flair. Farm-to-table is seamlessly integrated into Willett's menu, from the pickled garnishes she preserves herself to the seasonal produce she buys every week from local farmers' markets. Celebrating her 10-year anniversary in 2012, Felicia Suzanne's is one of a handful of this author's top picks. Renovated on the original location of the historic Peabody hotel, Felicia Suzanne's has it all: a sophisticated bar, a charming fountain patio protected by old brick buildings, and a menu that elevates Southern cooking from satisfying to sublime. Don't miss the restaurant's house-smoked salmon deviled eggs with Arkansas caviar, pepper-crusted salmon with sweet corn étouffée and tomato jam, or Friday-only lunches, where 25-cent martini specials are a great way to jump-start the weekend. If you like the pickled martini garnishes, check out Chef Willett's new line of condiments, pickles, and chow chow sold at the restaurant and online. Also see Chef Willett's recipe for **Bacon, Lettuce & Fried Green-Tomato Salad** on p. 266.

Flight Restaurant and Wine Bar, 39 S. Main, Memphis, TN 38103; (901) 521-8005; flightmemphis.com; Global; $–$$$. Three years after its opening, Flight is still wowing customers and critics. Voted one of the country's top 100 restaurants in 2012, the down-town hot spot offers flights—a trio of plates or pours—for salads, entrees, desserts, wines, vodkas, whiskeys, and cordials. Take heed: A flight of food is no small-plate sampling. The Feathered Flight, for example, includes a gorgeous trio of chicken, truffle-potato waffle, and mushroom cream sauce; quail with chipotle corn bread and tasso gravy; and a muscovy duck breast with butternut squash confit. Be sure to toss in a Fire and Ice flight of Pinot Noir served with a nifty descriptive menu of the wine trio. All menu items also are available in entree or small-plate portions, but why not play along? The restaurant is popular, so call ahead for dinner

HOMEGROWN CHAIN: JACK PIRTLE'S CHICKEN

Yes, it's true. The chicken on the logo sports a wacky blue cowboy hat, but don't dismiss Jack Pirtle's Chicken as ordinary until you hear the engaging story of Jack Pirtle, a working man who made good. A mechanic, millwright, and brakeman for the railroad, Pirtle didn't get into the restaurant business until his early 40s. When he built his first restaurant in 1957, he catered to blue-collar workers like himself, offering steak sandwiches and foot-long hot dogs, and staying open 24 hours to accommodate the nearby Firestone plant. A fortuitous meeting with Colonel Sanders pulled him into the fried chicken business. He adopted the colonel's signature recipe, but broke ties with the chain in 1964 because he didn't want to standardize his menu. Today, the company operates eight locations in the Memphis area, and the restaurants don't waiver from their original intent to provide fast and affordable food. The menu features burgers, hot dogs with slaw, smoked sausage, and chicken sold in different combinations, including a 12-piece Family Deal with biscuits, corn on the cob, chicken, gizzards, and Jack Pirtle's legendary sweet tea. For a complete listing of locations, check the company's website at jackpirtleschicken.com.

reservations. Ask for a cushy leather booth on Flight's 2nd-floor balcony where you can admire the restaurant's crystal chandelier and the view outdoors.

Grawemeyer's, 520 S. Main St., Memphis, TN 38103; (901) 526-6751; Cafe; $. Named after the Pullman railroad sleeper cars, The Pullman Hotel was built in 1912, one of many small hotels located around Central Station to accommodate travelers and railroad workers. Downtown residents Mark and Cynthia Grawemeyer have spent years renovating the Pullman building, and the 1st floor is now a restaurant, bakery, and bar offering families and urbanites breakfast in morning, a quick lunch midday, and drinks and dinner at night. The couple also owns **Rizzo's Diner** (p. 49) around the corner, and Rizzo's chef Michael Patrick is overseeing the kitchen here as well. The menu includes casseroles, pizzas, blue plates, seasonal specials, and some quirky picks like a bologna sandwich on white bread and a loaded baked potato stuffed with turkey, sour cream, butter, and cheese. Look for the building's apple-green trim and be sure to notice the restaurant's beautiful art Deco tile.

Gus's World Famous Fried Chicken, 310 S. Front St., Memphis, TN 38103; (901) 527-4877; Fried Chicken; $. Visitor alert: Don't mistake Gus's typical roadhouse style as another ho-hum chicken joint. This single-story brick building with the red-and-yellow sign might serve the best fried chicken on the planet. Ask anyone waiting in line on a busy weekend night, or step inside and smell the spices, a secret family recipe from Gus's original location in Mason, Tennessee. Soaked in buttermilk, the chicken at Gus's emphasizes thick, crusty skin, so here's how to order: Pick a 3-piece plate of white or dark meat. When it arrives at the table, peel a chuck of chicken from the bone and wait a minute while the spicy steam escapes. Now dig in and don't skip the white bread served with every plate. Be sure to drink a cold beer and notice the restaurant's mismatched decor. Traditional Southern sides are also on the menu, including baked beans, fried okra, hush puppies, and slaw. In 2011, a third Gus's opened at a busy East Memphis intersection. The building is new, but reinterprets the roadhouse vibe in a pleasing way, and the chicken recipe is the same. Here are Gus's other locations: 730 S. Mendenhall Rd., Memphis, TN 38117, (901) 767-2323; 520 US 70 West, Mason, TN 38049, (901) 294-2028.

The Happy Mexican, 385 S. 2nd St., Memphis, TN 38103; (901) 529-9991; happymexican.com; Mexican; $–$$. Located in a triangular single-story building where two roads fork, the original Happy Mexican is fun and colorful from the get-go. *Memphis Flyer* readers regularly name the restaurant's monster margaritas as the best in Memphis. See for yourself on Saturday, when $7.99 buys the Ultimate, a mix of Chinaco tequila, triple sec, orange juice, sour margarita mix, and a splash of Coke. Toss in the restaurant's better-than-average chips and salsa and you might consider skipping dinner. Don't. Like most Tex-Mex restaurants in America, the menu spans pages of burritos, chimichangas, enchiladas, tacos, vegetarian entrees, and combo dinners. Go straight to Happy Fajitas, a sizzling mix of chicken, shrimp, and steak served with rice, beans, lettuce, guacamole, sour cream, pico de gallo, grilled veggies (tomatoes, onions, and peppers), and tortillas, of course. For a lighter but equally good choice, order chicken soup, a fragrant bowl of simmered broth, rice, onions, tomatoes, fresh chiles, and tender chicken strips. Owner Larry Gonzales says his recipe for success is simple: "We know how to do Mexican," and "We are a happy place." The Happy Mexican also operates four other locations: 6080 Primacy Pkwy., Memphis, TN 38119, (901) 683-0000; 2760 N. Germantown Pkwy., Memphis, TN 38133, (901) 382-3202; 7935 Winchester Blvd., Memphis, TN 38125, (901) 751-5353; 5723 Raleigh La Grange, Memphis, TN 38134, (901) 388-4910;

Itta Bena, 145 2nd St., Memphis, TN 38103; (901) 578-3031; itta benamemphis.com; Upscale Southern; $$$. On the street where the blues were born, music gets funky and drinkers get happy, so food options lean toward gastro pub and soul food. Itta Bena, named after B. B. King's birthplace in Mississippi, offers something different: upscale Southern dining on the 3rd floor of the **B. B. King's Blues Club** (p. 198). The restaurant feels like a secret speakeasy with entertainment and a great window view of the action on Beale Street. Local greats like Susan Marshall sing at the piano, while the Itta Bena kitchen plates Southern favorites updated with contemporary (and local) ingredients. The scallops, for instance, are served over mascarpone cheese grits and finished with a sweet corn–crab cream sauce with wilted spinach. Daily specials pull out all the stops. A recent favorite is this appetizer called Good Times Roll: pan-seared tortillas with pulled barbecue pork and candied onion–lime salsa.

Kay Kafe, St. Jude Children's Hospital, 262 Danny Thomas Blvd., Memphis, TN 38103; (866) 278-5833; Cafe; $. Memphians are justifiably proud of St. Jude Children's Hospital, and they show their appreciation by volunteering for St. Jude in a myriad of ways. The latest group of volunteers is working a 2-acre garden to grow herbs and produce for the hospital's cafeteria. Under the tutelage of Executive Chef Miles McMath, the gardens are the lynchpin of a revamped menu at Kay Kafe emphasizing nutritionally rich, locally grown foods. Volunteers—many who work at St. Jude—grow produce all year long with a greenhouse, hoop houses, and more than 60 raised beds. The cafe's menu reflects the farm-fresh focus and McMath's culinary expertise with multiple food stations serving American and international foods. Chicken salad and chicken and waffles are two favorites. Kay Kafe is open every day to patients, families, employees, and the public.

Kooky Canuck, 97 S. 2nd St., Memphis, TN 38103; (901) 578-9800; kookycanuck.com; American; $$. While the name Kooky Canuck is a little silly, the menu is serious eating, as in a 4-pound Kookamonga burger on a fresh-baked bun. (The restaurant also serves a 6-pound King Kookamonga if you dare.) While most sensible eaters share the monster servings, some try to win the Kookamonga challenge: Eat the 4 pounder in less than 60 minutes, and it's free. A warning for potential competitors: It takes 23 hours of playing tennis to burn off the burger's 12,400 calories. Fortunately, not everything at Kooky Canuck is oversize, but the menu still tends toward hearty not healthy. The 6-ounce flank steak is served in a cast-iron skillet with beans and blue-cheese mashed potatoes. Peach, apple, or chocolate chip cobblers also are cooked in skillets and topped with a generous side of ice cream. Then there's the restaurant's signature *poutine,* a fast-food favorite in Quebec combining hand-cut fries, cheese, and a house-made brown gravy. Open 7 days a week until early morning, Kooky Canuck is also popular for watching the University of Memphis Tigers or grabbing a cold beer after work. The restaurant serves Canadian favorites like Moosehead and LaBatt Blue along with Fat Tire on draft and signature cocktails.

Lunchbox Eats, 288 S. 4th St., Memphis, TN 38103; (901) 526-8820; lunchboxeats.com; Cafe; $. Located just south of the FedEx Forum, Lunchbox Eats sells the kind of sandwiches we wish our parents packed for brown bagging to school. Plus, the menu plays off elementary school with such charmers as After School Scooby Snack and Field Trip Greens. Chef Kaia Brewer mixes gourmet with soul for sandwiches that are like blue plate specials upended by bread. The Graduation Burger, for instance, puts a slice of juicy meat loaf, mashed potatoes, tomato gravy, and crispy Tabasco onions between slices of toasted white bread. The Homeroom Chicken & Grits is chicken tenders, Muenster cheese, and whole-grain honey mustard between two cheddar-cheese waffles. Chalkboard specials also suggest more traditional blue plates like hamburger steak, along with surprises like duck gumbo, fish tacos, and frog legs. Homemade lemonade is another treat, especially in unusual flavors such as prickly pear, pink guava, and blueberry. True to its school-day theme, Lunchbox Eats closes at 3 p.m. Mon through Fri but stays open until 7 p.m. Sat.

The Majestic Grille, 145 S. Main St., Memphis, TN 38103; (901) 522-8555; majesticgrille.com; American; $$. Nearly 100 years ago, the Majestic No. 1 Theater was a downtown beacon for entertainment and hospitality. Today, proprietors Patrick and Deni Reilly continue the tradition with an American menu that tweaks Italian. Aged steaks, ranging from hanger to filet mignon, are served with Majestic butter and garlic mashed potatoes. Signature flatbreads are another house specialty, with can't-miss combinations like smoked salmon with red onions, capers, spinach, and mozzarella. The restaurant's weekend brunch is always busy because breakfast favorites are amped up just enough. (A 3-egg frittata with andouille sausage, white cheddar, and Parmesan cream is one example.) The ambience of the Majestic Grill is equally pleasing. Booths line one wall, a bar (with 5 draft beers) lines the other, and an open kitchen anchors the back. Above the kitchen floats a 15-foot movie screen with a continuous silent feed of classic cartoons on the weekends and black-and-white films during the week.

McEwen's on Monroe, 120 Monroe Ave., Memphis, TN 38103; (901) 527-7085; mcewensmemphis.com; New American; $$. Located near attractions and hotels, McEwen's feels like a neighborhood tavern without all the ruckus. A comfortable bar spans one side of the restaurant, and a dining area fills the other. A wine cellar in the basement is a third option for up to 20 people who want to party in private. Chef Keith Bambrick favors local ingredients and skews his menu to different appetites and price points. Small plates are affordable but substantial, like the saffron lobster risotto with fresh green peas. Downtown workers like lunch at McEwen's because the service is fast, and most dishes ring in under $10. My favorites: spicy black bean bisque and grilled yellowfin tuna with kimchee, cucumbers, and sweet ginger mayo on a Kaiser roll. Dinner trends upscale with beautifully plated seafood and steaks, such as a 16-ounce New York strip with roasted peach and bourbon butter and Yukon Gold potato and arugula hash. Either way, save room for McEwen's banana cream pie, a signature dessert well worth the calories.

Pearl's Oyster House, 299 S. Main St., Memphis, TN 38103; (901) 522-9070; pearlsoysterhouse.com; Seafood; $–$$. Located about midway down South Main Street, Pearl's Oyster House is half bar, half restaurant. Both work just fine because the restaurant's exposed brick and mellow oak flooring complement all moods. So does the restaurant's seafood-centric menu. Start with Pearl's Hot

Shucks or other fresh oysters from the Gulf of Mexico prepared in multiple ways, then move on to a create-your-own combination dinner from fried shrimp, coconut shrimp, shrimp scampi, salmon, pasta jambalaya, catfish, crab cake, seafood Alfredo, or lobster tail. Not a decision maker? No problem. Go with house favorites like peel 'n' eat shrimp, fish tacos, Louisiana seafood gumbo, or an amberjack po' boy, grilled or blackened. Pearl's also has a good kid's menu for $6 (hands up for chicken tenders) and a nice selection of sides that includes green beans, okra, stone-ground grits, and Italian spinach.

Rizzo's Diner, 106 G. E. Patterson, Memphis, TN 38103; (901) 523-2033; American; $–$$. Tucked in a historic shotgun space with a large storefront window, Rizzo's Diner marries flavor and affordability into one fine plate of food. Under the direction of Chef Michael Patrick, the downtown diner serves classy comfort food that is easy on the pocketbook and pleasing to the palate. Menus for lunch, dinner, and Sunday brunch are limited, but deciding what to order is still difficult. It all sounds so good. Two suggestions are scallops and cheddar grits served with greens and lemon beurre blanc, and the G. E. Patterson Burger, a hefty beef patty with oven-roasted tomatoes and Italian-Creole aioli on a soft, not-too-thick hoagie roll. Also check the restaurant's Facebook page for daily soups, such as roasted tomato bisque, and blue plate specials with seasonal veggie sides. Rizzos' signature dishes also are fun and tasty. Cheeseburger soup is an updated take on Patrick's childhood favorite, and the Lobster Pronto Pup is made with chunks of fresh lobster fried light and crispy.

Trolley Stop Market, 704 Madison Ave., Memphis, TN 38103; (901) 526-1361; trolleystopmarket.com; Home Cooking/Pizza; $. An apt description for Trolley Stop Market is farm-to-family table because Jill and Keith Forrester, the restaurant's owners, are farmers from Arkansas who believe locally sourced food should not be elitist or expensive. Their restaurant, located next to a downtown trolley stop, is an extension of the locavore mantra "Know your farmer, know your food." Many of the restaurant's products come from the couple's farm, where they grow an abundant selection of flowers and heirloom vegetables, which are also sold at Trolley Stop and at local farmers' markets. Most menu ingredients are locally sourced, so sandwiches, plate lunches, and pizzas swing with the seasons. There are so many standouts, it's difficult to pick a few, but here goes: Black & Blue Burger, pimento cheese and bacon on Texas toast, vegan quesadilla, Denno's Pizza Hoagie, house-made potato salad, chocolate-covered strawberry cake, or any of Jillbilly's gourmet specialty pizza pies. Trolley Stop also has daily specials like shrimp and grits, vegan nights, boutique beers, and an eclectic assortment of locally made goods, including cosmetics, ceramics, and locally grown rice from Arkansas.

The Arcade, 540 S. Main St., Memphis, TN 38103; (901) 526-5757; arcaderestaurant.com; Diner; $. The Arcade restaurant, the oldest restaurant in Memphis, has seen it all, including frequent visits by Elvis, who had a favorite booth now adorned with Elvis photos. Founded in 1918 by Greek immigrant Speros Zepatos, the restaurant is still family owned, surviving the neighborhood's heyday, decline, and rebirth with its soul and decor intact. Refurbished in the 1950s with boomerang Formica tabletops and tricolored Naugahyde booths, the diner is a favorite set for moviemakers. Discovered initially by Jim Jarmusch for his film *Mystery Train,* The Arcade also has figured prominently in many other films, including *The Firm, Walk the Line,* and *Great Balls of Fire.* Happily, the food in The Arcade is as authentic as its architecture. Daily specials serve meat loaf, turkey, and Southern-fried chicken; the cheeseburger is excellent, and the diner's generously sized breakfasts are served all day. Sweet potato pancakes are a signature dish, along with creamy chocolate milk shakes that need both a spoon and a straw.

The Butcher Shop Steakhouse, 101 S. Front St., Memphis, TN 38103; (901) 521-0856; thebutchershop.com; Steak House; $$–$$$. For most of its 30-plus-year history, The Butcher Shop has been a dinner-only venue serving grain-fed Midwestern beef that is aged four weeks and cut in-house. Recently, the restaurant introduced Fresh Burger Fridays, a one-day-a-week lunch special that puts

Charlie Vergos' Rendezvous: Walk out of The Peabody & Follow Your Nose

Who would think the magic of a barbecue pork rib could lead a waiter from Memphis to Air Force One four different times?

Certainly not Percy Norris, who started working at Charlie Vergos' Rendezvous in 1968 when an order of ribs cost $1.50.

"I've waited on Jimmy Carter and his family, Bill Clinton and his family, and Al Gore and his family," Norris says, rattling off a list of politicians and celebrities that also includes George Bush, Mick Jagger, Diana Ross, Michael Jackson, and Bill Cosby. "If they come to Memphis, they come here."

These days, a full rack of ribs costs almost $19, and pitmasters at the Rendezvous run through about 6,000 pounds of pork ribs every week.

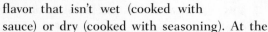

It's no wonder. On a busy Saturday night, several thousand people find their way down an alley near The Peabody to the most famous barbecue restaurant in the world. Many are ordering ribs "Vous-style," a signature savory flavor that isn't wet (cooked with sauce) or dry (cooked with seasoning). At the Rendezvous, ribs are slow-cooked over oak charcoal and hickory with a secret recipe of spices and then basted with a vinegar solution before they are served. Sauce, for those who insist, is served at the table.

Operating since 1948, the Rendezvous's origins are humble and have nothing to do with barbecue. Vergos started with ham and cheese sandwiches (they are still on the menu), catering to railroad and bank employees who worked the second shift. He fired up his first fire pit in the late 1960s about the time Norris started waiting tables.

"Being a waiter was an upstanding job to have in the community," Norris recalls. "We wore pressed shirts and shined shoes. We had to look spiffy."

The menu was simple: ribs or chopped shoulder. "We didn't write anything down," Norris says. "We just hollered in the orders."

From the beginning, customers valued waiters who were professional and genuine. And Rendezvous waiters stuck around. In addition to Norris, half a dozen other waiters have worked at the restaurant for more than three decades. Six more have served ribs for at least 20 years. "We call them the youngsters," Norris says, laughing.

For him, the success of the Rendezvous is a simple panacea: food plus service. "There's a mystique to longevity, to guys working in the same place for so many years," Norris says. "It makes people trust us and the restaurant."

Charlie Vergos' Rendezvous, 52 S. 2nd St., Memphis, TN 38103; (901) 523-2746; hogsfly.com; Barbecue; $$.

the leftover ends from the hand-cut steaks to good use. The menu (burgers, chips, and drinks) needs no frills because the ground beef is fresh and flavorful. Located in a circa 1890 building, The Butcher Shop is spacious enough for large parties and a 6-by-10-foot brick pit in the middle of the dining room. During the 1980s, customers cooked their own steaks over hickory charcoal. While that's still an option, most customers these days leave the grilling to the chefs and focus instead on the restaurant's salad bar, which is included with all entrees, along with baked potato and Texas toast. For an extra splurge, try The Butcher Shop's house-stuffed potato, seasoned with the restaurant's secret spices. The Butcher Shop also operates a second location at 107 S. Germantown Pkwy., Cordova, TN 38018; (901) 754-4244.

Chez Philippe, 149 Union Ave., Memphis, TN 38103; (901) 529-4188; peabodymemphis.com/dining; French; $$–$$$. Secluded on the 3rd floor of The Peabody hotel, Chez Philippe serves French cuisine freshened up with seasonal ingredients and a touch of Southern whimsy. A longtime favorite for special occasions, Chez Philippe is the only *Forbes* four-star restaurant in the Mid-South. From Wiesel crystal wine glasses to impeccable service, Chez Philippe is classic fine dining. With 22 tables on 3 different levels, dinner at Chez Philippe feels both intimate and opulent due to an international wine list and an excellent fixed-price menu offered in 3-, 5-, and 7-course tastings. Born in Gillette, Wyoming, Chef de Cuisine Ryan Spruhan adapts French classics in signature ways. For instance, instead of sole Véronique, he serves Flounder Bearnice with a wild Muscadine *gastrique* and pecans from Louisiana. Chez Philippe serves dinner Wednesday through Saturday, along with a 3-course afternoon tea offering pastries, scones, and tea sandwiches like fig and prosciutto on pumpernickel bread.

Paulette's, 50 Harbor Town Sq., Memphis, TN 38103; (901) 260-3333; riverinnmemphis.com; American; $$–$$$. From a quaint house on Madison Avenue, Paulette's anchored Midtown's Overton Square entertainment district for more than 30 years. Since 1974, Paulette's hung on to a successful French format that wooed customers with a romantic setting and warm popovers served with strawberry jam. But in 2011, citing an old building and slow traffic, owner George Falls relocated Paulette's to the River Inn at Harbor Town. Regulars worried about the restaurant's move to a downtown boutique hotel, but Paulette's is flourishing under Chef Scott Donnelly, who serves French-style American classics like pan-seared seafood and pepper-crusted filet mignon sautéed in butter-cream sauce. Paulette's desserts are as tempting as its entrees. Try the restaurant's hot chocolate crepe, a decadent fall into pecans, ice cream, walnut cream, chocolate shavings, and chocolate sauce.

A&R Bar-B-Cue, 22 N. 3rd St., Memphis, TN 38103; (901) 524-5242; aandrbbq.com; Barbecue; $. A friend who knows his barbecue swears the dry pork ribs at A&R are the best in Memphis. It's a big statement, but plenty of other folks agree. Pit cooked, the barbecue at A&R comes in many different ways, reflecting the restaurant's growth from a fast-food take-out window in 1983 to 4 restaurants for dining and catered parties. Started in 1983 by Andrew and Rose Pollard, the menu these days is a barbecue smorgasbord of pork and beef ribs, pulled shoulder, turkey legs, turkey breast, beef brisket, spaghetti, catfish, and smoked sausage and hotlink sandwiches. There are turkey and beef burgers, too, along with decadent sides like fried pickles and fried okra. It's difficult at A&R to save room for dessert, so go ahead and over-indulge. Homemade fried pies come in apple, peach, and sweet potato, or try a hunk of chocolate, lemon, or strawberry cake with colorful mix-and-match icing. Other A&R restaurants are located at 1802 Elvis Presley Blvd., Memphis, TN 38116, (901) 774-5907; 3721 Hickory Hill Rd., Memphis, TN 38115, (901) 365-9777); 7174 Highway 64, Memphis, TN 38133, (901) 266-0545

Alcenia's Desserts and Preserves, 317 N. Main, Memphis, TN 38103; (901) 523-0220; alcenias.com; Soul Food; $. With its beaded room dividers and potted plants, Alcenia's feels a little like a quirky aunt's kitchen. But there is nothing offbeat about the restaurant's food, which delivers exactly what the menu promises: "Soul from our hearts to your stomach." Yes, ma'am! Owner/Chef B. J. Chester-Tamayo cooks with her grandmother Alcenia's recipes, selling signature preserves and jellies (apricot, peach, pear, and fig) along with pickled tomatoes and chow chow by the pint. The restaurant's bread pudding with sauce is almost legendary in Memphis, although I prefer the custard pie. Tuesday through Friday, Alcenia's serves home-style meat and veggie plates (chicken, chops, catfish) with rolls or corn bread. On Saturday, the restaurant rolls out a $10 brunch with omelets, pancakes, chicken and waffles, and salmon croquettes. Pecan, sweet potato, and custard pies, along with regular and chocolate pound cake, are sold whole or by the slice all week.

Cozy Corner, 745 North Pkwy., Memphis, TN 38105; (901) 527-9158; cozycornerbbq.com; Barbecue; $. Plenty of restaurants help put pork ribs on the Memphis food map, but Cozy Corner with its retro paneling and homey feel takes a detour with a couple of barbecue specialties. Locals love the restaurant's Cornish hens, and with good reason. Smoked slowly to burnish the skin and then doused with barbecue sauce, the hens are so succulent you might give up pulled pork for good. The hens are served with plastic utensils, but use your fingers instead to get at the extra moist meat near the bone. Other Cozy Corner signatures are grilled rib tips and barbecue spaghetti that has the texture of soft Asian noodles. Still, my nod goes to the family-run restaurant's reinvention of its $4 bologna sandwich. Thick-sliced and rubbed with spices, the bologna is barbecued and served on a bun with sauce and slaw.

Dejavu, 936 Florida St., Memphis, TN 38106; (901) 942-1400; deja vurestaurant.org; Creole/Soul Food/Vegan; $. Chef Gary Williams is a larger-than-life personality who fills his Dejavu restaurant with customers who are crazy about his Creole and vegan soul food. Dejavu is located in a renovated brick building that was once a small church in the warehouse district behind D. Canale Beverage. Take the time to find it. Catfish and tilapia are deep fried, grilled, or blackened, and served with sides like grilled cabbage, candied yams, smothered okra, fried plantain, and spinach with lots of lemon. Big Keith's Bayou Classic tops tilapia with a creamy reduction of fresh lump crabmeat, crawfish, and shrimp. Other Creole favorites include jambalaya, alligator stew, andouille sausage po' boys, and cold cans of New Orleans's own Big Shot soda. Vegan dishes shape an unusual aside to the Creole menu. Veggie rolls are stuffed with curry cabbage, carrots, and raisins and fried to a golden brown, and the mock chicken salad will tempt even hard-core skeptics. Dejavu's desserts (both vegan and regular) include chocolate cake with strawberry sauce and Bananas Foster.

The Little Tea Shop, 69 Monroe Ave., Memphis, TN 38103; (901) 525-6000; Home Cooking; $. Operating since 1918, the longevity of The Little Tea Shop is reason enough for visiting. Located at its current location since 1935, the restaurant caters to workers, serving lunch only Mon through Fri. Its vintage appeal begins with a neon cursive sign that includes this tagline: HEALTHY HOME COOKING: DELICIOUS, NUTRITIOUS, REASONABLE. Inside, plate lunches offer all the standards: cobblers, chicken potpie, candied yams, black-eyed peas, and turnip greens topped with fresh tomatoes and sliced onions. On Tuesday, the restaurant serves white-meat chicken seasoned with a secret mix of spices and deep-fried mahogany brown. On Friday, the special is catfish. Proprietor Suhair Lauck hands pencils and paper menus to customers when they sit down. It's fun to check off entrees and sides as if they were sushi. A basket of corn-bread sticks also comes to every table, so crumble a little on your beans and greens, Southern style.

Miss Polly's Soul City Cafe, 154 Beale St., Memphis, TN 38103; (901) 527-9060; misspollysmemphis.com; Soul Food; $. Miss Polly's yellow-and-red sign at the south end of Beale Street features a sassy cartoon chicken with a spoon, an apron and the words LOVE, PEACE AND CHICKEN GREASE. How can you not walk right in? Start with fried green tomatoes or fried dill pickle chips, then move on to a chicken platter served with 8, 12, or 16 pieces with jalapeño corn bread and country-style sides. The spicy chicken at Miss Polly's is marinated for 24 hours, so it's a kicked-up mate to Belgian waffles with white gravy, butter, and syrup. There is, of course, another

Cooking With the King: Where to Eat When Visiting Graceland

Psst. It's time to dispel a food myth about Elvis Presley. Peanut butter and banana sandwiches weren't his favorite meal. He preferred bacon, and a lot of it.

The ultimate night owl, Elvis liked to sleep until late afternoon when his cook, Nancy Rooks, brought breakfast for dinner to his bedroom. Typically, the tray included a pound of bacon fried extra crispy, coffee, toast, pancakes, and eggs. Peanut butter and banana sandwiches were more of a late-night snack for Elvis, but they make a quick lunch option at **Rockabilly's Burger Shop** for the more than 700,000 visitors who come to Graceland every year. Rockabilly's, a retro '50s diner located in Graceland Plaza, serves the sandwich the Elvis way: white bread, peanut butter, and bananas grilled in butter. Rockabilly's also serves a trademark burger, hot dogs, and smoked Cajun sausage baskets.

The Graceland Plaza includes two other places to eat, along with Sirius/XM Elvis Radio, where you can stop by the studio and share a favorite Elvis story. The **Chrome Grille** serves meat loaf and mashed potatoes, another Elvis favorite, along with catfish dinners and Southern-fried chicken tenders. **Shake, Split & Dip** scoops up traditional ice-cream favorites like sundaes, house-made fudge, and single or double dips in waffle or sugar cones.

For authentic Memphis wings, don't miss **BJ's Wings and Things** across the street from Graceland Plaza. Sold drive-thru only, BJ's Wings are tasty and cheap. Individual wings sell for 49 cents Monday through Wednesday, a good time to sample all 6 sauces ranging from seasonal to suicidal. Honey Mild, my favorite, falls somewhere in the middle.

To find the barbecue landmark in the Graceland loop, look for a pink Cadillac and follow it to **Marlowe's Restaurant and Ribs.** Better yet, call ahead for a free limo ride to the family-owned restaurant, where Missy and Pete Gigliotti use recipes like their grandmother's marinara sauce and their father's fall-off-the-bone barbecue ribs. Featured on Guy Fieri's *Diners, Drive-ins and Dives,* Marlowe's mixes Elvis kitsch (they even have a gift shop!) with barbecue done many ways: ribs, chopped pork, beef brisket, shrimp, chicken, and spaghetti. There are Elvis tie-ins on the menu, too, such as the Blue Suede Burger topped with blue cheese and fried onion rings.

Another *Diners, Drive-ins and Dives* pick is located nearby. Owner Lou Martin specialized in smoked turkey legs, a fair-food favorite in Memphis, before opening **Uncle Lou's Southern Kitchen.** He adapted a fried-chicken family recipe, adding a honey-flavored glaze he calls "sweet, spicy love sauce." Other signature dishes are honey-buttered biscuits and the Monster Burger, 3 beef patties layered with 5 slices of cheese on a Kaiser bun. While contemplating how to tackle the burger, be sure to notice the charming wall map of America covered with colorful pushpins from the restaurant's customers.

BJ's Wings and Things, 3824 Elvis Presley Blvd., Memphis, TN 38116; (901) 396-4688; bjsbuffalostylewings.com; Chicken Wings; $.

Chrome Grille (Diner), *Rockabilly's Burger Shop* (Burgers), *Shake, Split & Dip* (Ice Cream & Shaved Ice/Soda Fountain), *3773 Elvis Presley Blvd., Graceland Plaza, Memphis, TN 38116; (901) 332-3322; $.*

Marlowe's Restaurant and Ribs, 4381 Elvis Presley Blvd., Memphis, TN 38116; (901) 332-4159; Barbecue; $–$$.

Uncle Lou's Southern Kitchen, 3633 Millbranch Rd., Memphis, TN 38116; (901) 332-2367; unclelousfriedchicken.com; Soul Food/Fried Chicken; $.

approach to Miss Polly's: Skip the chicken and head straight for the hot-buttered fried pies cooked in cast-iron skillets with scoops of vanilla ice cream. Open late on Friday and Saturday, Miss Polly's is a convenient stop for nursing a hangover or fueling up for another round of drinks.

Willie Moore's Family Restaurant, 109 N. Main St., Memphis, TN 38103; (901) 521-4674; Soul Food; $. After a fire destroyed Willie Moore's longtime restaurant on 3rd Street near Crump, loyal customers worried that they would never again eat Moore's pig feet and neck bones, a house specialty. Fortunately, the well-known king of soul food resurfaced two months later in a new location in the Claridge House building. For now, his chitlins are on hold, but the rest of his menu served cafeteria style is ready for visitors and office workers looking for a hot plate lunch. While most soul food restaurants feature daily specials throughout the week, Moore's traditional Southern menu stays pretty much the same every day: a dozen meat and fish dishes plus 15 or so sides, including catfish, meat loaf, sweet potatoes, pork chops, beans, peas, and greens. Be forewarned: Portions for both meat and vegetables are enormous. The restaurant is closed Sat but open Sun from noon to 5 p.m. During the week, the restaurant is open from 11 a.m. to 5 p.m.

Specialty Stores, Markets & Producers

Big Ono Bake Shop, 116 Front St., Memphis, TN 38118; (901) 590-4910. Feel like a trip to Hawaii that's easy on the pocketbook? Stop by Big Ono Bake Shop at the corner of Front and Gayoso and say hi to bakers Howard Montgomery and Jody Lees. Then dig into a Lava Roll, an island specialty made by slathering the dough with Plugra, a European-style butter with a higher fat content than American brands. *Ono* is the Hawaiian word for "delicious," and that pretty much describes the scones, pastries, stuffed cupcakes, and hula bread made at this small-batch bakery. Big Ono also sells its baked goods at **Miss Cordelia's** grocery (p. 68), **Easy-Way Produce** (p. 165) stores, and the seasonal farmers' markets. Better yet, stop by the bakery after 2:30 p.m. when prices are reduced 50 percent. Don't be late; the bakery closes at 3 p.m.

Bluff City Coffee, 505 S. Main St., Memphis, TN 38103; (901) 405-4399; bluffcitycoffee.com. A neighborhood favorite in the South Main arts district, Bluff City Coffee understands the happy morning triptych of freshly brewed java, house-made pastries, and free Internet. Take a little time and enjoy deciding between single-serve yogurt cakes (cherries and peaches are mixed in the dough), scones, turnovers, muffins, and duffins, a specialty of the house that crosses muffins and cake doughnuts. Breakfast sandwiches include standbys such as chicken and biscuit or lighter fare like a mini frittata. Lunch sandwiches tick toward gourmet: The hummus is topped with bacon, roasted red peppers, and feta cheese, and the turkey on a made-from-scratch baguette comes with Dijon mustard, green apples, and provolone. Bluff City recently relocated its baking operation to a large commercial kitchen downtown, expanding soup, sandwich, and pastry options. Bagels, breads, and cookies are made in-house as well, and owner David Adams plans additional locations.

Center for Southern Folklore, 1235 S. Main St., Memphis, TN 38103; (901) 525-3655; southernfolklore.com. Walk into the colorful Center for Southern Folklore and the store's assortment of blues music memorabilia and Southern kitsch will upstage lunch plans until you spot the handwritten menu behind the counter. Next thing you know, you'll want a meal or snack to taste Miss Ella's home cooking. The purpose of the center is to preserve Southern music and traditions, and for Ella Kizzie, there's no better tradition than food. Her peach cobbler, seasoned greens, hot-water corn bread, lemon chicken drummies, and Southern-style mac 'n' cheese have an almost cult-like following. A good time to see for yourself is during the center's brown-bag lunch concerts on Thursday or Friday afternoons. Also check the store's calendar for cooking demonstrations or attend the Southern Folklore Music Festival on Labor Day weekend to learn how to make indigenous recipes such as fry bread from Tennessee's Choctaw Indians.

City Market Groceries and Deli, 66 S. Main, Memphis, TN 38103; (901) 729-5162; citymarketmemphis.com. Buckets of fresh flowers flank the front doors of this compact urban grocery, stocked with essentials for cooking and fun stuff for snacking. In addition to staples like pasta, dog food, and canned goods, the market mixes in produce, organic items, ethnic foods, and a nice assortment of local products, such as corn chips, guacamole, and salsa from **Las Delicias** (p. 141), one of the city's favorite Mexican restaurants. For the time-strapped, the City Market deli makes traditional deli sandwiches such as roast beef or chicken salad along with stew, grilled salmon, curry chicken, and five-layer cakes. There are also soups, salads, and panini. The Trolley Special, a stack of sun-dried tomatoes, basil, and mozzarella on rosemary bread, is a standout. The deli's smoothie menu moves from Tropical Summer Splash to Go Green, a healthy concoction of spinach, celery, banana, and pineapple. Get orders to go, or eat in and people watch from the counter and stools that line the market's floor-to-ceiling windows.

Cucina Breads, (901) 355-1207; cucinabread.com. Sherri McKelvie says she started baking bread 20 years ago as a way to pass the time when she was snowed in a cabin in Oregon. We are glad the cabin was stocked with yeast. She later came to Memphis to bake for City Bread, and when that business closed she started her own, supplying artisan breads to local restaurants. A few years ago, McKelvie started selling at the downtown **Memphis Farmers Market** (p. 67) during the summer. Off-season, she sells at the

Tsunami Winter Farmers Market (p. 121) in Cooper-Young, building an enthusiastic following for her baguettes, focaccia, almond croissants, and crusty European *boules*. Get up early if you want a loaf because Cucina Breads sell out quickly; slice into one and you will know why. Her breads taste great and look beautiful, filling her table with wonderful flavors like semolina, rosemary, honey whole wheat, jalapeño cheddar, cranberry walnut, and (my favorite) chocolate cherry.

Frank's Main Street Market and Deli, 327 S. Main, Memphis, TN 38103; (901) 523-0101. Operated as a liquor store since the 1930s, Frank's converted to a grocery and deli in 2008. Painted liquor ads still cover the store's brick façade, but inside, the grocery upholds its slogan as "The Little Store with a Great Selection." Before Frank's added groceries, residents in the neighborhood had to drive to a store. Now they can have groceries delivered, along with deli meats smoked in the market's basement. Smoked turkey, chicken, and brisket can be purchased by weight to go, but don't skip the deli's sandwiches. You'll need both hands to eat a half. Frank's I.B.M. (Italian Business Man) is pepperoni, Genoa salami, capicola, and provolone stacked so deep it's a wonder any businessman makes it back to work without a nap. The turkey breast sandwich is equally good, combining bacon, chipotle mayo, and all the trimmings. Coolers line both side walls at Frank's (this was a liquor store, after all) stocking everything from Cheerwine and soft drinks to seasonal brews and imports like Samuel Smith Oatmeal Stout. If you need snacks, milk, or pasta, Frank's has staples, too.

Front Street Deli, 77 S. Front St., Memphis, TN 38103; (901) 522-8943. A tiny hole-in-the-wall at the corner of Union Avenue and South Front Street, this deli is a charming one-man band. Owner Lee Busby makes and wraps sandwiches and opens and closes shop. He also treats regular customers like family, which is one reason they comprise most of his business. Parking is scarce, but plenty of workers can walk to the deli for tuna, hot dogs, salads, beer, homemade desserts, and breakfast biscuits with egg, bacon, and cheese. Tourists also stop by to sit at the window counter made famous by Tom Cruise and Holly Hunter in a scene from Sydney Pollack's film *The Firm*. Busby doesn't take credit cards, just cash or checks, and don't visit much past 2 p.m. Typically, Front Street Deli closes for the day after lunch. The deli also has a second location at 3301 Winchester Rd., Memphis, TN 38118; (901) 794-6655.

Memphis Farmers Market, Central Station at S. Front Street and G. E. Patterson; memphisfarmersmarket.com. Established in 2006, the Memphis Farmers Market is on a mission: Bring fresh and healthy food to as many people as possible. Every Saturday from early April through October, the market transforms the pavilion behind historic Central Station into an energetic community of shoppers, chefs, vendors, and volunteers united by the local food mantra. This market has it all: fruits, vegetables, meat, cheese, honey, seafood, flowers, prepared foods, baked goods, garden plants, live music, food trucks, cooking demonstrations, activities for children, and free sitters for dogs. Supporters come from all over Memphis, so the market is a great place for people watching as well as shopping. When the market closes in the fall, organizers continue community outreach, beating the drum for healthier foods in home kitchens and school cafeterias. Local chefs also sponsor a popular series of dinners throughout the year featuring one-of-a-kind menus prepared with local food. The market is open from 7 a.m. to 2 p.m. Get there early for the best selection in produce and parking.

Miss Cordelia's and Cordelia's Table; 737 Harbor Bend Rd., Memphis, TN 38103; (901) 526-4722; misscordelias.com. Located at the northern edge of Mud Island on the Mississippi River, Harbor Town is a pedestrian-friendly urban village with small town charm. Miss Cordelia's is the neighborhood's social and retail hub, packing groceries and fresh food into a tight but inviting space. Yes, there are necessary national brands, but the store's character comes from its commitment to locally sourced products and a fresh meat and seafood counter specializing in hand-cut steaks and suppliers who raise their animals responsibly. Cordelia's Table is the market's adjoining cafe, offering a cornucopia of food to go and a bustling deli business for paninis, salads, and house-made soups. Tables clustered on the cafe's porch are fun for coffee (Cordelia's serves 6 varieties) and cake. Since its opening in 1996, Cordelia's has featured classic Southern layer cakes from Sugaree's, a small-batch bakery in New Albany, Mississippi.

South Memphis Farmers Market, 1400 Mississippi Blvd., Memphis, TN 38106; somefm.org/. Located near South Parkway in South Memphis, this seasonal market brings produce and local food to an urban neighborhood with limited fresh food choices. Operating May through October the market is open every Thursday from noon to 6 p.m. thanks to a jumpstart from St. Andrew AME Church and more than two dozen community organizations, including students at the University of Memphis. The market started small in 2010 with a handful of vendors in the parking lot of a former fish market. Part of a community development plan to build relationships and healthy lifestyles, the market continues to thrive with additional vendors, activities for children, cooking and canning demonstrations, and a full-time coordinator. An extensive renovation of a retail space, kitchen, and restrooms is also in the works.

Urban Treats, 903 Walker St., Memphis, TN 38126; (901) 774-3074. Talk about a fortuitous meet-up—this pairing of community outreach and local food is inspiring and delicious. In the spring of 2011, students from a nonprofit culinary arts training program with the Boys & Girls Club of Greater Memphis visited the **Cooper-Young Community Farmers Market** (p. 113). It was a yahoo! moment. The students, ages 16 to 21, discovered the unending possibilities of locally grown fruits and vegetables. Back in their kitchen, they started churning out fresh, uninhibited products like orange-spiced apple bread. Under the label Urban Treats, their products started appearing in independent markets. By the holidays, they were a full-blown catering company, taking orders for red velvet cookies and banana-nut-chocolate bread. Their savory products are as successful as their sweets. In fact, the label's cilantro lime pesto is a personal favorite. The engaging young people even produce a weekly cooking show, airing Wednesday evenings on TTC Food TV. Check the label's Facebook page for an updated list of products.

Wayne's Candy Company, 164 E. Carolina Ave., Memphis, TN 38126; (901) 527-4370; waynescandyco.com. Feel like getting in touch with your inner child? If so, pull up to the downtown dock of Wayne's Candy Company. Take a minute to notice the white warehouse with bright blue trim (it's the real deal) and then push open the door to the largest single location of warehoused candy in the country. Yes, that's a difficult fact to confirm, but one look around is its own verification. Stacked boxes are everywhere with all the candy you know and love: American standards like Hershey's mini bars as well as novelty brands, beef jerky, Cajun Chef pickles, and an amazing selection of nostalgia candy such as Pixy Stix, Necco Wafers, and break-your-teeth Atomic FireBalls. Wayne's stocks more than 3,000 items in 30,000 square feet, and it's all for sale. Just be sure to bring cash (no credit cards accepted), come early, and give a shout-out to Pop Rocks. The showroom opens at 6 a.m. and closes promptly at 3:45 p.m.

Midtown Memphis

Midtown Memphis is a neighborhood of contrasts, moving from stately turn-of-the-century homes to humble shotgun bungalows. At the center of Midtown is sprawling Overton Park, home to the Memphis Brooks Museum of Art, the Memphis College of Art, the Memphis Zoo, and one of the few remaining old-growth forests in Tennessee. The forest is a historically protected arboretum, but similar native hardwoods grow majestically in almost every Midtown neighborhood. First-time visitors should see for themselves and plan a leisurely drive through Midtown's Central Gardens, especially in late May when the hydrangeas are peaking and the crepe myrtles are starting to bloom.

Like the people and houses that make up its neighborhoods, restaurants in Midtown are an eclectic lot. Some, like Pho Hoa Binh on Madison, are small and family run. A few are funky joints like Payne's, renowned for its chopped barbecue sandwich and secret sauce. Others like Restaurant Iris showcase the finest cuisine in the city, mixing regional influences with big-city trends. Neighborhood boundaries also vary because few people agree on where Midtown begins and ends. For the purposes of this book, restaurants are included in the Midtown chapter if they fall within this general rectangle: the city's medical district to the west, the railroad tracks to the south, East High School to the east, and Jackson Avenue to the north.

Within those Midtown boundaries are three main east–west arteries: Poplar Avenue with its many charming apartment buildings from the 1920s; Union Avenue, the neighborhood's prominent commercial thoroughfare; and Madison Avenue, a combination of residences, businesses and restaurants.

Midtown also has two distinct restaurant and entertainment districts with storied personalities and histories: Cooper-Young and Overton Square. Cooper-Young is a historic residential neighborhood with a Saturday farmers' market and number of restaurants clustered near the intersection of South Cooper Street and Young Avenue. The neighborhood is particularly busy on weekends because revelers of all ages have many options for food and drink. The success of Cooper-Young over the past 20 years mirrors the decline of Overton Square, once the heartbeat of Midtown entertainment during the 1970s and '80s. Fortunately, Overton Square has seen its glory days come, go, and come back. A $35 million redevelopment project will be in full swing by 2013, rewarding the district's longtime tenants with new amenities, a hotel, and a rebranded theater district. Popular new eateries already have moved into the corner of Madison and North Cooper Street, including YoLo Frozen Yogurt and Gelato and Local Gastropub, whose original location is in downtown Memphis.

Abyssinia Restaurant, 2600 Poplar Ave., Memphis, TN 38112; (901) 321-0082; Ethiopian/Mediterranean; $–$$. Abyssinia is located in an outdated office building on a busy part of Poplar, so it's easy to miss. I ended up there one Monday night after trying two Thai restaurants that were closed. It was a lucky stumble. Abyssinia is the only Ethiopian restaurant in Memphis, offering unusual mixtures of lentils, meat, and vegetables that are also fun to eat. The no-frills restaurant is all about the food served traditionally on large platters with *injera,* a type of Ethiopian flatbread used instead of utensils to scoop up the food. Immigrants Yilma Aklilu and Seble Haile-Michael opened the restaurant in 2000 after fleeing political persecution. Seble learned to cook in Ethiopia from her grandfather, so her spice blends are new to many Memphis customers. Popular dishes include *yetsome beyaynetu,* a gourmet combination of vegetables with lentils and red sauce, split peas, and yellow sauce, collard greens and beets, to name a few. Lamb *fitfit* is another good dish made with onion, garlic, ginger, jalapeño, turmeric, and a spicy clarified butter that is scrambled with injera and softened with juice from the meat. Abyssinia also has a lunch buffet, served daily and priced under $10.

Bari Ristorante, 22 S. Cooper St., Memphis, TN 38104; (901) 722-2244; barimemphis.com; Italian; $$. This lovely Italian restaurant specializes in the fresh food cuisine of Puglia, and it is as charming inside as it is from the street. Housed in a 2-story brick building from the early 1900s, Bari has a cozy separate bar where bartenders mix a perfect blood-orange martini to complement Calbrese salami shaped like a rosebud and a trio of Italian cheeses. Owned and operated by Jason and Rebecca Severs (he's the chef, she's the manager), Bari has an all-Italian wine list, a commitment to local vendors and seasonal specials such as fresh Louisiana shrimp sautéed with organic Roma tomatoes, garlic, and basil. Bari's regular menu features plenty of other seafood, such as handmade cavatelli (a rolled pasta that looks like mini gnocchi) with fish, mussels, and calamari in a light tomato sauce. The antipasti at Bari also are excellent, offering such choices as calamari, smelt filets, and sardines lightly breaded, fried, and served with salt and lemon. The menu is vegetarian friendly, and Severs will cook off-menu on request. Simply put, Bari is an outstanding restaurant because it sticks to what it does best: combining simple, fresh ingredients into memorable plates. The Severs also own **Three Angels Diner** (p. 99), a more casual and family-friendly restaurant located on historic Broad Avenue in Midtown's emerging arts district.

Beauty Shop, 966 S. Cooper Ave., Memphis, TN 38104; (901) 272-7111; thebeautyshoprestaurant.com; Global/New American; $$. In 2003 trailblazer Karen Carrier poured her creative energy into the Beauty Shop, a restaurant in Cooper-Young that was a hair salon in the 1960s. (Its most famous customer, BTW, was Priscilla Presley.) In keeping with her trademark style, Carrier incorporated the salon's fixtures, including hair dryers and washing sinks, into the restaurant's decor. She also layered in hand-blown glass lights, midcentury-modern finishes, and a touch of kitsch for a symbiotic fusion of place and taste. Consider, for example, the Beauty Shop's re-creation of lunchtime American classics: House-made chips come with chipotle aioli; the club sandwich stacks house-cured salmon with red onion, guacamole, tomato, and mustard cream; and the cobb salad forgoes ham and turkey for crispy duck, mango, avocado, green beans, and Gouda goat cheese. Even the milk shakes at the Beauty Shop take exotic turns with flavors that change occasionally. (Recent examples include strawberry, balsamic vinegar, and cracked pepper.) Similar fusion flavors extend to dinner dishes such as Caribbean voodoo stew, and to Sunday brunch where customers line up for fried chicken and pecan waffles with eggs and a side of gravy. See Carrier's recipe for **Thai-Style Beef Salad with Chipotle Honey Vinaigrette** on p. 268.

Bhan Thai, 1324 Peabody, Memphis, TN 38104; (901) 272-1538; bhanthairestaurant.com; Thai; $–$$. Thai food is my favorite Asian cuisine, influenced largely by a tiny joint on Lincoln Boulevard in Venice, California, where I stopped twice a week for steaming bowls of *tom yum guy* to go. When I moved to Memphis 20 years ago, I was disheartened by the city's limited Thai food until 2002, when Bhan Thai opened in a refurbished turn-of-the-century home on

Homegrown Chains: Sekisui

While many restaurateurs have impacted the culinary scene in Memphis, none can make *this* claim except Jimmy Ishii: He brought sushi to Memphis. A native of Koru, Japan, Ishii attended St. Louis University, where he worked at a hibachi restaurant called Robata. When Benihana offered him a job, Ishii left school and moved to Memphis. He spent seven years at Benihana, working his way to head chef, but left in 1989 to open the first Sekisui on Humphrey's Boulevard in East Memphis. Customers crowded into Sekisui from the start, intrigued by slipping off their shoes to sit on pillows and ordering exotic plates expertly prepared by the master sushi chef Ishii hired from the West Coast. The skill of Sekisui's sushi chefs continues to attract customers who appreciate the restaurant's diverse menu of nigiri, rolls, and sushi combinations. In fact, Ishii put popular rolls suggested by customers on Sekisui's permanent menu to celebrate the chain's 15th anniversary. (One to try: Christy's roll made with prime tuna, crunchies, and cream cheese on the inside; avocado, smelt roe, cayenne, and sweet soy reduction on the outside.) Today, Ishii also operates Sekisui restaurants in Birmingham, Alabama; St. Louis, Missouri; and Chattanooga, Tennessee. In Memphis there are six Sekisui locations, including one in Midtown with a sushi bar that circles a moat. Chefs supply an ongoing parade of sushi so customers can pluck out a favorite while watching the pretty dishes float by on the water. Other locations spread from downtown to the suburbs, and menus and hours change from one Sekisui to the next. For more complete information, go to the chain's website at sekisuiusa.com/go.

Peabody. Oh happy day! Not only were the dishes authentic, but they were plated with an artistry new to me. Chef Alex Kamsrijan sculpted vegetables into delicate florets, garnishing intensely flavored ingredients with storybook whimsy. The same detail continues today, one of many reasons Bhan Thai is the perennial favorite for best Thai food in Memphis. While it's difficult to pick favorites, a few dishes stand out. Start with Andaman Secret, an off-menu appetizer of mussels, squid, shrimp, vegetables, and cilantro in basil sauce. Move on to red snapper fried golden, garnished with garlic, fresh pepper, and basil leaves and seasoned with tamarind hot-and-sour sauce. Homemade noodles shape the base of *chang mai* served with chicken or tofu in northern Thai curry sauce. Vegetarians will appreciate the restaurant's many meatless dishes, including starters like son-in-law eggs, which are deep fried and topped with sauce and crispy scallions. Everything else at Bhan Thai also adds up. The service is exemplary, and an outdoor patio gets rocking on warm summer nights.

The Brushmark, 1934 Poplar Ave., Memphis, TN 38104; (901) 544-6225; brooksmuseum.org/brushmarkrestaurant; New American; $–$$. Only one thing is wrong with the Brushmark. Except for special events, the restaurant only serves lunch on weekdays, brunch on Saturday and Sunday, and dinner on Thursday from 5 to 9 p.m. Located inside the Memphis Brooks Museum of Art, the restaurant typifies how perfect a limited menu can be. Credit belongs to Chefs

Wally Joe and Andrew Adams, who also steer their own restaurant in East Memphis called **Acre** (p. 127). Start with the Brushmark's signature Senegalese peanut soup and follow up with a mushroom flatbread sandwich with *tonkatsu*, garlic confit, jasmine rice, and edamame. I always learn a little something from the menus at the Brushmark, and tonkatsu is a Japanese deep-fried cutlet. Tonkatsu sauce (a type of Japanese Worchestershire made with pureed apples) also shows up for brunch. This time it is part of a blue-corn waffle plate with barbecue pork and jicama pineapple slaw. More traditional eaters can also be dazzled by the Brushmark's menu. The pastrami Reuben is house-cured brisket, and the grilled cheeseburger is dressed up just a tad with cornichons and roasted garlic mayo. On nice days, eat on the Brushmark terrace to enjoy the impressive trees in Overton Park, and after lunch, walk over to the Levitt Shell amphitheater, where a young Elvis Presley held his first concert.

Cafe Eclectic, 603 N. McLean Blvd., Memphis, TN 38107; (901) 725-1718; American/Cafe/Bakery; $. Comfortable cafe restaurants driven by local and organic foods are like a breath of fresh air in Memphis, where for decades plate lunches directed cafe menus. At Cafe Eclectic, the food is healthy and local but still familiar. Plus, they serve breakfast, lunch, dinner, and brunch. Lunch is a sure bet for chicken potpies, mac 'n' cheese and specials like fried cod sandwiches with homemade remoulade and a side of spring greens. Or try a bacon spinach salad with pear, pecans, feta, and bacon-sherry vinaigrette. Breakfast and brunch can include a wait at peak times, but hang in there. The stuffed french toast and buckwheat pancakes are excellent. So is the homemade Greek yogurt with honey, walnuts, and pomegranate syrup. The popular cafe also has an old-fashioned soda fountain with selections like s'more sundaes or malted milk shakes topped with whipped cream. Still, the cafe has more: a scratch bakery with house-made doughnuts, cake du jour, and scones. Don't miss my favorite scones: blueberry lemon made with lemon peel, wild blueberries, and a tangy lemon glaze. Vegans can also rejoice because Cafe Eclectic serves vegan blueberry and peach pie by the slice. In addition to its original Midtown location, Cafe Eclectic has a second restaurant in Harbor Town: 111 Harbor Town Sq., Memphis, TN 38103; (901) 590-5645.

Cafe 1912, 243 S. Cooper St., Memphis, TN 38104; (901) 722-2700; cafe1912.com; Bistro; $$–$$$. The entrance to Cafe 1912 opens directly into the dining room, and on busy nights, middle-age hipster types tumble in like it was a friend's Christmas party. A small but busy kitchen is visible from the door, adding to the restaurant's din of dishes and conversation. Fashioned after a French bistro in a building from 1912, the restaurant is a charming cache of Main Street America updated with food and drink for the new millennium. Filet and strip steaks are served with a choice of sauces, including chimichurri, a mix of olive oil, lemon, shallots and herbs. Nightly specials circle in, but stick with the standard menu of crepes, entrees, and burgers. The Maytag blue-cheese burger with bacon and roasted garlic aioli is sandwiched between ciabatta and served with a heaping side of shoestring pommes frites. For lighter fare, try the cafe's fried oyster salad on a bed of mixed greens. Oysters are fried with an expert's touch: crispy and golden on the outside and succulent in the middle. The salad also includes a splay of thinly sliced pears to balance the oysters' briny bite. For a quick meal and drinks, check out the cafe's backroom bar, where pours of a dozen different house wines are $6.50, and Belgian-style beers are priced about the same.

Cafe Society, 212 N. Evergreen St., Memphis, TN 38112; (901) 722-2177; cafesocietymemphis.com; Continental; $$–$$$. Chef-Owner Cullen Kent mixes Belgian and French influences into seafood, beef, and chicken dishes at this popular neighborhood restaurant in Midtown's Evergreen Historic District. Kent is a graduate of Le Cordon Bleu in Paris, and his French finesse shines through in perfect sole meunière, fricassee of escargot with wild mushrooms and chorizo, and filet of beef with warm mustard-tarragon potato salad. Lunch, served Monday through Friday, is a simpler affair with excellent sandwiches such as house-cured salmon and brioche grilled cheese, and braised brisket French dip. A nice way to get to know Cafe Society is to settle into its gorgeous mahogany bar where you can admire the restaurant's ambience and watch people come and go. Better yet, attend monthly wine tastings held the last Tuesday of every month by John Vego of **Buster's Liquors** (p. 231). Typically, the tastings cost $25, which covers cheese and half a dozen wines. Kent also prepares $5 small plates for the event. When the weather is nice, eat on Cafe Society's small sidewalk patio for a charming introduction to one of the prettiest neighborhoods in Memphis.

Cortona Contemporary Italian, 948 S. Cooper St., Memphis, TN 38104; (901) 729-0101; cortonacuisine.com; Italian/Pizza; $–$$. More than a dozen restaurants have failed to make a go of it at this northeast corner of Cooper and Young, despite the neighborhood's staying power. So before Cortona opened in early 2011, the priest from a nearby church sprinkled the restaurant with holy water. Almost two years later, Cortona is still busy and popular. Could it be the blessing? Perhaps, but more than likely the restaurant's success rests with Chef-Owner David Cleveland, who named Cortona after the Tuscan town where he spent two years cooking. While his food is Tuscan inspired, Cleveland tends to skip heavy sauces for more modern interpretations of Italian classics. His mushroom torta, for example, is a savory torte drizzled with balsamic-vinegar reduction and plated with arugula and Gorgonzola. Cleveland also hand cuts lasagna noodles from pasta sheets, creating a luscious foundation for meat sauce, fresh herbs, and a creamy blend of fontina and whole-milk mozzarella. His light walnut cream sauce cradles chicken and asparagus ravioli garnished with pesto, pine nuts, and Reggiano cheese. Even the desserts at Cortona are familiar but not predicable. Yes, tiramisu is on the menu, but so is triple-threat chocolate cake and almond torta with chocolate mousse and caramel. Cortona duplicates much of its dinner menu for lunch, which is a nice option for big appetites midday. The restaurant also offers Sunday brunch, weekday happy hours, and a small corner patio for people watching.

The Crazy Noodle, 2015 Madison Ave., Memphis, TN 38104; (901) 272-0928; Korean; $. Several good restaurants have come and gone where The Crazy Noodle now serves a streamlined menu of Korean noodle dishes. But owner Ji Choi can probably make this venture work because her sister's **Kwik Chek** (p. 89) deli next door is a fixture in Midtown. Choi also is an expert chef, tweaking her noodle bowls with unexpected flavors and pricing her dishes at $10 or less. This is a winning combination for noodle-starved foodies in Memphis who are effusive in their praise of Choi's big bowls served in pretty containers with lids. Try *jam-bong,* a spicy chicken broth with squid, shrimp, carrots, mushroom, zucchini, cabbage, and onions, or *yuk-gae-jang,* a delicious beef broth with sliced beef, turnips, and bean sprouts. The Crazy Noodle also serves half a dozen hot- and cold-noodle dishes. The spicy red pepper sauce on the bibim seafood noodle is excellent. Side dishes are limited but good. Vege-jean turns chopped root vegetables into crispy Korean latkes, and the tofu salad is a pretty picture on a plate.

Dō, 964 S. Cooper Ave., Memphis, TN 38104; (901) 272-0830; dosushimemphis.com; Sushi; $–$$. Karen Carrier's Tokyo-style sushi bar is an upbeat example of how fun food can be, especially when shared with someone special. A favorite for hipsters of all ages, Dō squeezes in an eclectic mix of decor and seating in a small space. Four-tops and white gauze curtains run along one wall, a bar fills up another, and vintage-furniture finds decorate the window bay. Then there's the long plank table in the center of the room, where no one's a stranger by their second Champagne Dream, a lovely concoction of Champagne, vodka, and plum sake. Expect a similar personality from Dō's inventive menu of nigiri, sushi rolls, noodle bowls, tempera, and bento boxes. The restaurant offers daily specials based on seasonal produce and the creative whims of the kitchen. Personal favorites include BBQ eel nigiri and the rich and buttery Andre roll, a combination of bacon, cilantro, jalapeño, Tabasco, and a type of escolar called walu. The menu also offers plenty of dishes for meat lovers, who should not miss the beef sashimi or the Kobe beef noodle bowl, a Thai-inspired combination of panang curry, coconut milk, lemongrass, and leaves from kaffir limes. Carrier also owns the **Beauty Shop** (p. 74) next door, so save room for a slice of the restaurant's strawberry or caramel layer cake. Since the restaurants share a kitchen, you can order dessert without changing tables.

Fresh Slices Sidewalk Cafe & Deli, 1585 Overton Park Ave., Memphis, TN 38107; (901) 725-1001; freshslicesrestaurants.com; Cafe/Deli; $–$$. Fresh Slices has three locations, but first-time visitors should eat at the original location on Overton Park Avenue. Part of a cute strip of brick storefronts, the restaurant is located on one of the most beautiful residential streets in Memphis, where many homes date to the early 1900s. The cafe's sidewalk patio with oversize umbrellas is a perfect place to appreciate the neighborhood and to study the menu, which is extensive. In fact, this is what Susan Ellis of **Hungry Memphis** (p. 11) had to say after a recent visit: "If you can't find anything to eat at Fresh Slices, just forget it and go home. You are impossible." For sandwiches, the menu lists more than 30 varieties, so indecisive types might head directly for the final choice: a "big boy" beef hot dog topped with diced onions, diced peppers, and sweet relish, and served with seasoned fries. Operating since 2004, Fresh Slices has featured dozens of dishes from the start, and some are better than others. Entrees ring in around $12 and include seafood, chicken, pasta, and steak. Some trend Caribbean, such as coconut-crusted tilapia with Creole rice and black bean and corn relish. Youngsters will like the kid's meals, which include all the expected favorites with chips for $3.50. In addition to the original cafe, Fresh Slices also has cafes at 8556 Macon Rd., Cordova, TN 38018, (901) 756-8774; and 6600 Stage Rd., Bartlett, TN 38134, (901) 388-0270.

Fuel Cafe, 1761 Madison Ave., Memphis, TN 38104; (901) 725-9025; fuelcafememphis.com; New American/Vegetarian/Vegan; $–$$.

Fuel Cafe is a bit of a misnomer. The name Fuel derives from its location, not its healthy food. The building at the corner of Madison and Auburndale was built in the 1920s as a gas station, and the famed Mobile Pegasus adorned the top of the building for decades. It was converted into a restaurant in the late '90s, attracting several different occupants until early 2010, when Fuel opened with an updated interpretation of an American cafe. While some of the food at Fuel reflects traditional cafe fare, the menu is chef driven and all natural: meat and poultry are grass fed; seafood is wild caught; and dishes change seasonally. About half of Fuel's customers are vegetarian or vegan, so Chef Andrew Armstrong's menu goes well beyond grilled cheese. Try the eggplant caviar, quinoa, and red bean chili, or vegetarian walnut and cheese "meat loaf" with mashed potatoes and mushroom leek gravy. Meat eaters will be happy, too, especially when they bite into the Fuel bison burger and hand-cut fries served with this trio of dipping sauces: white truffle Parmesan, red pepper rouille, and sweet chile. Dinner entrees stay affordable but showcase Armstrong's talent to elevate home cooking. Here are a few current favorites: chicken paillard niçoise with lemon tapenade, cherry tomatoes, haricots verts, and fingerling potatoes, with a handcrafted ice pop for dessert. Fuel also serves Saturday brunch and operates an extremely popular food truck by the same name (p. 24).

Golden India, 2097 Madison Ave., Memphis, TN 38104; (901) 728-5111; goldenindiarestauranttn.com; Indian; $–$$. When it comes to Indian cuisine, an American gold standard is tandoori and tikka, specifically chicken in a traditional yogurt-based marinade that is cooked over red-hot charcoals in a traditional tandoor oven. Golden Indian's tandoori and tikka chicken dishes hit all the right notes, especially when eaten with freshly steamed basmati rice and garlic naan or *deema,* a type of naan stuffed with minced lamb. Chef's specials from north Indian are also good. Try lamb, chicken, or beef *karahi,* a Pakistani specialty that derives its name from the traditional wok-like pot used to cook it. While buffets are typical at Indian restaurants, the midday spread at Golden Indian is exceptionally good and served all week, offering more than 20 vegetarian and meat dishes with chutneys, condiments, breads, and desserts for $8.50. (Children eat for $5.) The restaurant also serves a nice selection of beer and wine, but don't overlook the nonalcoholic choices, especially Indian coffee and mango lassi. A longtime tenant of historic Overton Square, Golden Indian is a charming space for some, a little funky for others. Most customers agree, however, on the restaurant's service, which is efficient and friendly.

Imagine Vegan Cafe, 2156 Young Ave., Memphis, TN 38104; (901) 654-3455; Vegan; $. At first glance, Imagine Cafe looks a little like a coffeehouse. There's a sandwich board on the sidewalk listing specials, local giveaway literature stacked on the corner of the bar, and Christmas lights strung loosely from the ceiling. But then you notice the toddlers running around and think, "Wait, this place is wholesome." I'll say. Although the menu uses descriptions like chicken, steak, and cheese, Imagine Cafe is strictly vegan, specializing in comfort food favorites such as country-fried seitan with gravy, mac and vegan cheese, eggless egg salad, smoked sausage and peppers, beef tips and onions, fried chicken nuggets, and peanut butter–soy-milk shakes. Although Imagine had a bit of a shaky start when it opened in 2011 next to Cooper-Young's Goner Records, owners Kristie and Adam Jeffrey quickly found their stride. At the cafe's one-year anniversary buffet, customers packed the restaurant for a vegan menu that reads like a throwback to favorite kid foods. (Can you say pigs in blankets?) Sides include lots of fresh veggies, and desserts are exceptional thanks to vegan baker Karina Khan's layer cakes, cupcakes, and brownies. Imagine also serves Sunday brunch and a good selection of craft beers such as Rouge Dead Guy, Abita Turbodog, and Saranac Caramel Porter. There's no wine, but you can bring your own for a reasonable cork fee.

India Palace, 1720 Poplar Ave., Memphis, TN 38104; (901) 278-1199; indiapalacememphis.com; Indian; $. The colorful tile mural on the exterior of India Palace is a convincing draw, especially for first-timers. So is the friendly greeting at the door and the flawless service that carries through the entire meal. Inside, the restaurant is spacious, spotlessly clean, and decorated with large murals of elephants, which seem to fascinate toddlers while their parents stay focused on the lunch buffet. The buffet at India Palace is almost legendary with workers, and for good reason. The food is hot, fresh, and there's no waiting. Plus the $9 buffet offers several varieties of naan, assorted appetizers such as samosa and chicken *pakoras,* perfect basmati rice, and an endless choice of vegetarian and meat-centric dishes. If you like your Indian food extra spicy, skip the buffet and order off the menu. The kitchen is happy to kick up the heat. Like most Indian restaurants, the menu at India Palace can be daunting, so head directly for the chef's specialties, which are cooked in Indian iron skillets called *karahi.* The chicken *fraizee,* a house specialty, is also excellent, especially when accompanied by *karahi aloo palak,* a freshly chopped spinach cooked with potatoes, onions, tomatoes, and spices.

Jasmine Thai and Vegetarian Restaurant, 916 S. Cooper Ave., Memphis, TN 38104; (901) 725-0223; Thai/Vegetarian; $-$$. Jasmine Thai is a small gem of a place tucked in a converted house in Cooper-Young. Large parties should call ahead to save tables, but otherwise the restaurant is a perfect drop-in spot for Thai and vegetarian dishes that are consistently good. Owners Pam and Justin Fong started their restaurant in the early '90s in the Memphis suburb of Bartlett. They added a vegetarian menu a few years later and eventually moved to Midtown, where many of their customers lived. Thanks to the couple's vegetarian focus, even the restaurant's meat and seafood dishes are loaded with fresh veggies, so side dishes are superfluous. Instead, order sweet-and-hot tofu curry or house *lad na,* a satisfying bowl of drunken noodles with, among other things, beef, chicken, black beans, peppers, and bamboo shoots. On my last visit, I asked Pam to explain the ingredients in Jasmine's dim sum dipping sauce. She sent her husband to the table (he's the main chef) who gave me a mini cooking lesson. A few minutes later, Justin reemerged from the kitchen to show me how his thumb is imprinted on his wooden wok ladle from so many years of cooking. Could there be any more endearing exchange with a chef than that?

Kwik Chek, 2013 Madison Ave., Memphis TN 38104; (901) 274-9293; Korean/Greek/Deli; $. My college-age daughter said this when she heard about the *Food Lovers' Guide to Memphis:* "Don't forget about Kwik Chek." Leave it to young people to find the best $6 meal in Memphis. From the outside, Kwik Chek looks like a run-down convenience store, potholes and all. Inside, the place still feels confusing: beer cases on one wall, a checkout on the other, a deli counter along the back, and a few tables and quickie-mart snacks in the center. Even the menu has a bit of a personality disorder. There are Korean dishes like *pajeon* (egg pancakes with vegetables and shrimp) and bibimbap; hoagies like the Turk (turkey, provolone, bell pepper, onion, tomato, lettuce, Parmesan, and lemon-herb dressing); and Mediterranean favorites such as gyros and falafels. Kwik Chek has Philly steak and tuna salad, too, but even these American classics taste better than average because they are made to order with secret add-ons. At Kwik Chek, most menu descriptions include the words *spice, sauce,* or *dressing,* and these flavorful mash-ups keep the food unique.

La Baguette, 3088 Poplar Ave., Memphis, TN 38111; (901) 458-0900; Cafe/Bakery/Bread; $–$$. La Baguette French Bread Shop is a mixed bag, depending on expectations. For some customers, the bakery's mix of tarts, éclairs, and special-order cakes are as close to Paris as they care to get. For others, the bread and pastry fall short. Either way, most folks value the bakery's affordable selection of day-old products and the hot cross buns sold only during Lent. And in Memphis, where independent bakeries are few and far between, La Baguette fills a niche. The bakery, operating since 1976, also doubles as a popular cafe, especially for lunch when business workers and homemakers with kids crowd in for quiche, soups, salads, and sandwiches. Soups change day to day, but order spicy tomato or corn chowder if they are available. Sandwiches are priced under $5 and include house-made versions of these Southern classics on baguettes: egg and olive, chunky pimento cheese, and chicken salad topped with scallions and sliced almonds. While the bakery opens to the parking lot, the restaurant's cute cafe tables meander down the interior corridor of Chickasaw Oaks Mall, making lunch feel a little like a midday visit to the French Pavilion at Epcot Center.

Memphis Pizza Cafe, 2087 Madison Ave., Memphis, TN 38104; (901) 726-5343; memphispizzacafe.com; Pizza; $–$$. At the bottom of the take-out menu for Memphis Pizza Cafe are small block letters that say VOTED MEMPHIS' BEST PIZZA. A listing of 18 consecutive years follow the headline, beginning with 1994, not long after the restaurant opened in historic Overton Square. While other restaurants in Memphis serve better pizzas, Memphis Pizza Cafe undoubtedly has the most loyal local following. Maybe it's because every teenager in town knows somebody who works at one of the cafe's five locations or because families flock to the restaurants for fast meals after soccer games. An integral part of the community, Memphis Pizza Cafe also gives back, participating in a number of annual events for local non-profits. The restaurant prides itself on fresh ingredients, offering dozens of toppings for thin-crust pizza with house-made dough. The no-sauce pizza is particularly good. Memphis Pizza Cafe also serves the standard selection of subs, along with meatball and provolone and blackened chicken and cheddar. Over the years, the restaurant has opened four suburban locations, but the original restaurant in Midtown is the one to visit, especially when servers open the restaurant's charming french doors to help soften the summer heat. Other Memphis Pizza Cafes are located at 5061 Park Ave., Memphis, TN 38117, (901) 684-1306; 7604 W. Farmington, Germantown, TN 38138, (901) 753-2218; 797 W. Poplar Ave., Collierville, TN 38017, (901) 861-7800; 5627 Getwell Rd., Southhaven, MS 38672, (662) 536-1364.

Pho Hoa Binh, 1615 Madison Ave., Memphis, TN 38104; (901) 276-0006; Vegan/Vietnamese; $. From the outside, Pho Hoa Binh is easy to skip, especially for newcomers who might be put off by the chunks of asphalt missing in the parking lot. Push through any hesitation and order lemongrass tofu to go, even if you're not a vegetarian. Your order will be double bagged and knotted, but the dish will still fill the car with such an intoxicating fragrance that you will be struggling to untie the bag for a taste test by the second stoplight. The secret to Pho Hoa Binh's tofu is this: It's double fried and drenched with lemongrass, so the flavors are layered into every bite. The tofu is also included in the restaurant's lunch buffet, which is much loved in Memphis because the food is consistent, and the cost is $6. Vegans will appreciate Pho Hoa Binh's dozen or so seitan dishes, including barbecue (of course!), kung pao, and curry. Overall, the small family-run restaurant offers almost 200 choices, so there are plenty of dishes with beef, chicken, pork, squid, and crab. A few to try: pho thai, a wonderful beef noodle soup with plenty of cilantro, mint, and jalapeños; pepper steak; chicken with vermicelli, lemongrass, onions, and fish sauce; and green shell mussels.

Restaurant Iris, 2146 Monroe, Memphis, TN 38104; (901) 590-2828; French/Creole; $$–$$$. Every spring, amateur photographers submit their favorite photos of Tennessee's state flower to Restaurant Iris in hopes of winning a dinner for two. Customers vote online for their favorite iris pic, and the friendly competition is a nice metaphor for Kelly English's personality and position. English is the city's most celebrated chef both locally (best chef, best restaurant, and best service for three consecutive years) and nationally (James Beard Award semifinalist and *Food and Wine* best new chef). English is also a hell of a nice guy who works hard to promote Memphis restaurants and local food purveyors. A native of Baton Rouge, English worked with New Orleans celebrity chef John Besh before moving to Memphis in 2008 to open Restaurant Iris in the home of the former La Tourelle, a storied French restaurant where some of the city's best chefs trained. English continues the reputation of the converted Queen Anne home near Overton Square, with signature French/Creole dishes like his lobster "knuckle sandwich" with tarragon and tomatoes. Restaurant Iris serves dishes both a la carte and as a 5-course "degustation" menu with wine pairings. Dishes use local and seasonal ingredients to showcase English's love for traditional Louisiana cooking. Begin with a salad of brussels sprouts, bacon, and sherry, and continue with Gulf speckled trout amandine or soft-shell crab with *maque choux,* oyster mushrooms, and sauce Choron. Another win-win choice is Kelly's "surf and turf," a New York strip stuffed with fried oysters and blue cheese; meat-loving friends laud this dish more often than any other steak in the city. See Chef English's recipe for **Amandine of Gulf Flasher & Cauliflower Puree** on p. 276.

Saigon Le, 51 N. Cleveland, Memphis, TN 38104; (901) 276-5326; saigon-le.com; Vietnamese/Chinese/Thai; $–$$. Thick menus with covers and color photos are both awesome and intimidating. Will taste translate from laminated promises to dishes on the table? Will decisions about what to order change with every page? Yes and yes at this popular Vietnamese restaurant located across the street from **Viet Hoa** (p. 122) supermarket on a scruffy stretch of Cleveland Street. Unlike some Asian restaurants with menus that seldom change, Saigon Le keeps inventing new dishes, like crispy tofu with jalapeños and twice-cooked white noodles with beef, pork, shrimp, and chicken. Maybe the recipes are being discussed by the women at the back booth peeling their way through a bottomless bowl of carrots. Or maybe the folks in the kitchen just like to cook new things. Either way, a meal at Saigon Le is an adventure, especially if you try the kung pao's spicy pepper sauce, the oversize pancake appetizers, or anything on the Vietnamese side of the menu. Here are a few dishes to discover: tofu curry; catfish soup; sliced beef with vermicelli, vegetables, lemongrass, and fish sauce; and clear noodle soup with barbecue pork, squid, shrimp, and crab.

Soul Fish Cafe, 862 S. Cooper, Memphis, TN 38104; (901) 725-0722; soulfishcafe.com; Po' Boys/Plate Lunches; $. Sometimes a name says it all. So goes Soul Fish, an unpretentious cafe with soul food like vegetable plates and fish food like blackened tilapia. Soul Fish opened in a non-description cinder-block building in 2006, and customers loved the place from the start. My daughter, who lives in Brooklyn, heads to Soul Fish as soon as she arrives home and orders the same thing for every visit: a fried catfish po' boy with lettuce, tomato, and house-made remoulade. The remoulade is exactly right, one of several unexpected extras that moves Soul Fish beyond predictable. Other surprises include seasoned cornmeal, fresh and tangy pico de gallo, homemade croutons, and mashed potatoes that are better than mom's. The veggie plates are good, offering seasonal add-ons to menu standards like Cajun cabbage, pickled green tomatoes, and sweet-potato fries. Along with catfish and tilapia, the restaurant serves two smoked pork tenderloin po' boys: the Memphis with bacon, coleslaw, and barbecue sauce and the Cuban with ham, pickles, mustard, Cuban mayo, and swiss cheese. Service is efficient and upbeat at Soul Fish, especially when servers are suggesting root beer floats or a slice of caramel pecan pie. In addition to the original location in Cooper-Young, Soul Fish has a second restaurant at 3160 Village Shops Dr., Germantown, TN 38138; (901) 755-6988.

Stone Soup Cafe & Market, 993 S. Cooper, Memphis, TN 38104; (901) 922-5314; stonesoupcafememphis.com; Cafe/Plate Lunches; $. It's always great to see a start-up hit a home run with a second restaurant. Such is the story with Sharon Johnson, whose bakery and lunch cafe called Buns on the Run closed a few years ago. For her new venture, she teamed up with Emily Bishop and moved to a more prominent location across the street from the Saturday farmers' market in the same Cooper-Young neighborhood. Located in a converted cottage, Stone Soup Cafe has the same homey feel as the bakery but offers expanded menus for breakfast and lunch.

Eating Vegan in Memphis: It's Not As Hard As Visitors Might Think

In a city like Memphis, where greens are cooked with bacon and butter rules, can vegans eat out? Absolutely, says Bianca Phillips, author of a new cookbook called *Cooking Crunk: Eating Vegan in the Dirty South*.

"People assume that it's hard to find vegan food in the barbecue capital of the world," Phillips says. "But over the past few years, vegan options at Memphis restaurants have exploded."

Consider the one-year anniversary party for **Imagine Vegan Cafe** (p. 86), the city's only all-vegan restaurant located in the Midtown neighborhood of Cooper-Young. To celebrate, owners Kristie and Adam Jeffrey staged an all-you-can-eat vegan buffet with such comfort foods as spinach dip, pigs in blankets, mac and cheese, and raspberry tarts. The party was so well attended that many customers ate standing up.

"If I had one final day to eat in Memphis, I'd start with Memphis Slam at Imagine Cafe for brunch," Phillips says, describing a plate of biscuits, tofu scramble, sausage, gravy, and cheese sauce, all vegan versions, of course.

In addition to Imagine, a handful of more upscale eateries, including **Ciao Bella Italian Grill** (p. 132) in East Memphis, prepare vegan entrees by request. Memphis chefs enjoy cooking special dishes for vegans, Phillips says: "It gives them a chance to showcase their creativity."

A sampling of some of the most popular restaurants with vegan food follows. For a complete guide, check out the dining listings on Phillips's blog called *Vegan Crunk* (vegancrunk.blogspot.com).

Cosmic Coconut (p. 162) is a vegan juice bar serving smoothies made with coconut milk, homemade soups, and healthy snacks like kale chips and coconutties, an addictive cookie ball made with cashews, almonds, and cocoa.

Dejavu's (p. 58) menu is a bit far-fetched, but it's all good: soul food, Creole food, and vegan food. Vegan options include mock chicken salad and spinach-mushroom quesadillas dressed up with News Orleans spice.

Fuel Cafe (p. 84) is an American diner where carnivores (try the bison burger) can eat alongside vegan friends. Popular vegan dishes include nachos topped with quinoa chili and tofu-stuffed manicotti.

Muddy's Bake Shop (p. 171) is a from-scratch bakery where vegan cupcakes have cute names such as Vegan Almond Brothers (almond cake with almond icing). Muddy's also makes vegan pies with hand-rolled dough and fruit fillings such as roasted apples and toasted pecans.

Pho Hoa Binh (p. 91) serves a tofu-heavy lunch buffet for about $7. Other excellent dishes include kung pao tofu with peanuts and pea pods and lemongrass tofu, an almost legendary dish in Memphis that is fragrant and crispy.

R. P. Tracks (p. 218) is a student hangout for the University of Memphis, so it makes sense that its signature dish is "world famous barbecue tofu." Even better, the barbecue tofu comes in a myriad of ways: nachos, burritos, sandwiches, and quesadillas.

Three Angels Diner (p. 99) is a farm-to-table restaurant with a vegetarian twist. Popular vegan dishes include mock egg salad; tofu scramble with red pepper, Portobello mushrooms, and smoky paprika; and a daily selection of veggies for the diner's plate lunches.

Open from 7 a.m. to 3 p.m. (except for Sunday when it opens at 9 a.m.), Stone Soup Cafe serves fresh homemade food with a touch of Southern whimsy. Breakfast includes excellent biscuits and gravy, quiche lorraine, and standout crepes filled with sweetened cream cheese and toppings like fresh blueberries, peanut butter, and banana. Lunch offers the full complement of salads (try the stuffed tomato), sandwiches (available on gluten-free bread), and plate lunch specials like roasted pork loin and lasagna. The cafe's list of vegetables is always impressive because choices move beyond fried okra and greens. Typical veggie specials included corn salad, cucumber salad, and carrot-raisin salad all on the same day. After eating, be sure to wander down the hall to the cafe's market to admire the scrumptious bakery case filled with assorted goodies all locally made.

Sweet Grass, 937 S. Cooper, Memphis, TN 38104; (901) 278-0278; Low Country; $$. At a dinner party last summer, I made osso bucco with **Newman Farm** (p. 254) Berkshire pork. Guests heaped on the praise, including this memorable comment: "Your osso bucco is better than Sweet Grass's." I mention the compliment because the spontaneous reference illustrates the shining halo that stays wrapped around Ryan Trimm's Sweet Grass, voted best new restaurant by every publication in Memphis when it opened in 2010. Sweet Grass is named after the fragrant perennial that grows along the Carolina coast, a fitting reference for Trimm's low-country-style cuisine made with local ingredients. While many chefs in Memphis incorporate Southern influences into their cooking, no one serves Carolina specialties with Trimm's singular focus. I've tried a number of Trimm's small, medium, and large plates, and I've been more than pleased with every dish. Start with oyster stew or mussels with sweet peppers, pickled onions, tomatoes, and fresh sorrel. Follow with shrimp and grits combined with sea scallops, house-made sausage, and Benton's country ham. Save room for deep-dish sour-cream apple pie and share if you must. Sweet Grass is also popular for craft beers, classic cocktails, and appetizers after work. Sunday brunch is busy but worth the wait, especially if a house-made Bloody Mary with pickled okra helps pass the time. The brunch menu is more lunch than breakfast, but who needs cereal on Sunday? Try this hefty and flavorful plate instead: 2 poached eggs layered with a crab cake, fried green tomatoes, and lemon-basil hollandaise sauce. See Chef Trimm's recipes for **Frogmore Stew** on p. 278 and **Shrimp & Grits** on p. 279.

Three Angels Diner, 2617 Broad Ave., Memphis, TN 38112; (901) 452-1111; threeangelsdiner.com; Diner/Vegetarian/Vegan; $. Three Angels Diner is closed on Mon, so next-door neighbor Babak Tabatabai got busy, building the diner a new shingled awning to get ready for a visit from Guy Fieri with *Diners, Drive-ins and Dives*. The gesture says a lot about the charm of the neighborhood and the diner's place in it. Since opening in 2010, Three Angels has introduced many customers to the Broad Avenue arts district and new food niche: healthy comfort food. Some customers know owners Jason and Rebecca Severs from **Bari** (p. 73), their popular Italian restaurant in Midtown. Others are drawn to the couple's commitment to sustainable practices. They buy local, recycle cooking oil, and tote kitchen scraps to the **Urban Farms** (p. 121) compost pile located nearby. Even more customers come for the food, a great-tasting mix of updated diner classics. Lunch plates, for instance, change with the seasons, offering vegetables like roasted brussels sprouts and green beans sautéed with white wine vinegar. The burgers, made with responsibly raised beef, are hefty, and the condiments are house-made. Named after the Severses' children, Three Angels does have a family bonhomie, offering kid-friendly foods like macaroni and cheese, icebox pie, and blueberry pancakes for Sunday brunch. Happily, the restaurant also has a full-service bar and stays open late. Even parents need a cocktail, right?

Tsunami, 928 S. Cooper, Memphis, TN 38104; (901) 274-2556; tsunami memphis.com; Pacific Rim/Seafood; $$–$$$. I have a handful of taste memories that never fade: the first time I ate a Pepperidge Farm Milano cookie; the first time I dipped a fresh California artichoke in warm butter; and the first time I ate roasted sea bass at Tsunami when the restaurant opened in 1998. Long before sea bass become the darling of modern American menus, Chef Ben Smith prepared the perfect plate, stacking the fish on black Thai rice with a drizzle of beurre blanc. His signature dish is still on the menu (and on the cover of *The Tsunami Restaurant Cookbook*), but don't think Smith is stuck in the past. Instead, he updates his original seafood focus with local purveyors, seasonal ingredients, and new menu twists. He recently added *izakaya* to his selection of small plates. Izakaya is a type of Japanese tapas bar, and Smith's spin includes wasabi deviled eggs, blue cheese potato croquettes with Sriracha cream, and rice vermicelli with shrimp in spicy coconut broth. Smith parlays similar creativity into his entrees, including the restaurant's vegetarian options like goat cheese and fried eggplant napoleon with roasted red pepper sauce and basil oil. (Even eggplant haters should give this dish a try.) An anchor of the Cooper-Young neighborhood, Tsunami has seen both high-end and casual restaurants come and go. It remains unfazed, offering its distinct enclave for a romantic dinner, cocktails at the bar, or late-night appetizers on a small sidewalk patio.

20/20 Diner, 1245 Madison Ave., Memphis, TN 38104; (901) 722-3289; Cafe; $. 20/20 Diner is located on the fourth floor of the Southern College of Optometry, but the cafe's predictability stops with its name. Instead of standard fare, Kathy Katz makes soups, salads, and sandwiches from scratch that are unique enough to keep lunch interesting. Katz's African peanut soup and roasted red-pepper hummus are customer favorites, and her daily specials offer such dishes as a Greek burrito: spinach, feta, and Parmesan wrapped in filo dough, baked and topped with marinara sauce. Vegetarians will appreciate the cafe's many options, including its pimento cheese that sets a new standard for a Southern favorite.

In addition to cheddar and pimentos, Katz adds house-made mayo, green onions, and cream cheese to her pimento for a spread that makes crackers seem superfluous. Many people skip 20/20 Diner because they assume it's an in-house cafeteria for students and faculty. It's not. Just be ready to show your driver's license to the security guard on the first floor and then take the elevator upstairs. Another option is to find Katz at the **Memphis Farmers Market (p. 67)** on Saturday or the Wednesday **Farmers' Market at the Garden** (p. 164) in East Memphis. Along with her spreads, hummus, and pimento cheese, Katz sells take-and-bake dishes such as spanakopita and lasagna.

Landmarks

Bogie's Delicatessen, 2098 LaSalle, Memphis, TN 38104; (901) 272-0022; bogiesdeli.com; Deli; $. JoLynn Greer started working at Bogie's Deli in the early 1990s when it was owned by Robert and Elizabeth Renfro, transplants to Memphis from Virginia Beach. The couple missed eating at a New York–style deli, so they opened their own, serving Boar's Head meats, and soups, salads, and desserts from favorite family recipes. When the Renfros decided to sell the business, the Greer family jumped in to keep Bogie's locally owned. The Greers continue the Renfros' "everything is homemade" mantra and use many of the couple's original recipes. Every morning restaurant chefs make water bagels and boil farm-raised chicken breasts for Bogie's popular chicken salad. Then they use the chicken broth for pastas and daily soup specials such as chicken wild rice. Bogie's shrimp, tuna, pasta, fruit, and broccoli-bacon salads, sold by the sandwich or the pound, are favorites with regular customers. Explains Greer, "A local doctor eats here almost every day, and he always orders the same thing: a turkey chef and a small fruit salad." While the original Bogie's is in East Memphis, on Mendenhall Rd., first-time visitors should stop by the Midtown location, which has a nice front porch shaded by a perky aqua awning. Plus, the location shares a parking lot with Malco's Studio on The Square, a favorite local theater. Other locations include: 715 S. Mendenhall Rd., Memphis, TN 38117, (901) 761-5846; 80 Monroe Ave., Memphis TN 38103, (901) 525-6764; 2028 W. Poplar Ave., Memphis, TN 38017, (901) 854-8555.

Broadway Pizza House, 2581 Broad Ave., Memphis, TN 38112; (901) 454-7930; broadwaypizzamemphis.com; Pizza; $–$$. Broadway Pizza opened in 1977, the same year Elvis died, but the timing doesn't dampen the restaurant's heartfelt connection to the King of Rock 'n' Roll. Lana Cox, the founder of Broadway Pizza, delivered pizzas to Elvis as a teenager from a place called White's on Jackson Avenue. When Cox opened her own restaurant, she put a drawing of Elvis on the front of her laminated menu, a decision she was later forced to defend in court. She eventually won the copyright case, but the settlement included one stipulation: The menus must stay

ELVIS, PIZZA & BARBECUE: COLETTA'S RESTAURANT PERFECTS A MEMPHIS TRIFECTA

Here's something to get your hands around in addition to a fat slice of barbecue pizza from Coletta's Restaurant: Priscilla Presley was probably one of the first pizza delivery girls in Memphis.

At the time, Jerry Coletta was a young man working at his family's restaurant after college. He and his wife, Diane, still operate Coletta's, but Jerry is more than happy to sit down in the restaurant's Elvis room and reminisce about his most famous customer.

He remembers Priscilla and her friend Sandy Schilling, the wife of Memphis mafia member Jerry Schilling, stopping by Coletta's several times a week to bring pizza home to Graceland. "They were so beautiful," Coletta says. "All the guys in the restaurant would go crazy when they came in."

Coletta's pizza was so popular at Graceland that Elvis asked for a restaurant charge account, and Col. Tom Parker paid the bills every month. "We sent a bill, and the colonel mailed back a check," Coletta says. "I probably should have held on to a few of them."

Occasionally, Elvis visited Coletta's late at night and sat in the room now decorated with photos and memorabilia, including an Elvis-era menu, when regular pizzas cost $1.75, meatball subs cost 40 cents, and a slice of pie cost a quarter. "We'd close the room's doors so he could have some privacy," Coletta says. "But when Elvis went to the bathroom, he'd have two bodyguards, one on either side."

Even without the Elvis connection, Coletta's is a landmark restaurant in Memphis with an impressive history of hard work and tenacity. Coletta's grandfather, an Italian immigrant, started the business in 1923 as an ice-cream parlor. During the early 1950s, his father, Horest Coletta, switched from ice cream to Italian food, serving traditional family recipes and introducing Memphis to its first restaurant pizza.

"Sailors would come in from Millington and ask for pizza," Coletta says. "My dad didn't know what pizza was, and neither did most people in Memphis."

To stimulate interest, Horest developed what became Coletta's trademark dish: a deep-dish barbecue pizza. From the start, customers loved the combination of house-made sauce and a generous topping of smoky barbecue. In fact, the barbecue pizza is still earning accolades more than 60 years later. In a March 2012 issue, *Parade* magazine included Coletta's barbecue pizza in its Pizza Hall of Fame, along with nine other restaurants from across the country.

The unexpected publicity is pulling in out-of-town visitors, and some may be a little startled by Coletta's well-worn exterior and its retro bar that feels like a wine cellar at Disneyland. If so, remember this: Coletta's is the oldest continuously operating restaurant in Memphis, and its accoutrements are as authentic as the family's hospitality and kitchen's pulled pork.

Coletta's Restaurant, *1063 S. Parkway East, Memphis, TN 38106, (901) 948-7652; and 2850 Appling Rd., Memphis, TN 38133, (901) 383-1122; Italian/Pizza; $.*

in the restaurant. "Everyone wants to take one, but we have to say no," says daughter Dewana Ishee, who carries on her mother's devotion with Elvis memorabilia in the restaurant, including a karate belt worn by the King himself. These days, Ishee's children and husband help her run the family business, which is the bellwether of a neighborhood that has seen its ups and downs. For the past few years, artists and hip proprietors have turned historic Broad Avenue into an emerging arts district. Happily, Broadway stays exactly the same, serving 30 different pizza combinations on garlic butter crust, house specialties like Southern fried catfish, and homemade pies and cakes.

Dino's Grill, 645 N. McLean Ave., Memphis, TN 38107; (901) 278-9127; dinosgrill.com; Italian / Plate Lunches; $. When a member of my book club suggested Dino's Grill for an upcoming meeting, the group got almost rapturous. Everyone, it seems, had a fond connection to Dino's, a Memphis tradition since it opened in 1941 on the downtown corner of Main Street and Beale. In 1972, Dino's moved to its present Midtown location, bringing along long-standing family recipes for traditional Italian dishes and meat-and-threes. These days, Dino's is a neighborhood restaurant in the truest sense: kicked back, consistent, and filled with regular customers who like all the options. And there are plenty. Open 7 days a week, Dino's serves breakfast, lunch, dinner, and takeout. Breakfast starts at 7:30 a.m. with homemade biscuits and all the trimmings. Lunch offers sandwiches such as Italian steak and peppers plus plate lunches and $5 specials (on Wednesday, for example, $5 buys a burger, drink, and fries). Dinner includes Italian dishes like stuffed jumbo shells with a side of spaghetti or toasted ravioli, Dino's signature dish. The ravioli is stuffed with ground chicken and spices and made fresh every day. Dino's also sells uncooked ravioli, which is a nice to-go meal along with a quart of the restaurant's Sunday gravy. Better yet, pull up a chair and stay a while for all-you-can-eat spaghetti offered every Thursday night.

Molly's La Casita, 2006 Madison Ave., Memphis, TN 38104; (901) 726-1873; mollyslacasita.com; Mexican; $. Let's cut right to the chase on Molly's. Yes, the tamales are homemade, but so are the margaritas, and it's the salty-rimmed margaritas that many Memphians treasure, especially on Margarita Monday when La Casita Margaritas are discounted all day. The secret margarita recipe came from Molly Gonzales, the restaurant's founder and namesake, who had her first restaurant across the river in West Memphis in the early 1950s. In 1974, she opened Molly's in the original Toddle House on Lamar Avenue. Gonzales relocated the restaurant to its current location in 1982, establishing her Tex-Mex favorites in a pink adobe building on Madison Avenue. Gonzales learned to cook from her father, and many of the family's recipes remain on the menu today. House favorites include Red Snapper a la Casita with rice and spicy green beans, and shrimp tacos in lightly grilled tortillas. The surprise ingredient in the tacos is chipotle ranch dressing. As with most Tex-Mex restaurants, the menu covers all the bases: tacos, burritos, chimichangas, and fajitas, but Molly's offers more sauce choices than most: cheese, chili gravy, ranchero, mole, salsa verde, sour cream, and a tomato cream called salsa rosada. Molly's also feels lived in like a favorite armchair, which makes everything on the menu taste better.

Wiles-Smith Drug Store, 1635 Union Ave., Memphis, TN 38104; (901) 278-6416; Soda Fountain/Milk Shakes & Malts; $. Anyone who has ever swiveled on a chrome lunch-counter stool while munching tuna and toast can appreciate the appeal of a drug store soda fountain. At Wiles-Smith, the oldest independent pharmacy in Memphis, the experience couldn't be more authentic. The lunch ladies are friendly, the yellow countertop is Formica, and the milk shakes are served in a cold metal canister with a thick layer of frothy bubbles. The drug store serves shakes in four flavors (choco-late, vanilla, strawberry, and cherry), along with cherry or vanilla Cokes, ice cream floats, sundaes, and $4 lunchtime favorites such as chicken salad, fried egg, and corned beef on rye. Before leaving, be sure to say hello to pharmacist Charles Smith. He's been behind the counter for more than four decades, but almost closed up shop a few years ago after a string of burglaries. Luckily, friends and neighbors rallied, opening an emergency fund to help Smith stay in business. These days, Wiles-Smith opens 6 days a week at 10 a.m., but occasionally closes early (2 p.m. on Wed, 3 p.m. on Sat), and only accepts cash or checks.

 **Barbecue & Blue Plates**

The Bar-B-Q Shop, 1782 Madison Ave., Memphis, TN 38104; (901) 272-1277; dancingpigs.com; Barbecue; $–$$. This longtime barbecue joint is an institution in Memphis that will make you happy from the time you push open the door until you sink into a barbecue sandwich served on Texas toast. It takes gumption to pull barbecue off a bun, but the Bar-B-Q Shop has plenty of chutzpah. They did, after all, name their award-winning sauce Dancing Pigs and made versions available in mild, hot, and dry. The dry version won a "fiery food" challenge a few years ago, beating out 600 other entries. The restaurant's hot sauce has plenty of supporters, too, including a judge in the *Memphis Flyer*'s annual barbecue sandwich competition who wrote, "The sauce is incredible. Punishing fire; perfect sweetness. A balancing act Philippe Petit might be proud of." Sold online and at Kroger grocery stores throughout Memphis, Dancing Pigs sauce is the backbone for pork or beef barbecue sandwiches and ribs, wet or dry. The restaurant also barbecues chicken, spaghetti, brisket, and nachos and serves the requisite sides of beans and slaw.

Bob's Barksdale Restaurant, 237 Cooper Ave., Memphis, TN 38104; (901) 722-2193; Plate Lunches/Breakfast; $. For more than three decades, Bob's Barksdale Restaurant has been turning out plate lunches that are Southern and iconic, much like the magnolias that shade nearby streets. Country-fried steak is on the menu every day, but other specials rotate: meat loaf on Monday, Greek-baked chicken on Tuesday, stuffed bell peppers on Wednesday, beef tips over noodles on Thursday, and salmon croquettes on Friday. Vegetable sides also change daily and include favorite standbys such as buttered carrots and turnip greens. In addition to lunch, Barksdale serves oversize breakfasts that pull in loyal weekenders for hotcakes, biscuits, maple syrup, and red-eye gravy, all made from scratch. Omelets are fat and fluffy, and onions and melted cheese wrap the hash browns in a warm and delicious jacket of calories. The restaurant closes after lunch, but in the evening, passersby should step through the scruffy sidewalk garden and look through the plate-glass window. When Barksdale is closed, the retro appeal of its ragtag photos and mahogany paneling is almost as satisfying as a catfish plate.

Central BBQ, 2249 Central Ave., Memphis, TN 38104; (901) 272-9377; cbqmemphis.com; Barbecue; $. You don't have to be a jam-band fan to appreciate Central BBQ, located just west of the Liberty Bowl with a roof that looks like a checkerboard, only red and white. But if you follow Phish or Widespread Panic, you'll definitely enjoy Central's tie-dye T-shirts and the twentysomething party vibe on the restaurant's spacious deck, especially on a pretty day. Open since 2002, Central is lauded locally and nationally for its succulent ribs, broad menu, and 4 different kinds of sauce. In addition to ribs and shoulders, Central has a handful of other delicious standouts: smoked sausages; dry-rub wings; peanut butter pie; thick-cut and seasoned potato chips; turkey sandwiches pulled in the manner of pork; and 8-inch portobellos marinated, grilled, and topped with slaw, sauce, and smoked Gouda. Central also is green-fork certified, meaning, among other things, no plastic bags. Instead, servers package bulk and to-go orders in brown paper sacks stamped with Central's well-known logo, a big-ear pig with a loopy smile. Central BBQ is popular, and the lines can get long, so don't forget about the restaurant's second location (4375 Summer Ave., Memphis, TN 38122; 901-767-4672). Central BBQ also plans a third location downtown in the South Main Historic Arts District, where its tie-dye food truck (p. 24) shows up at the **Memphis Farmers Market** (p. 67) on Saturday.

CK's Coffee Shop, 1698 Poplar Ave., Memphis, TN 38104; (901) 276-6737; Breakfast; $. For young people in Memphis, CK's Coffee Shop is a rite of passage, much like a first kiss, only more adult. CK's is where teenagers first miss curfew to hang out with friends or mitigate a hangover with scrambled eggs and toast. Plenty of adults like the coffee shop, too, especially if they are looking for an inexpensive meal after midnight or a bottomless cup of coffee for less than $2. Open around the clock, CK's has been around

since 1940. In 2011 investors bought most of the chain and buffed them up a bit with an expanded menu that dumped the '60s-era color food photos. Sadly, many of the stores shut down quite suddenly the following year, leaving longtime workers unemployed and loyal customers disappointed. Fortunately, three CK's locations remain, offering fast and affordable grill standards like chili cheeseburgers, crispy hash browns, and breakfast served all day. In addition to Midtown, other coffee shop locations are: 1642 East Shelby Drive, Memphis, TN 38116, (901) 396-1061; 5370 Winchester Road, Memphis, TN 38115, (901) 363-1238.

Payne's Original Bar-B-Que, 1762 Lamar Ave., Memphis, TN 38114; (901) 272-1523; Barbecue; $. Here's a great surprise for a barbecue-loving date. Go to Payne's for the best chopped pork sandwich in Memphis. Dinner is easy on the pocketbook, and there's no need to dress up. Located in a converted gas station on Lamar Avenue, Payne's couldn't be any more real. On the building's front wall, painted white cinder blocks make a screen of concentric squares. The design is very midcentury modern, but that's as fancy as Payne's gets. Inside, a few tables are scattered about. Behind the counter, the recessed pit and the cleaver rule. Sandwiches are chopped to order with the skin on, so chewy dark crust is mixed in with the lighter meat. Sandwiches come with Payne's special sauce, which is thinner and tangier than most. Payne's slaw is also unique and, like the rest of the menu, replicates family recipes from the 1940s. Made with mustard and green cabbage, the slaw has a neon glow that can be a little startling. Flora Payne, the restaurant's charming proprietor, is happy to explain the slaw, along with the history of Payne's, which was started in 1972 by her late husband, Harold and his mother.

Specialty Stores, Markets & Producers

Cooper-Young Community Farmers Market, 1000 S. Cooper St., Memphis, TN 38104; cycfarmersmarket.org. Located in the parking lot of First Congregational Church, the Cooper-Young Farmers Market is only a short block away from the neighborhood's popular restaurant district. A relative newcomer, the market found its stride when it decided to stay open every Saturday from 8 a.m. to 1 p.m. throughout the winter months. Started by Lori Green from Downing Hollow Farm as an alternative to the **Memphis Farmers Market** (p. 67) downtown, the market has a bit of a rogue edge, attracting smaller local growers and start-up artisans who like all the fun. About 30 growers and purveyors participate every week, providing baked goods, prepared foods, farm-fresh eggs, responsibility raised meat, fruits, vegetables, and flowers that are locally grown and often organic. About a dozen artisans also circle in with crafts and cosmetics, and local musicians perform every week. The Cooper-Young market is serious about its mission to bring fresh food to underserved communities. It is one of several markets in

Memphis participating in a matching funds program called Double Green: The market matches SNAP benefits dollar for dollar up to $10 a day for fruit and vegetable purchases. Credit and debit card users are also eligible.

Fork It Over, 2400 Union Ave., Memphis, TN 38112; (901) 278-0028; forkitovercatering.com. Michelle Campbell started Fork It Over in a modest yellow bungalow on the edge of Cooper-Young, delivering prepared meals once a week and selling entrees and sides to go on-site. Four years later, she moved to a much bigger kitchen at Lindenwood Christian Church to accommodate her runaway catering business and to feed the 140 children who attend the church's day-care center. She's still delivering to customers who order from weekly menus online and selling prepared meals to busy parents when they pick up their children. She's also started a take-and-bake for fresh entrees that can be popped in the oven at home or frozen for later meals. Campbell's menus tend to add pizzazz to updated home cooking. For example, she encrusts her beef tenderloin with horseradish and serves pork medallions with olive-caper sauce. Freshly prepared side dishes such as succotash, Italian spinach, and smashed red potatoes with herbs also are good because they are self-confident enough to remember their place on table.

Java Cabana, 2170 Young Ave., Memphis, TN 38104; (901) 272-7210; javacabanacoffeehousse.com. For more than 20 years, Java

Cabana has been brewing an elixir of coffee, community, and music. Think Woodstock meets Elvis, a relationship cultivated by founder Tommy Foster's unabashed love for the King. In fact, the back room of Java Cabana was an Elvis wedding chapel with an Elvis impersonator on hand for the nuptials. In 1998, Mary Burns, who had started Java Cabana's poetry readings, purchased the business, and she still runs the place today. The coffeehouse has a settled-in hippie patina, which makes it a favorite set for local filmmakers. Musicians and poets also flock to Java's Thursday night open mike, where the audience can be kicked back or a little raucous depending on their caffeine intake. The coffee at Java is organic fair traded and is served in a typical menu of lattes and espressos. Java also offers some excellent specialty drinks, including Drama Queen (raspberry mocha topped with crushed peppermint and chocolate) and Funky Monkey (steamed milk with banana, chocolate syrup, double espresso, and fresh cream). The food menu is short and sweet, offering breakfast (french toast, veggie omelet), sandwiches (tuna salad, veggie sloppy joe), and desserts (coconut cake, scones, and vegan cookies).

Makeda's Homemade Butter Cookies, 2370 Airways Blvd., Memphis, TN 38114; (901) 745-2667; makedascookies.com. Travelers heading to or from Memphis International Airport should schedule an extra 10 minutes for a stop at Makeda's Homemade Butter Cookies, located on Airways Boulevard just north of I-240. Since 1999, members of the Hill family have been baking melt-in-your-mouth butter cookies from a dressed-up version of their grandmother's recipe. The business is named after Makeda Hill, who died from leukemia at age 7, and the family's loving memories of Makeda saturate their baking and friendly customer service. Don't expect monster mall cookies at Makeda's. Instead, the cookies, priced 6 for $5, look and taste like dessert from a family potluck. In other words, they are moist and on the thin side because they are made with plenty of butter. These days, Makeda's sells 16 kinds of cookies, including pecan peanut butter (unbelievable!), oatmeal raisin walnut, and double chocolate chip. Along with large cookies individually wrapped, Makeda's sells bite-size cookie trays, cookie bouquets, and all-occasion baskets. The bakery also has a mail-order business (cookies are baked and shipped the same day) and a second location in southeast Memphis at the Hickory Ridge Mall, 6063 Hickory Ridge Mall, Memphis, TN 38115; (901) 367-8799.

Mary Carter's Decorating Center, 3205 Summer Ave., Memphis, TN 38112; (901) 452-1233; bakingstuff.com. Decades before Pinterest, Mary Carter's Decorating Center had a DIY groove, selling paint in the summer and supplies for making candy and decorating cakes when the weather turned cold. About 25 years ago, big business bought out the Mary Carter paint franchise, but the Faherty family held on to their small cottage on Summer Avenue and kept selling decorating supplies for food. In a commercial neighborhood now dominated by body shops and junk stores, family members continue to educate home bakers and candy makers about caramel clusters, molded chocolate, and colored fondant. Merchandise also is sold online, but a visit to the store is much more inspiring. Park behind the building and enter through the back door, where boxes, bags, stickers, and ties turn a small room into a Martha Stewart wonderland of gift-giving possibilities. Tools of the trade dominate the store's front room: stencils, wedding cake toppers, cookie cutters, cake pans (there are even skulls), and cupcake sprinkles in every imaginable shape and color. Novice and experienced customers feel comfortable at Mary Carter's because friendly employees patiently explain how to make everything from suckers to peppermint crunch. Proprietor Kathy Faherty also schedules classes in the store's teaching room, especially around the holidays. They are free of charge and fill up fast.

Mary's Gluten-Free Goods, 1954 Felix Ave., Memphis, TN 38104; (901) 550-8043; marysglutenfreegoods.com. The testimonials on the website for Mary's Gluten-Free Goods confirm this: People who eat gluten-free diets miss fried egg sandwiches on english muffins. Fortunately, Mary Durham has spent almost 30 years perfecting gluten-free baking, and her english muffins are an exceptionally good stand-in for the originals. So are the rest of her products, which include a diverse assortment of cookies, breads, cakes, and cupcakes. Durham started baking at home for her own diet restrictions, so her recipes are tried and true, moving beyond the basics with such tempting treats as lemon pecan squares, a thin glazed shortbread layered with brown sugar, pecans, and coconut. In addition to english muffins, Durham offers an excellent sandwich bread, dinner rolls, and egg- and dairy-free baguettes. Cupcakes are equally good, especially the strawberry and pumpkin spice. Look for Mary's dinner rolls at **Tsunami** (p. 100), sandwich rolls at **Stone Soup Cafe** (p. 95), and her complete menu of products at the **Memphis Farmers Market** (p. 67) on Saturday. During the fall, winter, and spring, Durham also sells Mary's Memphis Crunch, a chocolate-almond toffee that is buttery and delicious.

Otherlands Coffee Bar, 641 S. Cooper St., Memphis, TN 38104; (901) 278-4994; otherlandscoffeebar.com. Otherlands Coffee Bar was the first place my daughter wanted to shop for her friends when she was a tween. At the time, I wondered, how she even knew about the place? But I enjoyed the shop's merchandise mix of cat coin purses, bamboo sporks, tie-dye scarves, and sock monkeys as much as she did. Many young people, it seems, gravitate to Otherlands with predictable ease, moving from frappes and cell phones to laptops and espresso. These days, the sprawling coffee bar looks like the college apartment everyone wishes they had: multicolored walls and thrift-store finds pulled together like an Anthropolgie store. There's even the lingering scent of incense until a barista whips up a strong iced latte with a flavor shot of chocolate. The only difficult part of Otherlands is deciding on a beverage. In addition to hot, cold, and frozen coffee drinks, the bar serves smoothies, chai tea, flavored steamed milk, and fresh-squeezed lemonade. For food, there are simple sandwiches, homemade soups, and breakfast, including "the best cinnamon toast in the South." When visiting, be sure to read the bulletin boards, especially the one devoted to local art and music. You may see a little self-promotion because Otherlands also hosts live music many weekend nights.

Republic Coffee, 2924 Walnut Grove, Memphis, TN 38111; (901) 590-1578; republiccoffeememphis.com. What's not to love about a coffeehouse that operates from 6 a.m. to midnight with free wireless, live music, and food made from scratch? Open since 2003, Republic Coffee turned a run-down brick building on a busy street into a comfortable gathering spot for people of all ages. More spacious than most coffee venues, the cafe has booths, freestanding tables, and comfy chairs so it works for either informal meetings or solitary musings on a laptop. Experienced baristas work with coffees from around the world for a drink menu of frappes, mochas, iced coffees, espressos, and smoothies that is much larger than the typical Starbucks. Baristas are also happy to accommodate individual whims no matter how arcane. While the coffee drinks are excellent, it's the food at Republic that sets it apart. Salmon, chicken, bacon, mushrooms, and tofu are smoked over hardwood in-house for a variety of breakfast and lunch sandwiches. The Pedro can reel in any skeptic with its smoky tofu, slaw, and chipotle sauce on toasted ciabatta bread. Sides are also excellent (get the carrot soufflé), and breakfast plates are served all day. Try the Vegas house special: double-smoked bacon, scrambled eggs, and a fresh bagel seared in butter and topped with cream cheese and clover honey.

Sharon's Chocolates & Bread Cafe, 2881 Poplar Ave., Memphis, TN 38111; (901) 324-4422; sharonsmemphis.com. Sharon and Michael Fajans dipped in and out of the local farmers' markets before opening a retail store for their artisan breads and hand-crafted chocolates. The cafe also sells sandwiches and pizza, but first things first. Sharon's truffles, made with a custom blend of European chocolates, are divine and show the love and experience of a longtime chocolatier. Their smooth crunchy shells in milk, dark, or white chocolate hide creamy ganache in natural flavors that change day to day. A current favorite: dark chocolate infused with orange and decorated with a tiny curl of candied orange peel. Sharon's husband, Michael, handles the baking, and his scrumptious parade of Italian bread, focaccia, ciabatta, and *boules* shape the foundation of the cafe's menu. On a recent visit, here's how a customer explained her decision not to buy a loaf of rosemary focaccia: "Usually, I eat the entire focaccia before I get home and then tell my family Sharon was out, but tonight I have to zip up a dress." Along with the heavenly combination of bread and chocolates, the couple make meatballs and Italian sausage from scratch (you can taste the fennel) and pizza dough every day. The Sicilian-style pizza dough is crispy with a little bounce in the middle, shaping a delicious tableau for toppings like sausage and green olive or chicken italiano, a warm and satisfying mix of chicken breast, pepperoni, peppers, onions, and mozzarella.

Tsunami Winter Farmers Market, 928 S. Cooper St., Memphis, TN 38104 (Tsunami parking lot). As the winters grow more temperate, Mid-South farmers are embracing cold-frame farming to keep locally grown produce available year-round. But most outdoor farmers' markets in Memphis shut down in October. So Van Cheeseman of Flora Bluebird Farm asked Chef Ben Smith if he could use the parking lot of **Tsunami** (p. 100) restaurant on Saturday mornings for a small market with handful of hearty participants. Smith agreed. Located in the heart of the Cooper-Young neighborhood, the Tsunami winter market quickly established an enthusiastic following of local chefs and locavores. Customers appreciate the ease of one-stop shopping for cheese, eggs, produce, coffee, pork, and beef and the personal relationships with vendors that aren't so easily made at more crowded summer markets. Vendors have time to chat, explaining a new recipe for swiss chard or how to prepare pork belly for a special occasion dinner. Plus, there's a camaraderie between vendors and customers who are wrapped up against the cold and whining about what to do with yet another bag of sweet potatoes.

Urban Farms Market and Farm, 2977 Broad St., Memphis, TN 38112; (901) 257-9627; bdcmemphis.org/urban_farms.html. Located in a former corner gas station in the underserved community of Binghampton, Urban Farms Market is like the Little Engine That Could: determined, tireless, and loved. In 2010, the Binghampton Development Corporation leased 3 acres of land once used to grow cotton to give people in the neighborhood access to fresh food. Volunteers and residents pitched in resources and time to develop an urban farm where kids plant their own gardens and more experienced growers provide vegetables for the Urban Farms Market nearby. Today, the partnership between farmers and residents continues to thrive, thanks largely to the market's slow but steady growth as a community center and grocery. During the spring and summer, workers pull stands outdoors to showcase locally grown produce. On Saturday, the market's parking lot feels like the heartbeat of the community. Kids wander in and out of the store, now fully stocked with cage-free eggs, staples, fruits, vegetables, and a private-label coffee called Urban Joe. Behind the store, a seasonal nursery stocks heirloom vegetable plants and compost from the farm sells for $2 a bucket. Volunteers teach residents how to grow food in their yards, and some are already selling herbs back to the market. Part of the market's mission is to encourage these types of food-based start-ups, so Urban Farms also sells locally made pickles, preserves, and baked goods. Open from early spring through Labor Day, the market pulls in commuters at its busy intersection of Tillman and Sam Cooper Boulevard. The farm, which welcomes visitors, is located a few blocks away, off the Greenline bike path at 198 Wills St.

Viet Hoa, 40 N. Cleveland St., Memphis, TN 38104; (901) 726-9388. Memphis writer Chris Davis calls Cleveland Avenue the gateway to the East, and Viet Hoa is his favorite market along the ethnic strip. Davis should know since he's bold enough to buy the market's more exotic prepared foods, such as deep-fried chicken feet.

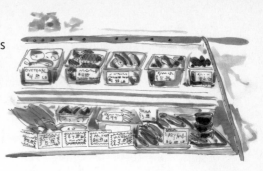

"You also can get whole cooked ducks for $15," he says. "Whether I'm cooking in my comfort zone or going on a foodie adventure, I leave happy and considerably less poor than if I'd gone to Kroger." The prices are affordable at this full-service market that also offers a decent selection of Mexican foods, a fresh-meat counter, and a butcher who is more than happy to shave soup beef super-thin. The no-frills spread of seafood is odd or awesome depending on how you roll. Heads-on fish are iced next to live fish, lobster, and king crab swimming in large tanks. The market also sells aisles of packaged and canned groceries, seasoning blends, rice, bulk tofu, housewares, and bottled drinks like toasted coconut. The produce section is a nice place to wander and marvel at the exotic fruits and roots and to find great buys on veggies. On a recent visit, I paid 85 cents for a bottle of water, $1.73 for a heavy bag of baby bok choy, and a dollar for a dozen limes. Owner Tommy Fan recently opened another market in southeast Memphis called VH Foods. It's located in a former Kroger with 50,000 square feet for produce, international groceries, and a hot lunch bar: 3565 Riverdale Rd., Memphis, TN 38115; (901) 547-5887.

Yippie Hippie Foods, PO Box 40263, Memphis, TN 3817; (901) 491-3329; yippiehippiegranola.com. When Malcolm Ervin couldn't find a good low-sugar, low-fat, high-protein breakfast, he invented his own. At first, he packaged his Yippie Hippie granola in quart mason jars and gave them away to friends. Next, he and his wife Jennifer moved to a small commercial kitchen, and then a bigger one. Now they are selling granola every week at the **Memphis Farmers Market** (p. 67) and recently snagged Whole Foods as a corporate customer. So in the crowded field of granolas, what makes Yippie Hippie special? The packaging is colorful, and so are Malcolm and Jennifer's personalities. But even more important, the couple sells a healthy granola that actually tastes good. Made in small batches with rolled oats, nuts, and seeds, the granola is mixed with a blend of hemp, rice bran, and walnut oil, and sweetened with agave nectar, raw honey, and maple syrup. There's even a little cinnamon, lemon juice, and amaretto liqueur in the recipe so the granola is a delicious way to increase fiber and protein. For breakfast on the run, Yippie Hippie makes granola bars in 6 flavors that also pack a 7-gram protein punch.

East Memphis

Located between Midtown and the I-240 loop, East Memphis is a sprawling residential homage to the optimism and architecture of postwar America. Shaded by red oaks and magnolias, East Memphis neighborhoods represent the sensibilities of the 1950s with blocks of three-bedroom ramblers built for blue-collar families along with sprawling colonial and ranch-style houses for more-affluent professionals.

Even today, these neighborhoods have a baby-boomer feel of a time when kids rode bikes to the shopping center or stole through sewers to explore a different part of town. My own home near Audubon Park was built by the owners of a quintessential midcentury steak house called The Embers. Most middle-age adults raised in Memphis can recall special-occasion dinners at The Embers on Park Avenue, where the martinis were cold, the baked potatoes were loaded, and the steaks were grilled medium rare. While the Embers fell to commercial development years ago, other landmark restaurants in East Memphis carry on. Folk's Folly, Pete & Sam's, Jim's Place, and the city's first Asian restaurants along Summer Avenue are still family run, continuing long-standing relationships between proprietors and customers who visit regularly.

No better example exists in East Memphis than Mortimer's, a restaurant with a historical cachet few can match. Sara Bell opened Mortimer's in the early '80s, naming it after her father who ran a much-loved restaurant on Poplar Avenue called The Knickerbocker. At Mortimer's, Bell still serves some of the recipes from her father's restaurant, which was located across the street from Sekisui Pacific Rim, the flagship restaurant of Jimmy Ishii who first brought sushi to Memphis in the late 1980s.

In many ways, Sekisui Pacific Rim illustrates the juxtaposition of old and new that is luring young energetic chefs to the city's most stable suburbs. Fifty years ago, restaurants in East Memphis hugged the retail centers along Poplar and Park Avenues, while Asian restaurants scattered haphazardly along Summer Avenue. Today's restaurants mimic the same trajectory, but with considerably more panache. Along the Poplar corridor, chef-driven restaurants like Interim, Acre, Circa, Napa Cafe, River Oaks, Grove Grill, and Andrew Michael Italian Kitchen are reinventing American cuisine with regional and continental twists. And on Summer Avenue, proprietors are energizing strip centers with authentic Mexican food that is unpretentious and affordable. A weekly farmers' market, ethnic grocery stores, and a wave of independent butchers are also expanding the popular palate and making the East Memphis food scene inclusive and fun.

Acre, 690 S. Perkins, Memphis, TN 38117; (901) 818-2273; acre memphis.com; New American, $$–$$$. Perhaps no restaurant in Memphis has been more eagerly anticipated than Wally Joe's Acre. A coming together of vision and talent, Acre opened in May 2011 after a 2-year renovation of a midcentury home near Theatre Memphis. From the start, Acre hit all the right notes. Inside, the restaurant feels like an elegant Aspen ski lodge. Outside, red oaks shade a garden patio protected by stacked stone walls. And then there's the kitchen, where Executive Chef Andrew Adams and a constellation of culinary stars turn out dishes like sea scallops with bok choy, bone marrow, eggplant, and black bean sauce, and my new favorite: fluke seviche. Joe describes Acre's style as a melting pot of global flavors and seasonal ingredients. Together the influences turn fine dining at Acre into a worldwide adventure of flavor and fun. Happily, the vacation extends to the restaurant's bar, where bartenders mix artisan cocktails with house infusions that are both naughty (fig and fennel moonshine) and nice (pear or apple vodka). See Chef Adams's recipe for **Tomato Tartare with Chickpea Panisse, Chèvre & Baby Arugula** on p. 264.

Amerigo, 1239 Ridgeway Rd., Memphis, TN 38119; (901) 761-4000; amerigo.net; Italian, $–$$. When Amerigo opened in 1999, my daughter attended school across the street. We visited Amerigo regularly for the restaurant's family-friendly Italian food and early-bird specials. I especially loved Amerigo's arugula salad tossed with flame-grilled apples, roasted walnuts, Gorgonzola, and Gorgonzola vinaigrette. Not long ago, I revisited Amerigo and was happy to see the salad still on menu, along with other dishes I remember, like cedar wood–roasted salmon and mashed potatoes with leeks and Asiago cheese. Why mess with a good thing, right? Happily, Amerigo's brick oven is still turning out great-tasting food, such as cheese fritters and gourmet pizzas topped with spinach and house-smoked chicken. The menu also includes more steak entrees, crowd-pleasers like lasagna, and at least a dozen pastas such as wild-mushroom ravioli and gluten-free spaghetti. Special events are another option, pairing unique menus with tastings for tequilas or martinis.

Andrew Michael Italian Kitchen, 712 W. Brookhaven Circle, Memphis, TN 38117; (901) 347-3569; andrewmichaelitaliankitchen .com; Italian; $$–$$$. Boyhood friends Andrew Ticer and Michael Hudman are the darlings of the Memphis food scene for many reasons, including their unabashed love for heritage Berkshire pigs and their restaurant's fresh food focus. The chefs' success came quickly. In 2009, they opened Andrew Michael Italian Restaurant with an inauspicious start chronicled in the Food Network's *The Opener*. Less than three years later, the James Beard Foundation named Ticer and Hudman semifinalists for Best Chef in the Southeast, and the chefs have opened a new gastropub across the street called **Hog**

& Hominy (p. 214). Simply put, Ticer and Hudman are damn good chefs, combining a tradition of family cooking (Maw Maw's Ravioli) with locally sourced and seasonal ingredients (house-made gnocchi, shrimp, pork belly, crowder peas, and basil *panna gratta*). The restaurant serves dishes traditionally as starters, pastas, entrees, and desserts, so an evening meal can be a martini and small plate at the bar or a leisurely multicourse love affair. Adventurous customers should try "No Menu Monday," when the whims of the kitchen appear magically on your plate.

Booksellers Bistro, 387 Perkins Extension, Memphis, TN 38117; (901) 374-0881; thebooksellersatlaurelwood.com; Cafe; $-$$. What's more risky these days than an independent bookstore? How about an independent bookstore cafe? Memphis almost lost this longtime neighborhood cafe when its bookstore, formerly called Davis Kidd, went belly up. But after community support and a new investor, the bookstore and cafe bounced back with a new name, and they are better than ever. The bistro divides its menu into midday and evening options and includes a sprinkling of recipes from celebrity chefs. Good luck getting past the appetizers, especially the bistro's signature bowl of tomato–blue cheese soup, a sure cure for any ailment. Other good starts are the Mediterranean platter to share (the white bean and feta dip is excellent) and the warm brie drizzled with caramel, topped with toasted almonds, and served with pear slices. Wraps, burgers, stuffed

HOMEGROWN CHAIN:
YOLO FROZEN YOGURT & GELATO

Think the frozen yogurt buzz is dying down? Then stop by **YoLo Frozen Yogurt & Gelato** where self-serve yogurt pumps and a remarkable buffet of toppings dazzle customers with a colorful parade of decision making. Consider this sampling of yogurt toppings: praline, granola, sprinkles, Skittles, Snickers, chocolate chips, cupcake bites, cashew crunch, butter cookies, animal crackers, Gummy Bears, Oreo crumbles, fresh fruit, and hot fudge sauce. Even more impressive, about two dozen toppings are locally sourced, a commitment that extends to the chain's green philosophy to recycle and reduce waste. Yogurt flavors are equally appealing and change by day and location, but birthday cake and cheesecake, two perennial teen favorites, pop up often. YoLo also serves a revolving selection of homemade gelato (pomegranate, salted caramel, Nutella!) along with a sumptuous line of goodies called YoLo Bakes. Look for popovers (called Pop Tarts here), scones, cupcakes, ice-cream cookies, and gelato cakes with buttercream frosting, to name a few. Started in 2010 by attorney Taylor Berger and entrepreneur Mike McCaskill, YoLo has charmed its customers and its community, waving the local flag and supporting schools and nonprofits. Already, the self-serve chain operates five stores in Memphis and has expanded into Asheville, North Carolina; Owensboro, Kentucky; and Jackson, Tennessee. For a complete list of YoLo locations, visit its website at yolofroyo.com.

croissants, tilapia sandwiches, Asian noodle salads, and one of the most popular quiches in the city make up the menu's middle. Evening selections get more fancy, offering crab cakes, Merlot duck, and a fried green tomato napoleon layered with goat cheese and sautéed spinach.

Casablanca, 5030 Poplar Ave., Ste. 7, Memphis, TN 38117; (901) 725-8557; casablancamemphis.com; Middle Eastern; $–$$. After a move from the Cooper-Young neighborhood in Midtown, Casablanca seems to have found a permanent home in East Memphis on the busy Poplar corridor near Whole Foods. Operated by Aimer Shtaya, Casablanca also is straying some from its roots. A new menu includes dishes like eggplant Parmesan, lasagna, and chicken fingers for the kids. While the children's menu is a plus, adults should probably stick with what Casablanca does best: a *shawerma* platter with chicken, beef, and lamb cooked in-house on a vertical spit and served with spicy sauce on the side. The couscous platter with leg of lamb is also excellent, as is the hummus chickpea spread served with fresh pita and grilled chicken. The restaurant's quiet, cool interior is another plus: pumpkin-colored walls, Persian rugs, and floor-to-ceiling shelves stocked with olive oil from Jerusalem made by the owner's father. The olive oil, bottled with a cork and available for purchase, is rich and flavorful. Casablanca caters, operates a busy to-go business, and has a second restaurant in Cordova at 1890 N. Germantown Pkwy., Ste. 99, Memphis, TN 38106; (901) 433-9712.

Cheffie's Cafe, 483 High Point Ter., Memphis, TN; (901) 345-0455; cheffies.com; Cafe; $. Cookbook author Jennifer Chandler is an exuberant cheerleader for simple and healthy food. Her cookbooks titled *Simply Salads, Simply Suppers,* and *Simply Grilling* are enthusiastic how-tos for families who think they are too busy to cook. Chandler's restaurant, Cheffie's Cafe, continues her fresh and simple mantra. Located 2 blocks from the Memphis Greenline, the cafe is a beacon of sorts for joggers and bicyclists who give Cheffie's a hip, Portland feel. So does the menu. Customers order at the counter in four steps. Salad or sandwich? Lettuce or bread? Protein? Toppings? Sounds easy enough until the toppings offer endless choices like chickpeas, peppers, marinated artichokes, and sliced pickles. An easy fix for too much decision making is Cheffie's signature menu, which includes these two combos: mixed greens with curried walnut-apple chicken salad and balsamic vinaigrette, and a roast beef sandwich with french-fried onions, sliced red onion, and horseradish. Cheffie's also serves wine, gelato, lemonade, and tea 3 ways: sweet, unsweetened, and pomegranate. See Jennifer Chandler's recipe for **White Bean Chicken Chili** on p. 281.

Ciao Bella Italian Grill, 565 Erin Dr., Memphis, TN 38117; (901) 205-2500; ciaobellamemphis.com; Italian/Greek; $–$$. Ciao Bella is tucked in the middle of a very ordinary shopping center, but don't be put off by the restaurant's lackluster curb appeal. Inside, Chef Jonathan Steenerson is up to something special, serving both Greek and Italian dishes that are tasty and unique. Consider, for example, mussels saganaki, where sautéed mussels, crushed red pepper, crumbled feta cheese, and Greek oregano mingle together in a tomato-seafood broth. Traditional Greek favorites like makaronopita, a baked macaroni and cheese pie, are also on the menu, along with gourmet pizzas, calzones, and Italian classics like lasagna and veal scaloppine. Pizzas are thin crust and baked with plenty of olive oil so they taste rich and buttery. Steenerson locally sources much of his meat and produce and remembers customers with dietary restrictions. A gluten-free pizza crust is in the works, and vegans who ask will be treated to dishes like fettuccine with chickpea and pine-nut pesto served in roasted acorn squash.

Circa, 6150 Poplar Ave., Ste. 122, Memphis, TN 38119; (901) 746-9130; circamemphis.com; French / New American; $$$. Pushing open the door to John Bragg's Circa is like stepping from the world we know to the world we want. From the first friendly greeting to the last bite of gâteau, Circa wraps guests in a luxurious cocoon of style and service. Designed by 3six0, a boutique firm affiliated with the Rhode Island School of Design, the award-winning restaurant is a monochromatic wash of grays, metallic finishes, and thoughtful details. Glass-orb chandeliers float above tables like a sea of bubbles, and serpentine wall screens double as artful racks for bottles of wine. The food and service at Circa are equally impressive, offering American dishes grounded in classic French technique. Bragg also plays to the Southern palate with such entrees as polenta-stuffed quail with chorizo, fingerling potatoes, and natural jus. Dinner is expensive, but lunch and Sunday brunch are half the cost. Circa's tuna salad niçoise is an exceptionally good lunch entree. Served on a square white china plate, tomatoes, pickled red onions, black olives, and potato salad anchor a fresh mound of greens. Seared tuna slices and a quartered egg rest on top, forming a perfect cap of protein for a light drizzle of dressing.

The Elegant Farmer, 262 S. Highland St., Memphis, TN 38111; (901) 324-2221; theelegantfarmerrestaurant.com; New American / Farm-to-Table; $$. Chef Mac Edwards has a sensible philosophy for The Elegant Farmer: "Take what God makes and don't screw it up." Amen. No chef in Memphis takes farm-to-table more seriously than Edwards, who shops several times a week at local farmers' markets for a menu of elevated comfort food. Voted best new restaurant by *Memphis* magazine in 2012, The Elegant Farmer is shifting Southern favorites in a more sophisticated and seasonal direction. Dishes are familiar with a twist, like a pair of farm-fresh deviled eggs seasoned with curry, or a center-cut pork chop brined, oven roasted, and crowned with spring-onion marmalade.

 The Elegant Farmer's menu is limited but feels large, thanks to extras like house-made pickles, pecan butter, and manager Leslee Pascal's luscious desserts. (Personal favorite: a 2-inch wedge of pound cake smothered with blueberries and dusted with confectioners' sugar.) When the weather is nice, sit

on the restaurant's outdoor patio, which has a Swiss chalet feel and flower beds of colorful, old-fashioned perennials. See Pascal's recipe for **Butter Pound Cake** on p. 287.

Emerald Thai Restaurant, 5699 Mount Moriah Rd., Memphis, TN 38115; (901) 367-2827; emeraldthairestaurant.biz; Thai; $. Is there any better antidote to a chill in the air than a hot steaming bowl of *tom yum guy*? I didn't think so until a recent visit to Emerald Thai, where instead of soup I ordered a salad called Spicy Shrimp and Squid Yum (number 24 on the menu). It was love at first bite, even though I'm not sure why this dish is called a salad. Instead of lettuce or noodles, the plate overflows with steamed squid and shrimp and a Thai spin on mirepoix: carrots, cucumbers, and red onions tossed with citrus, chile, and garlic dressing. Be sure to squeeze the juice from the plate's fresh lime quarters and then scoop up any leftover dressing with a spoon. Heavenly! For more than 15 years, the Praseuth family has been serving very good Thai food on a stretch of Mount Moriah Road better known for commercial car lots. The restaurant's green curry is exceptional, pooling into a fragrant sage sea for chicken, peas, carrots, mushrooms, eggplant, and zucchini. Like many family-owned Asian restaurants, beer is sold but wine is not. Wine drinkers, however, can bring their own bottle for a $5 cork fee.

Erling Jensen, 1044 S. Yates Rd., Memphis, TN 38119; (901) 763-3700; ejensen.com; Continental; $$$. Danish native Erling

Jensen came to Memphis in 1989 to head a popular French restaurant in Midtown called La Tourelle. Seven years later, he opened his own restaurant in East Memphis, where he continues to impress customers and critics with one of the finest restaurants in the city. Voted best chef in Memphis for 10 consecutive years, Jensen's continental cuisine is deft and delicious because he steps outside expected boundaries. His menu offers scallops, duck breast, and rack of lamb, along with an elk chop from Guadalupe and a bison rib eye rubbed with mole spice. For years, dinners at Erling Jensen have been notoriously expensive, and while standard menus are still pricey, the restaurant now serves fixed-price dinners on Friday and Sunday nights. The dinner and wine pairings on Friday look especially interesting, and they are a nice showcase for Nate Oliva, the restaurant's new chef de cuisine. In 2011, the restaurant also added a small intimate bar with an excellent small plate menu. The blackened buffalo burger with crispy Benton bacon and stilton cheese aioli is particularly good.

Fratelli's Cafe, Memphis Botanic Garden, 750 Cherry Rd., Memphis, TN 38117; (901) 766-9900; fratellisfinecatering.com; Cafe; $–$$. For people who think it's time to retire the panini, Fratelli's Cafe is a game changer. Located at the Memphis Botanic Garden, Fratelli's packs Mediterranean flair into a lunch-only menu of panini, focaccia, sandwiches, and salads made with organic greens. An established caterer, proprietor Sabine Baltz understands that a good sandwich needs a great spread. Her combinations are superb: fig and olive with turkey, roasted red peppers, red onion, and arugula; dill mayonnaise with chicken cordon blue; lemon aioli with eggplant and goat cheese; and pesto mayonnaise with Super Mario, a combo of Swiss cheese, ham, salami, mushrooms, and tomato. Baltz's dressings also give her salads appropriate zing. Try the pork tenderloin salad (pork, avocado, orange, spinach, roasted red peppers, and spicy orange aioli) and then head outdoors to wander in a field of daffodils or feed the giant koi in the garden's Japanese tranquility lake.

The Grove Grill, 4550 Poplar Ave., Memphis, TN 38117; (901) 818-9951; thegrovegrill.com; New American; $$–$$$. Anchoring the Laurelwood Shopping Center since 1997, The Grove Grill pioneered modern American cooking in Memphis, blending local ingredients and regional influences into a menu that's easy to love. The restaurant, owned by Chef Jeffrey Dunham and his wife, Tracey Dunham, featured low-country shrimp and grits from the start, and while the dish is still featured, the rest of the menu continues to evolve in sensible tweaks. Menu changes are creative but comfortable, like fig and Gorgonzola flatbread, house-made Guinness ice cream and Granny Smith apple mignonette for the restaurant's raw Gulf Coast oysters. Like most popular restaurants, the Grove Grill features chef dinners and wine pairings, including dinners in an intimate Chef's Table/In the Kitchen setting. Recently, the Grove introduced weekday specials with an Italian twist, including Chef Joshua Perkins's spaghetti carbonara made with pork belly, black pepper, and farm-fresh eggs. The restaurant's full menu is also served in the bar, which is a friendly and comfortable setting for regulars and newcomers.

Hollywood Pizza Shack, 4523 Summer Ave., Memphis, TN 38122; (901) 680-7900; hollywoodpizzashack.com; Pizza; $–$$. At first, the edge of a Lowe's parking lot seems an unlikely location for a pizza joint. But who doesn't get hungry running errands? So goes the strategy at the Hollywood Pizza Shack, where husband-and-wife team Bobby and Christy Brown turn out New York–style pizzas in 14- and 16-inch pies, along with calzones and subs in similar variations. Each pizza is made to order with regular or garlic-butter hand-crafted crust and a choice of standard toppings or more unusual fare such as pulled pork barbecue and roasted red peppers. The shack also serves pizza combinations like the Fiery Buffalo Chicken, a combination of grilled chicken breast, red onions, spicy buffalo sauce, and blue cheese. Prices are reasonable, especially on Wednesday night when the Shack offers a large pie with one topping for $10. Even better is the weekday lunch special: 2 slices and a drink for $5. Customers can eat in, take out, or call for free delivery with minimum orders.

Interim, 5040 Sanderlin Ave., Memphis, TN 38117; (901) 818-0821; interimrestaurant.com; New American; $$–$$$. My friend

Victoria works for a busy law firm, so she likes to steal away to the blue upholstered bar stools at Interim to lunch alone with a cobb salad and a generous pour of Pinot Grigio. Occasionally, she treats herself to an Interim burger, an addictive stack of responsibly raised beef, bacon, white cheddar, toppings, and garlic aioli on a Kaiser bun. For a more gregarious lunch, slip over to the dining room, where an open kitchen fuses table conversations with a sensuous display of seasonal dishes from Chef Jackson Kramer. In the "what's your favorite restaurant" game, Interim tops many lists thanks to Kramer's culinary training in Portland, Oregon, and his commitment to sustainable food. Using seasonal ingredients, Kramer develops complex flavor combinations like stuffed trout with basil-fennel orzo or chicken breast with ricotta-spinach tart, oyster mushrooms, and garlic cream. In addition to lunch and dinner, Interim also serves Sunday brunch. Offerings showcase a similar style, such as croque madame with smoked ham, fontina, fried farm egg, and Mornay sauce, along with a $5 menu for children.

Jr's Fish & Chicken, 3992 Park Ave., Memphis, TN 38111; (901) 320-1020; Fried Chicken/Middle Eastern; $. Can fried chicken coexist peacefully with an excellent gyro? Only time will tell at this small table and take-out restaurant, formerly called Castle Restaurant but repositioned as Jr's Fish & Chicken in 2012. The new owners are promoting both menus, which is good, because the gyro, a lovely grilled boat of a sandwich, combines beef and lamb cooked quickly on a hot grill then layered in pita bread with chunks of tomatoes, shredded lettuce, sliced onions, and a liberal dose of tzatziki. Grab plenty of napkins for working across the gyro three messy bites at a time. The restaurant also serves other Middle Eastern favorites such as falafel, shish kebab, and baklava along with chicken and fish specials like the Jr's Trio: two catfish filets, two wings, six shrimp, fries, coleslaw, rolls, and a drink for $9.99. Additional locations: 4109 Elvis Presley Blvd., Memphis, TN 38116, (901) 345-3333; 3087 S. Perkins Rd., Memphis, TN 38118, (901) 795-5255.

Juicy Jim's, 551 S. Highland, Memphis, TN 38111; (901) 435-6243; Pizza/Sandwiches & Subs; $$. From the street, Juicy Jim's looks more like a college bar than a restaurant, but the place sells more food than beer, says owner Jim Matson. Some of the party vibe comes from the pizzeria's location on the Highland Strip, a popular hangout for college kids from the University of Memphis. Matson stays open late to accommodate revelers who are so familiar with his menu that they order by number, not name. Hot and cold deli sandwiches run from $10 to $12 and are large enough to share. Matson also doesn't scrimp on ingredients, importing cold cuts from New York for such crowd-pleasers as the Hangover Stopper, a combo of steak, sausage, cheese, ham, onions, peppers, mushrooms, tomatoes, lettuce, and pickles. Matson likes the saying, "There is nothing little here," a motto that certainly extends to the restaurant's half-pound Black Angus burger sandwiched between fried onions and 2 slices of cheese. The big-is-better mantra also describes Juicy Jim's New Jersey–style pizzas, which are made in house with scratch dough and tomato gravy. The Hawaiian (mozzarella, ham, and pineapple) is particularly good.

Las Delicias Mexican Bar and Grill, 4002 Park Ave., Memphis, TN 38117; (901) 458-9264; Mexican; $. Voted best Mexican restaurant by several local publications in 2012, Las Delicias takes Tex-Mex standards to the next sphere, thanks to the whole Delicias package. The food is authentic, the margaritas are made with freshly squeezed lime juice, and the restaurant's charming owners, Leila and Antonio Martinez, coordinate fast and efficient service. Then there are the chips, flaky and crunchy at the same time and so good they are distributed locally at stores and farmers' markets. Served in bottomless baskets, the chips are the prelude to the restaurant's guacamole, a rapturous melody of chunky avocado, tomatoes, onions, cilantro, jalapeño, and more fresh lime. In fact, the guacamole is so good you'll want to skip the chips for a spoon, but try to hold back. There is plenty more to order. Try the *charros* beans, a heart-warming and soupy blend of pintos, cilantro, chorizo, and jalapeños, or any of the restaurants tacos, flautas, and fajitas served with handmade corn tortillas. Las Delicias also has two other restaurants: 3727 Mendenhall, Memphis, TN 38115, (901) 542-0170; 5689 Quince Rd., Memphis, TN 38119, (901) 800-2873.

Los Comales, 4774 Summer Ave., Memphis, TN 38122; (901) 683-9530; Mexican; $. The English translation of Los Comales is "griddles," but in Mexico *los comales* are the clay dishes used for making tortillas. The name pretty much sums up the authenticity of this unpretentious spot, one of several excellent Mexican restaurants that have popped up on Summer Avenue over the last few years. Friendly and stripped down, Los Comales has a counter where folks settle in for a beer after work. No wonder. Dos Equis is on tap, and the food is fresh and seasoned perfectly with cilantro, caramelized onions, and lightly grilled poblanos. Skip the standards (although the enchiladas are excellent) and try something new. At $2.75, the *chicharrón* (fried pork skin) *sope* stuffed with shredded lettuce, avocado, and tomatoes is a meal in itself, while the *hongos* (mushroom) *sope* is an equally pleasing vegetarian option. Seven Seas soup is a little more expensive, but plenty for two. When the steaming bowl arrives, take a minute or two to breathe in the tomato broth before fishing out chunks of carrots, calamari, shrimp, crab, baby clams, and sausage. A fiery bowl of chopped cilantro, jalapeños, and raw onions is served alongside, so customers can toss in a little extra heat.

Los Compadres, 3295 Poplar Ave., Ste. 101, Memphis, TN 38111; (901) 458-5731; Mexican/Cuban; $. In 2009, Los Compadres, a popular restaurant in Midtown, relocated a mile east. The move to a renovated storefront on Poplar continues to be a good fit. A friendly bar across the back of the restaurant is a good perch for eating and watching television, and an outdoor patio with shade umbrellas is nice when the weather warms up. The food is a notch above typical Tex-Mex, especially the *sopa de camarón,* a spicy bowl of shrimp, baby carrots, cauliflower, rice, cilantro, avocado, and lime. For an appetizer that's almost a meal, try *Choriqueso,* a mound of chips topped with chorizo, onions, tomatoes, jalapeños, cilantro, and *queso blanco* served sizzling hot in a cast-iron pan. Los Compadres also adds new items such as grilled fish filet with rice and beans and recently introduced a Cuban menu. For *carne a la juliana,* cooks marinate steak in Cuban herbs and then sauté the meat with onions and a trio of peppers. An excellent garlic roast chicken is also available, along with items that appear to be Cuban a la USA. Here's an example: A combo called Real, which is beef, chicken, chorizo, bacon, and pineapple, tops both a spaghetti dish and a home-made pizza.

Mango Restaurant and Ice Cream, 2733 Getwell Rd., Memphis, TN 38118; (901) 369-4334; mangomemphis.com; Middle Eastern/Mexican/Chicken Wings/Ice Cream; $. The influx of nationalities into Memphis is most evident in the city's growing number of ethnic grocery stores and casual restaurants that mix up cuisines from around the globe. Most of these places are no-frill settings in strip centers serving international dishes along with a few American favorites. Located south of American Way, Mango's one-page menu offers American food (BBQ wings, cheeseburgers, Philly cheesesteaks), Mexican food (gorditas, tortas, tacos, burritos), Middle Eastern food (shish kebab, gyro, falafel), and homemade ice cream for $2 a scoop. All items except the Mango Plate, which includes shish kebab, chicken, gyro meat, and salad, ring in under

THE TOP 10 SANDWICHES IN MEMPHIS: MAKING MUSIC WITH TWO SLICES OF BREAD

Most folks slap ham and cheese on bread for lunch and call it a day. Not so for Midtown foodie Joe Hayden, who thinks the sandwich, no matter how humble, deserves respect.

A journalism professor at the University of Memphis, Hayden grew up in a big family with an Italian mother who loved to cook. "She didn't like a lot of kids in her kitchen," Hayden says. "Sandwiches were something I could make and not get in her way."

So what makes an ideal sandwich for a man who eats one as often as possible? Construction is important, Hayden says. A good sandwich doesn't fall apart: "If you have to eat a sandwich with a knife and fork, it's a disappointing sandwich."

Flavorful fillings matter too, something Hayden showcases with The Joe, a sandwich he hopes to one day see on a restaurant menu. "Spread goat cheese on bread and then add oven-roasted chicken, roasted red peppers, and baby spinach," Hayden says. "It's delicious and beautiful. When you bite into it, it looks like Christmas."

While The Joe is a homemade favorite from Hayden's own kitchen, he's discovered plenty of other satisfying sandwiches at restaurants around town. He keeps an ongoing top-10 list, which for now includes these favorites:

Caprutto: Fratelli's Cafe (p. 136) delivers the holy grail of Italian ingredients—prosciutto, mozzarella, and marinated tomatoes—served with basil and pesto mayonnaise, the perfect complement.

Cuban Po' Boy: Soul Fish Cafe (p. 94) smokes its ham and pork tenderloin in-house, the top-shelf ingredients in its Cuban Po' Boy, along with pickles, mustard, Swiss, Cuban mayo, and a soft muffuletta roll.

Fried Egg Sandwich: Let's cut right to the chase: You will never eat a better fried egg sandwich than the bacon and avocado version served at **Sweet Grass Next Door** (p. 220).

Grilled Chicken and Pineapple: Pineapple is a miracle food (much like sour cream), which is why the grilled chicken sandwich at **Cafe Eclectic** (p. 78) is so satisfying. The provolone, spinach, and roasted tomatoes help, too.

Hey Zeus: An unassuming convenience store, **Kwik Chek** (p. 89) serves gourmet sandwiches like Hey Zeus, a Greek-influenced wrap with turkey, roast beef, feta, Italian seasonings, and lemon-herb dressing.

Jive Turkey Hoagie: The grilled chicken wrap at **Trolley Stop Market** (p. 50) is a good and healthy alternative, but for pure flavor, there's no substitute for the Jive Turkey Hoagie, a delectable combination of turkey, bacon, and avocado on a hearty bun.

Lobster Roll: Nestled in a Texas toast–style hot-dog bun, the lobster roll at **The Slider Inn** (p. 219) with mayo and lemon juice is fresh and delicious. The lobster is shipped in fresh from Maine.

Sam I Am: The neighborhood bar **Young Avenue Deli** (p. 222) serves several standouts, but Sam I Am is on top: turkey, bacon, and Gouda cheese get a twist of Memphis with barbecue sauce.

Special Gyro: The secret to the gyro at **Brother Juniper's** (p. 156) is the shiitake vinaigrette, which lightens up the combination of meat, spinach, tomatoes, and feta.

Tuscan Sun: No ingredient is boring when coupled with something else interesting. Case in point: the Tuscan Sun panini at **Cordelia's Table** (p. 68) made with chicken breast, provolone, roasted tomatoes, portobello, and pesto mayo.

$10. The large tamales filled with chicken or beef are particularly good, and the menu's accoutrements (tzatziki, hummus, red and green salsa) are fresh, house-made, and authentic.

Mosa Asian Bistro, 850 White Station, Memphis, TN 38117; (901) 683-8889; mosaasianbistro.com; Asian Fusion; $. Mosa Asian Bistro likes to mix up influences even with dessert. Instead of green-tea ice cream, the restaurant serves chocolate-covered strawberries, New York–style cheesecake, and owner Charlene Pao's homemade cupcakes. At $1.50 each, the cupcakes are irresistible. The red velvet comes with a swirl of buttercream icing and a sprinkle of rock sugar, and the chocolate with strawberry icing has chocolate chips hiding inside. Mosa has two locations, and both restaurants serve a fusion of Korean, Thai, and Japanese dishes priced mostly under $10. A good choice for lunch or dinner is the Jiao Zhe Bowl, a signature entree made with plump chicken pot stickers, homemade chicken broth, carrots, sliced Napa cabbage, and a hot dipping sauce. The menu also changes periodically at Mosa, adding new items like Yo Bing, which are toasted crepes with black bean, edamame, and corn relish, and Korean BBQ beef prepared mild, medium, or spicy.

Napa Cafe, 5101 Sanderlin Ave., Ste. 122, Memphis, TN 38117; (901) 683-0441; napacafe.com; New American; $$–$$$. The surge of new restaurants in East Memphis over the past few years makes it easy to forget the trailblazers who ushered in chef-driven cuisine. Don't overlook Napa Cafe, tucked in a shopping center behind the Racquet Club since 1998. Owned by Glenda Hastings, Napa Cafe is ideal for special occasions, private parties, or midweek lunches. The business blue plate lunch includes daily specials (firecracker chicken with pan gravy on Friday!) plus a mind-blowing meat loaf made with ground prime tenderloin and sun-dried tomato gravy. First courses are generally ample enough for a light meal, especially the restaurant's short-rib sliders with jicama and red cabbage slaw. Evening entrees like duck, tuna, salmon, and filet mignon are delicious but not overly fancy, so they are nice companions for Napa's extensive selection of wines. A winner of the *Wine Spectator* magazine Award of Excellence for 12 consecutive years, Napa aggressively promotes international and domestic wines with special menus and more casual wine tastings paired with appetizer plates. Look for new seasonal options from Chef Rick Saviori, bento boxes on both lunch and dinner menus, and major renovations to Napa's dining room and bar. See Chef Saviori's recipe for **Braised Pork Cheeks with Sweet Potato Puree** on p. 285.

River Oaks Restaurant, 5871 Popular Ave., Memphis, TN 38119; (901) 683-9305; riveroaksrestaurant.com; French/American; $$–$$$. Tucked in an asphalt island near the I-240, the unassuming exterior of River Oaks belies the exquisite cuisine served inside. The Maîtres Cuisiniers de France named Chef-Owner José Gutierrez chef of the year in 2011, and with good reason. A longtime chef at **Chez**

Philippe (p. 54) in The Peabody, Gutierrez opened and closed a downtown restaurant before moving east to River Oaks, where he gives classic French cuisine a bistro spin without sacrificing flavor, detail, or elegant plating. There's also a touch of whimsy to the dishes at River Oaks. The Wednesday-night fried chicken special is served family style with green beans and mashed potatoes, and at lunch, the chef's TV dinner includes delectable mini courses on a divided, four-square plate. Lunch at River Oaks can be quick and satisfying, but let dinner be leisurely and drawn out. Start with a thyme-lemonade cocktail and cheese beignets, a pâte à choux dough with Camembert, gruyére, and a little lemon zest. Move on to Duck Two Ways or a rib eye with pommes gratin, a fat and happy steak draped with a veil of truffle sauce and a bright green plume of lightly steamed broccoli. See Chef-Owner José Gutierrez's recipe for **Crispy Ahi Tuna with English Pea–Wasabi Puree & Orzo Pilaf** on p. 274.

Sekisui Pacific Rim, 4724 Poplar Ave., Memphis, TN 39117; (901) 767-7770; sekisuiusa.com; Japanese/Sushi & Sashimi; $–$$$. I have eaten more meals at Sekisui Pacific Rim than any other restaurant in Memphis. Can there be any more sincere endorsement than that? Yes, Jimmy Ishii's flagship restaurant is close to my home, but my affinity for SPR, as it is commonly called, goes well beyond geography. For me, SPR wraps everything I love to eat into a sophisticated but friendly package. I like the restaurant's Ocean Pyramid so much that I frequently get it to go, skipping the restaurant's techno ambience for my sofa at home where I quietly savor the impressive mound of short-grain rice, yellowtail tuna, bluefin tuna, and salmon topped with sliced avocado and caviar. Sushi rules at SPR, especially the rolls, which change regularly. Overall, the SPR menu is seafood-centric, but its grilled teriyaki burger with swiss cheese, sautéed mushrooms, and onions is my husband's favorite burger in town. SPR also serves a nice selection of sake, wine, and signature cocktails, and on Friday and Saturday, the restaurant and sushi bar stay open late.

Sharky's Gulf Grill, 6201 Poplar Ave., Memphis, TN 38119; (901) 682-9796; sharkysgulfgrill.com; Seafood/Sushi & Sashimi; $$. Memphis has the Mississippi River, but it's still landlocked. In fact, driving to the Gulf Coast takes 8 hours, which accounts for some of Sharky's success. The pastel-colored restaurant with its spacious bar and Louisiana shutters feels like eating at the beach. The menu helps, too, replicating many of the dishes Memphians associate with summer vacations to Florida and Alabama: rock lobster, peel 'n' eat shrimp, oysters on the half shell, steamed seafood platters with corn on the cob and red potatoes, fresh-catch specials grilled or blackened, and Chef Tim Foley's blue-crab bisque, a sinfully delicious recipe made with claw meat and Fairbanks cream sherry. Sharky's flies in fresh seafood every day, a nice boost for the restaurant's entrees and extensive sushi menu of raw rolls, fried rolls, and nigiri. Even Sharky's iceberg wedge has a Gulf Coast twist: Four flame-grilled shrimp top the salad along with the requisite blue cheese and bacon bits. Sharky's seafood focus extends to Sunday brunch and to its coastal cocktails, which include golden margaritas and martinis made with pineapple.

Landmarks

Edo Japanese Restaurant, 4792 Summer Ave., Memphis, TN 38122; (901) 767-7096; Japanese, $–$$. Not long ago, I overheard a twentysomething talking up a potential date. "Let's go to Edo," he said. I was flabbergasted that Edo is a date destination for young people. After all, it was the first Japanese restaurant in Memphis and is still operating at its original location on Summer Avenue. But what's not to love about the place for customers of any age? The decor has a vintage campy appeal, and some of the food is authentic to its original era. Plus there's sushi, which is a nice update, especially the banzai roll stuffed with crab and salmon and garnished with gorgeous vertical sculptures of cucumber wedges and radish sprouts. Shabu-shabu (translation: swish, swish) is another popular option because the veggie, tofu, and sliced-beef soup is cooked right at the table.

Folk's Folly Original Prime Steak House, 551 S. Mendenhall, Memphis, TN 38117; (901) 762-8200; folksfolly.com; Steak House; $$–$$$. Folk's Folly is the perennial winner for best steak in Memphis, so there is nothing foolish about its name or its menu.

When founder Humphrey Folk decided to convert an East Memphis residence into a steak house, his friends didn't think it would work. The name Folk's Folly recognized their good-natured ribbing. More than 30 years later, the restaurant is still popular for business dinners, special occasions, or date nights, serving prime cuts to please any appetite: petit filet mignon, porterhouse, monster cowboy rib eye, lollipop veal chops, and range-fed rack of lamb. The menu also has steak specials like the 16-ounce New York strip served with bacon and onion-fried potatoes. Vegetables are a la carte, including potatoes made nine different ways. (Hint: Try potatoes au gratin or garlic-and-leek mashed.) Don't overlook the restaurant's retro piano bar where fried dill pickles come with every drink. For grilling at home, investigate the Prime Cut Shoppe next door, open Mon through Sat until 6:30 p.m. The market sells prime cuts, seafood, sides, and the restaurant's legendary chocolate fudge brownie.

Jim's Place Restaurant and Bar, 518 Perkins Extension, Memphis, TN 38117; (901) 766-2030; jimsplacememphis.com; American/Greek; $$–$$$. In 1912, Greek immigrant Nick Taras opened the first Jim's Place in the basement of a downtown hotel at Monroe and Main. Since then, the restaurant has moved several times, but it is still family owned and operated. From the start, Jim's Place specialized in hand-cut steaks and popular Greek dishes, such as *souflima,* a family recipe of rotisserie-grilled pork tenderloin still served today. In 2011, Jim's Place moved from the family's 5-acre homestead to the center of East Memphis, renovating a prime location into a stylish urban steak house with a Peter Luger feel. Longtime chef Scott Ritchie is still in charge, preparing customer favorites like charcoaled jumbo shrimp basted in lemon-oregano sauce alongside new additions such as lamb burgers with grilled eggplant and tzatziki. Southern classics such as yellow coconut cake with creamy divinity icing are on the menu as well. In addition to the more formal dining rooms, the new Jim's Place offers a spacious and comfortable bar for grown-ups. It's lively but not too loud, and experienced bartenders know how to mix manhattans and martinis. The Taras family also operates a second restaurant with a similar menu called Jim's Place Grille in Collierville: 3660 Houston Levee, Collierville, TN 38017; (901) 861-5000.

Lotus, 4970 Summer Ave., Memphis, TN 38122; (901) 682-1151; Vietnamese; $. For almost 30 years, Vietnamese immigrants Joe and Hanh Bach have been operating Lotus with the friendly confidence that comes from decades of experience running a restaurant. Joe handles the front of the house, while Hanh works the back, simmering chicken broth for three days for Lotus Combination Soup or stuffing duck with a decadently rich mix of meat, olives, and vegetables. The restaurant is funky and sometimes the air conditioner barely works, but these are ambient inconveniences that make the food taste even better. Bring your own wine (Lotus is only open for dinner) and order *banh xeo,* a crepe that leans toward the French side of Vietnamese cooking. Hanh stuffs ground pork, chopped green onions, baby shrimp, and crunchy bean sprouts into a paper-thin rice-flour crepe fried extra crispy. Dipping each bite into the side of sauce is essential because the citrus flavor blends the crepe's filling into a lovely, harmonious whole.

Mortimer's, 590 N. Perkins St., Memphis, TN 38117; (901) 761-9321; ardentmusic.biz/mortimersrestaurant; American; $–$$. It's easy to zip by Mortimer's restaurant, especially since the entrance is in the back. But next time slow down and think about lunch or dinner, and here's why: Mortimer's is the real deal. Operated by Sara Bell since 1981, the restaurant is a throwback to a time when adults could smoke, drink, and eat with impunity. These days, there's no smoking in Mortimer's, but the decades of classic American food and drink are layered in the place, giving it a blue collar *Mad Men* feel. Much of the ambience comes from Mortimer's storied history, which stretches back to the mid-1950s when Bell's father, Vernon Mortimer Bell, owned the Knickerbocker, an East Memphis institution remembered for its scallops, steaks, and fancy scroll menus. Many of the Knickerbocker recipes (trout amandine!) are still served at Mortimer's, along with daily lunch specials like salmon croquettes. Eating in the restaurant bar is another good option, especially on Saturday nights when oysters on the half shell are iced, served with lemon wedges, and cost 40 cents each. While visiting, take a few minutes to appreciate Mortimer's vintage kitsch decor and the tribute wall to family member Chris Bell, whose band Big Star was a Memphis standard bearer for the power pop superstars of the 1980s.

Pete & Sam's, 3886 Park Ave., Memphis, TN 38117; (901) 458-0694; peteandsams.com; Italian; $$. Pete & Sam's has been the city's go-to Italian restaurant for engagement parties, birthday dinners, or fun evenings out for almost 65 years. In its current location since 1960, this no-frills favorite offers American-Italian classics like house-made minestrone, ravioli, and lasagna served Southern style with sweet spaghetti sauce. Yes, Pete & Sam's uses canned mushrooms, but the throwback taste adds a nifty retro appeal to the restaurant's ample portions and great dollar value. Dinner specials, for instance, include an entree, a single-serve thin-crust pizza, and a second side for about $13. There's a joi de vivre to Pete & Sam's, a legacy of founder Sam Bomarito who died in 2012 at the age of 89. His customers carry on, cranking up the volume, especially on weekend nights. The restaurant's BYOB policy contributes to the energy. Pete & Sam's sells only beer, but customers can bring wine for a $3 setup. Some even bring liquor, filling chilled mason jars with vodka and ice.

Wang's Mandarin House, 6065 Park Ave., Memphis, TN 38119; (901) 763-0676; wangsmemphis.com; Chinese/Tapas; $–$$.

Remember when going out for Chinese meant a fancy restaurant with opulent wall treatments and large upholstered booths? Wang's Mandarin House still offers that kind of style and service, which is probably why the restaurant is the perennial winner for best Chinese food in Memphis. Since 1982, Wang's has anchored the shopping center at Park and Ridgeway, serving Mandarin, Cantonese, Szechuan, and spicy Hunan dishes. The chef's specialties are particularly good, especially Happy Family, a spicy brood of beef, prawns, pork, and chicken in the chef's special sauce, and Wang's Mu Shu vegetables, wok tossed with wood-ear mushrooms and cabbage and served with Chinese pancakes and sweet plum sauce. For more updated dishes, try Wang's new sushi bar or its adjoining space where owner Shelly Ansley's daughter, Lisa, serves a menu of small plates and cocktails. The cold and hot plates run from $4 to $8 and mix up American and Asian influences. Try cold sesame noodles, truffle mac 'n' cheese, or tangy Thai lime chicken wings. All three are nice companions for cocktails such as Sake Blossom, which is as refreshing as the promise of its name. Wang's also has a second location downtown: 113 S. Main St., Memphis, TN 38103; (901) 523-2065.

Barbecue & Blue Plates

Blue Plate Cafe, 5469 Poplar Ave., Memphis, TN 38119; (901) 761-9696; Breakfast / Plate Lunches; $. Breakfast at Blue Plate Cafe is so satisfying that after I finish my meal, I want to head home and paint my kitchen sunshine yellow to honor the cafe's cheerful paint and the made-from-scratch banana pancakes served with crunchy peanut butter syrup. The cafe does have a hospitable history. It was built as a private home in 1954 by Kemmons Wilson, the founder of Holiday Inn, before settling into its restaurant role in the mid-1990s. Since then, Blue Plate Cafe has built a legion of loyal customers, even though the service is spotty and waits are common on the weekends. In Memphis, good comfort food is worth the wait.

At Blue Plate, eggs and omelets come with homemade biscuits and sawmill gravy, along with buttermilk pancakes, hash browns, or grits. There are also eggs Florentine, belgian waffles, and the house specialty: pancakes made with raisins, chopped pecans, and cinnamon. The cafe serves breakfast all day, and meat-plus-threes kick in at 11 a.m. All the standards are here, plus some extra vegetable choices such as baked apples, Jello and fruit salad, and white soup beans. For workers and visitors downtown, Blue Plate operates a second location in the business and hotel district: 113 Court Sq. South, Memphis, TN 38103; (901) 523-2050.

Brother Juniper's, 3519 Walker Ave., Memphis, TN 38111; (901) 324-0144; brotherjunipers.com; Breakfast; $. Flanked by a Laundromat and a Goodwill store, Brother Juniper's started as an artisan bakery to teach at-risk youth the values of hard work and fellowship. The original Brother Juniper was the cook for St. Francis of Assisi, which fits right in with the cafe's hippy-dippy vibe. So does the food. House-made pastries, biscuits, muffins, and loaf breads are wholesome and heartfelt, and the menu is diverse. Hate eggs? Try one of 5 different potato meals on a plate, like home fries topped with chorizo, green onions, green peppers, cheddar, and sour cream. Worship celebrity chefs? Go for the 3-egg open-face omelet named the San Diegan, featured in Rachel Ray's book *Best Eats in Town*. Hung over? How about 2 eggs scrambled with a little cheddar and ham. Too young to eat much? Brother Juniper's has pancakes, waffles, and a children's plate. Vegan? You're covered, too, with black-bean breakfast burritos or tofu scramble. No matter what's ordered, all meals include grits or home fries and biscuit or toast served with the restaurant's legendary fruit spreads, which are also sold online and at the restaurant.

Ching's Hot Wings, 1264 Getwell, Memphis, TN 38111; (901) 743-5545; Chicken Wings; $. The motto for Ching's Hot Wings is "Best Damn Wings Period." Most customers pretty much agree, especially players from the University of Memphis Tigers basketball team who say Ching's makes the best wings this side of Buffalo. Player testimonies abound in this sports-centric wing joint. Jerseys, posters, and more than 100 framed photos cover the restaurant's walls, and the memorabilia is fun to read while waiting for a hearty mix of drummies and two-prongers seasoned mild hot, extra hot, suicide, lemon pepper, dry hot, honey gold, honey hot, or honey extra hot. (My husband's favorite: honey gold.) Every order comes with a sweet croissant, carrots, and celery sticks and a choice of ranch or blue cheese dressing. Go with the blue cheese. Ching's is a family restaurant named after owner Josh Williams' grandmother, so don't be put off by the location's funky strip center. Inside, the wings are authentic, the service is fast, and the customers in line might include a local celebrity athlete.

Corky's Ribs & BBQ, 5259 Poplar Ave., Memphis, TN 38119; (901) 685-9744; corkysbbq.com; Barbecue; $. People in Memphis like to debate about where to find the best ribs, and Corky's is always a contender. For more than three decades, customers have flocked to Corky's multiple locations to "get some [sauce] on ya," an inevitability at this nationally recognized restaurant where the barbecue sauce is finger-licking delicious and the meaty ribs are slow cooked over hickory and charcoal for 18 hours. Corky's also serves classic Memphis dry ribs, along with pulled pork shoulder, chicken, turkey breast, and beef brisket. And then there are the extras: fried onion loaf, barbecue potato skins, smokehouse salad, and homemade fudge pie. Out-of-town visitors may have spotted Corky's franchises in other states. If not, consider sending a little taste of Memphis to friends and family back home. Corky's overnights gift packs with slabs, shoulders, and all the fixings. Options range from bottles of sauce and seasoning to the Memphis Throw Down, a party blowout for 20 that includes slabs, sauces, beans, and pies. Other local Corky's are located at 1740 Germantown Pkwy., Cordova, TN 38018, (901) 737-1988; 743 W. Poplar Ave., Memphis, TN 38017, (901) 405-4999.

Neely's Bar-B-Que, 670 Jefferson, Memphis, TN 38103; (901) 521-9798; neelysbbq.com; Barbecue; $. Several years ago, I visited Nashville's Grand Ole Opry Hotel for a food convention, primarily to see Pat and Gina Neely in action. The Food Network stars from *Down Home with the Neelys* were headliners for the convention, but I didn't understand their popularity until I sat with the adoring audience. "Good Lord," I thought. "This pair rode barbecue into the world of celebrity chefs." No kidding. These days, the couple has cookbooks, great television ratings, and a second show with Food Network called *Road Tasted with the Neelys*. Their launch, however, was humble: a small barbecue restaurant in downtown Memphis started in 1988 by Pat and his three brothers. Gina joined the team a few years later when the family opened a second restaurant in East Memphis. Both restaurants still operate today along with a third location in Nashville, offering exactly what the Neelys preach: the real deal. Voted best ribs in both Memphis and Nashville, the Neelys use a secret spice (surprise!) for beef ribs, pork ribs, and rib tip dinners. The restaurants also serve a few specialties, including hot wings, spaghetti, and Texas beef sausage topped with sauce and slaw. In Memphis, the Neelys' second restaurant is located at 5700 Mount Moriah Rd., Memphis, TN 38115; (901) 795-4177.

Three Little Pigs BBQ, 5145 Quince Rd., Memphis, TN 38117; (901) 685-7095; threelittlepigsbar-b-q.com; Barbecue; $. The barbecue history is layered into Three Little Pigs BBQ, a neighborhood favorite where customers contribute pig memorabilia to owner Charlie Robertson's extensive collection. Shelves line three walls to display the mementos, but customers focus more attention on the line that typically forms around dinnertime. The menu is pretty simple at Three Little Pigs: only chopped or pulled shoulder (no butts or ribs) and a trademark tangy barbecue sauce that leans toward the thin side. The sauce recipe, along with recipes for the restaurant's slaw and beans, came from Loeb's Barbecue, a now defunct chain of barbecue joints that in its heyday included more than 100 locations, including this spot near the intersection of Quince and White Station. Customers are almost fanatical about the beans at Three Little Pigs, made from scratch with chili powder, brown sugar, beans, and ground meat from the pork shoulders, which are pit cooked daily for 24 hours.

Tops Bar-B-Q, 3970 Rhodes Ave., Memphis, TN 38111; (901) 323-9865; topsbarbq.com; Barbecue; $. My introduction to brisket came from my New York mother-in-law, who in fine Jewish tradition cooks brisket as often as possible. That's why I never expected to see brisket at a barbecue joint. At Tops Bar-B-Q, the brisket sandwich, pulled into sweet smoky shreds and piled on a bun with mild or hot barbecue sauce, is a new addition to a menu that started in 1952 and has been smoking ever since. Pork shoulders at Tops are pit cooked for 10 hours over hardwood, charcoal, and green hickory at each of the chain's 14 locations. But the brisket is cooked in smokers, which probably explains the meat's extra smoky flavor.

Many barbecue restaurants in Memphis also sell beef barbecue, but at Tops, the beef is saved for burgers that are freshly ground and made to order with lettuce, cheese, and pickles. The beans at Tops are also delicious, flavored with bits of pork and an occasional chunk of bacon. Some Tops restaurants are drive-thru, but first-timers should skip convenience for the retro charm of an original location. The Tops brick-pit chimney near Getwell and Rhodes, for instance, is always warm to the touch, and its walk-up window still includes the restaurant's original buzzer.

Specialty Stores, Markets & Producers

Charlie's Meat Market, 4790 Summer Ave., Memphis, TN 38112; (901) 683-1192. A poster of a steer hangs on the wall at Charlie's Meat Market, detailing the location on the animal of different cuts of beef. It's a nice touch, but hardly necessary when a bevy of butchers are on hand to explain the difference between a skirt steak and a hanger steak. Charlie Hogan Jr. started Charlie's in 1967, and the business is still family run. An old-fashioned butcher shop in the best sense, the market offers expertise along with a remarkable assortment of beef and pork, all hand cut into a myriad of price points. Premium-cut and bacon-wrapped filets mignons, for instance, start at 4 ounces, a nice option for customers cutting back on their meat. Restraint, on the other hand, is difficult at Charlie's,

where freezers overflow with beef, pork, and poultry in bulk, and the shelves are stocked with an abundant assortment of marinades and grilling spices. While many customers stay focused on the market's steaks, roasts, and tenderloins, don't overlook the leftovers. Butchers grind beef, chuck, and round every day from the market's trimmings, and Charlie's Italian links and andouille sausages have a not-too-spicy appeal.

Cosmic Coconut, 5101 Sanderlin Ave., Memphis, TN 38117; (901) 729-7134; cosmiccoconut.com. Silly me. Until I visited the Cosmic Coconut, the only vegan juice bar in Memphis, I didn't get the coconut connection. It seems coconut milk and coconut meat are important substitutes for dairy, which isn't missed one bit in the bar's lovely list of smoothies and juices, available in 9-, 12-, and 16-ounce servings. Tucked in an out-of-the-way retail center, the juice bar has earned an enthusiastic following that is moving from niche to mainstream. An expanded menu of snacks and food helps. Coconutties sold three to a pack are a crossover favorite, a raw cookie made with cashews, almonds, carob, and sweeteners that tastes like a crunchy and delicious piece of chocolate cake. The bar also serves up coffees, cappuccinos, lattes, and frappes along with at least a dozen loose-leaf teas. Steel-cut oats with fresh fruit and soup specials like sweet potato lentil are giving customers more reasons to stick around and enjoy the ambience of Cosmic Coconut. The place is charming. Flats of wheatgrass fill a sunny window, tables and chairs are vintage finds, and the store's graphic wallpaper feels a little like the Jetsons.

Curb Side Casseroles, 5130 Wheelis Dr., Memphis, TN 38117; (901) 761-0287; curbsidecasseroles.com. Raising a house full of hungry kids and juggling two jobs? If so, Curbside Casseroles could be an important BFF. Singles and busy professionals will also appreciate the gourmet to-go casseroles sold Tuesday, Thursday, and Saturday from a small back house on a residential cul-de-sac. Open since 2007, Curbside jumped into the prepared-meal boom early, and their customers remain loyal, especially during the holidays when a green-bean casserole or pimento spread can be a lifesaver. Curbside sells dozens of dishes, from old-school classics like strawberry cake, stuffed bell peppers, homemade sweet pickles, and cheesy chicken enchiladas to more updated fare such as green chile stew and salmon with mango salsa. Desserts, sides, and entrees are frozen and ready to bake and come in three different sizes to fit any family or occasion.

Dinstuhl's, 436 Grove Park, Memphis, TN 38117; (901) 682-3373; dinstuhls.com. The arrival of April in Memphis is marked in many ways, but none is more fanciful than a visit to Dinstuhl's candies, where the store's merchandising duplicates the palette of spring. It's impossible to settle on one candy, so grab a basket and fill it up: buttercream eggs, milk chocolate bunnies on sucker sticks, orange jelly beans packaged like carrots, dark chocolate eggs wrapped in purple and pink foil, and ladybug sugar cookies iced in pastel hues. For more than 100 years, Dinstuhl's has sweetened up Memphis with hand-stirred candy made in small batches: truffles, turtles, caramels, molded chocolates, boxed chocolates, and house specialties like cashew crunch. The stores are sensory overload, especially during the holidays and when chocolate-dipped fruit arrives. Dinstuhl's sells pineapple and grapes dipped in milk chocolate year-round, but the strawberries don't arrive until Valentine's Day, the raspberries come in July, and the blackberries pacify the August heat. In 1983 Dinstuhl's moved its candy kitchen to an 11,000 square-foot space in Bartlett, where open houses with plenty of samples are held in December and March.

Farmers' Market at the Garden, 750 Cherry Rd., Memphis, TN 38117; (901) 576-4100; memphisbotanicgarden.com. I pick up my CSA on Wednesday afternoon at this neighborhood farmers' market, so it's difficult not to play favorites. Confession aside, even the vendors who participate in other venues admit the market at Memphis Botanic Gardens has an intrinsic sociability that makes farm-to-table shopping a pleasure. Certainly, the setting helps, offering a relaxed line of vendor tents and a pine tree grove to fend off summer heat. Shoppers also come in manageable waves for local produce, meat, flowers, garden plants, and artisan crafts instead of the mad crunch at the larger outdoor markets. In addition to produce vendors, the market hosts some of the best local producers in the city, including OC Vegan Foods, Groovy Granola, Peace Bee

Homegrown Chain: Easy-Way Produce

Visitors to Memphis might dismiss the bright orange Easy-Way stores as some sort of peanut/produce stand more suited for rural roads than busy intersections. Don't be fooled. Easy-Way Produce is one of the most treasured local chains in Memphis, started in 1932 by Pate Carter as a single downtown grocery. Still family owned and operated, Easy-Way shifted toward produce in the early '70s, an emphasis continued today at its seven locations. From the beginning, the stores promoted regional produce and competitive prices, showcasing Ripley tomatoes early in the season and discounting day-old produce instead of throwing it away. Some products are sold in bulk, like pecans, dry pinto beans, and individually wrapped chocolates made by the Amish in Tennessee. Groceries also reflect the chain's local commitment with an eclectic inventory from small producers: loaf bread, purple popcorn, Muscadine grape cider, dill pickles in gallon jars, and chocolate milk from a nearby dairy. For decades Easy-Way closed on Sunday, but most stores are now open 7 days a week. For a complete listing of locations, click on the Easy-Way website at easywayproduce.com.

Farms honey, and responsibly raised beef from Mathis Creek Farms. Another popular attraction is One Sharp Dude, a mobile sharpener who brings the edge back to scissors, garden tools, and kitchen cutlery.

Gibson's Donuts, 760 Mount Moriah Rd., Memphis, TN 38117; (901) 682-8200. Anchoring a small retail strip with a revolving retro sign, Gibson's is everything a doughnut shop should be: open 24 hours with deep discounts every night from 11 p.m. to 1 a.m. No surprise the college kids start pulling up at 10:30 p.m., forming a line out the front door by 11. For 45 years, the early, early morning shift has been baking trays of Gibson's doughnuts in dozens of varieties. Sprinkles, glazed, cake, filled, cinnamon, sugar, iced, and twisted, they are all here, including buttermilk drops, a relative newcomer recently featured on the Cooking Channel's *Cheap Eats*. A mainstay of New Orleans, buttermilk drops were the signature doughnut of a place called McKenzie's, which never reopened after Hurricane Katrina. Now Gibson's carries the baton in a nod to the family's own roots in the French Quarter. A couple of things make buttermilk drops unique. They don't have a hole in center; instead, the doughnuts puff up into a moist Southern white cake on the inside with a crunchy exterior. The exact cooking method is a trade secret, but oil temperature, the amount of oil in the fryer, and the temperature of the batter all count. (Secret batter ingredient: ice cubes.)

Holiday Deli & Ham Co., 585 Erin Dr., Memphis, TN, 38117; (901) 763-4499; holidaydeli.com. At Holiday Deli & Ham, the honey-glazed ham salad dips back to a time when every kitchen had a meat grinder and no part of a Sunday ham was ever wasted. Diced in perfect chunks, the deli's honey-glazed ham salad is mixed with celery, green onions, sweet pickles, and mayo and piled on bread with tomatoes and shredded iceberg lettuce. The ham salad has been on the deli's menu since it opened in 1993, along with other family recipes like Papa's Famous Pimento Cheese, a Southern classic done right. In addition to cold sandwiches, Holiday Deli offers a nice mix of hot sandwiches and panini, including Luke's Kickin' Chicken with chipotle BBQ sauce, cheddar cheese, and bacon. All sandwiches include a bag of Ruffles original chips and a wedge of dill pickle for about $7, so lunch is affordable and filling. The deli serves breakfast, too, starting at 6:30 a.m. during the week. (Recommendation: a stuffed breakfast quesadilla.) Breakfast and lunch specials like spicy cheese grits, fiesta black bean salad, and homemade taco soup cycle in every month, and the deli is a full-service caterer for platters, trays, and boxed lunches. Additional Holiday Deli & Ham restaurants are located at 2087 Union Ave., Memphis, TN 38104, (901) 881-6433; 7652 Poplar Ave., Memphis, TN 38138, (901) 869-6650; 3750 Hacks Cross Rd., Memphis, TN 38125, (901) 624-4848.

J. Brooks Coffee Roasters, 6073 Mount Moriah Rd., Memphis, TN 38115; (901) 488-7529; jbrookscoffeeroasters.com. While other cities are crowded with premium roasters, Memphis has only a few. J. Brooks is the newbie, but their flavorful brews are blended by pros. John Pitman and Ben Bondurant are experienced roasters who understand there's more to good coffee than turning on the pot. Their artisan roaster specializes in beans from around the world, offering blends, single origins, decaf, and espresso. Their blends are exceptionally good, because beans are individually roasted to their best flavor point and then combined with other beans into distinctive combinations. J. Brooks coffee is served at local restaurants, and 12-ounce bags are sold at specialty markets, the **Cooper-Young Community Farmers Market** (p. 113), and Superlo grocery. The roasters also are packaging private label blends such as the bold and flavorful blend Urban Joe sold at **Urban Farms Market** (p. 121) in Binghampton.

La Michoacana, 4019 Summer Ave., Memphis, TN 38122; (901) 555-1234. In Memphis, where air conditioners run six months a year, a *paleteria* called La Michoacana has turned the humble Popsicle into the city's rock star of refreshment. House-made at the store's original location on Winchester Drive, the all-natural *paletas* are made with fruit and cream in dozens of flavors. On any day of the week (52 weeks a year), there are about 60 flavors in rotation. The flavors change so quickly there are no labels in the store, but owner Rafael Gonzalez is happy to run through the list: cream pops like butter pecan, mocha, and pine nut, or frozen fruit bars like guava, watermelon, and pineapple. Listening to Gonzalez chant the names of the paletas in the cold case is a mesmerizing melody until he hits a chord you can't pass up. For me, it tends to be rum raisin or, more recently, rose petal and chocolate. The paletas also are affordable: $2 for a regular, or spend an extra dollar to get one dipped in chocolate, sprinkles, or chopped nuts. La Michoacana also operates a paleteria at 6635 Winchester Dr., Memphis, TN 38115; (901) 365-4992.

Lucchesi's Ravioli & Pasta Company, 540 S. Mendenhall, Ste. 3, Memphis, TN 38117; (901) 766-9922; lucchesis.com. The cheerful red-and-white awnings on Lucchesi's storefront foretell the personality of this Italian market and deli selling meats and cheeses from countries around the world and pasta and sauces made with family recipes. Lucchesi's makes and freezes more than two dozen entrees every day, including 5 kinds of lasagna, Italian meatballs, chicken cacciatore, veal Parmesan, and an impressive assortment of ravioli, including mushroom and four-cheese. There's an authenticity to Lucchesi's, and no wonder. The family has been making pasta for generations, starting with John P. Robilio, who immigrated to Memphis in 1909 to build a thriving grocery and import business that eventually became Ronco Pasta. These days, the family grocery includes homemade soups and desserts, an extensive deli for Italian-style sandwiches on artisan bread, and more traditional deli favorites like tuna salad and egg and olive. Lucchesi's also sells its popular take-and-bake pizzas made with the deli's special three-cheese blend.

Mediterranean International Grocery, 3561 Park Ave., Memphis, TN 38111; (901) 320-5799. The first time I pulled into the parking lot of Mediterranean International Grocery, I was a bit mesmerized by the large neon letters on the store's plate glass windows. The sprawling script advertised lamb and goat, Halal meat, and the best gyros and falafels in town. I wondered, Is there any food here I understand? And then I spotted this: organic chicken. Now we're talking, I thought, heading inside where owner Sami Abdelfattah explained how cage-free chickens from Crescent Foods are raised on vegetarian diets without hormones or antibiotics. I promptly purchased a roaster, along with a bag of large fava beans, a bag of basil seeds, and a small bucket of green olives packed with lemon slices, bay leaves, and yellow pepper. Plenty of the store's other groceries were also familiar and competitively priced: couscous, lentils, basmati rice, grapeseed oil, kitchenware, freshly made hummus, and hookahs lined up in a row. Abdelfattah opened Mediterranean Grocery in 1997, adding more international foods to the Middle Eastern mix as his business grew. The grocery also has a small restaurant with charbroiled kebabs made to order and plate lunches liked *adas polo,* a seasoned chicken served with basmati rice, lentils, and dates.

Memphis Marinades, memphismarinades.com. Meat marinades are a crowded field in Memphis, but grill maestro Jim Boland has something unique: dry marinades for beef, chicken, lamb, and pork. Called Memphis Marinades, these seasonings tenderize and flavor meat when mixed with water. It's an unusual concept that works. Boland spent more than a decade perfecting the marinades in his own kitchen and in barbecue cooking competitions around the world. He uses limes, lemons, and oranges in the marinades because the citrus adds nice flavor and helps lower the salt content. At about $7 a jar, they are affordable, easy to store, and 100 percent natural. Look for the marinades online and at specialty stores, including **Miss Cordelia's** (p. 68) grocery downtown and **Charlie's Meat Market** (p. 161) in East Memphis.

Muddy's Bake Shop, 5101 Sanderlin, Memphis, TN 38117; (901) 683-8844; muddysbakeshop.com. Memphis was a little late putting cupcakes on the table, which might explain the initial popularity of Muddy's Bake Shop when it opened in 2008. The bakery's staying power, however, rests squarely on the mixing bowl and marketing savvy of owner Kat Gordon, who has built an almost fanatical fan base for her from-scratch cupcakes like Prozac (chocolate/chocolate), Razzle Dazzle (chocolate/raspberry), and Frankly Scarlet (red velvet/cream cheese.) Gordon also is a charming advocate for ecofriendly practices, promoting clean packing and local ingredients such as cage-free eggs. Her bakery has a cute retro theme with a smattering of locally made products. Her menu of baked goods also keeps growing with seasonal specials for cookies, bars, and pies that change week to week. To accommodate her growth, Gordon moved her support bakery in 2012 to Midtown's emerging arts district on Broad Avenue. Watch for workshops, special events, and maybe a pop-up bakery. See Owner Kat Gordon's recipe for **Strawberry Rhubarb Pie** on p. 288.

Poplar Perk 'N, 4610 Poplar Ave., Memphis, TN 38117; (901) 433-9401. When a Facebook friend's lament alerted Jimmy Whidden that a coffee shop had closed at the corner of Poplar and Perkins, he stepped in with a plan. He came up with a cute name and hired experienced baristas who helped him locate a local fair-trade-coffee roaster named Gusta Java in Jackson, Tennessee. That was in 2009, and since then, Poplar Perk 'N has stayed amped up in a small corner location with a busy drive-thru and a few indoor and outdoor tables. Yes, there are nice baked goods and munchies to go with the drinks, but coffees, lattes, and smoothies are what matter here. Monthly drink specials keep the menu lively, such as the Pink Palace White Mocha, named after a local museum but beholding to strawberry syrup and white mocha sauce. Regulars seem to get a kick out of Poplar Perk 'N's quotes of the day, which are scrawled on a chalkboard in a sprawling handwritten script.

Ricki's Cookie Corner, 5068 Park Ave., Memphis, TN 38117; (901) 866-2447; rickiscookies.com. Long before *artisan* became a buzz word, Ricki Krupp turned out challah bread in her home kitchen along with her original "chipsticks," a chocolate-chip cookie bar that is soft, chewy, and memorable. In 2000, she kicked off the new millennium with a commercial kitchen in Eastgate

Shopping Center, expanding her offerings to include biscotti, cakes, chipsticks in new flavors, and half a dozen varieties of brownies. Challah bread remains a mainstay, offering unique options such as chocolate, cinnamon raisin, butter crust, whole wheat, and round challah for high holidays. A certified kosher bakery, Ricki's continues to celebrate Jewish holidays with traditional baked goods, such as hamantaschen for Purim filled with poppy seeds, chocolate, or fruit. A longtime favorite for corporate gift giving, Ricki's also maintains a busy mail-order business, offering cookies and brownies in an assortment of gift tins and samplers. The nearby Kroger and **Easy-Way Produce** (p. 165) stores also sell her products, but the best selection is at the bakery, where Krupp is typically on hand to offer samples and a friendly chat.

Shoaf's Loaf Organic Bakery, (662) 801-1822. A shift from corporate attorney to artisan baker is not a typical trajectory, but that's exactly what Sarah Tinkler did, joining her mom, Melinda Shoaf, to build a small-batch bakery for sticky buns, dinner rolls, cinnamon rolls, and rustic, hard-crusted *boule.* Tinkler uses freshly ground, organic whole wheat flour and seasonal produce for an ever-changing cornucopia of family recipes and her own kitchen experiments. The bakery's cinnamon rolls, for instance, mimic the seasons. Tinkler adds berries in the spring, peaches in the summer, and apples in the fall. In the winter, Tinkler also makes homemade

University of Memphis Vegetable Garden: Free Food & a Place to Relax

Blame it on the bedding plants yanked up and replaced at the University of Memphis every spring and fall.

So says campus veterinarian Karyl Buddington about her inspiration for the school's community vegetable garden, tucked between a parking garage and outdoor running track.

"The wasted time and money made me a little crazy," says Buddington, who is the university's director of animal-care facilities and heads the garden committee. "I thought we should be growing food."

Started in 2009 with money from student green fees, the project today includes the main Urban Oasis garden with 52 raised beds for produce and flowers, along with smaller gardens scattered around campus. In 2012, the school approved another $54,000 to develop an outdoor classroom and a series of seminar speakers, and the garden committee published the *Healthy Living Cookbook* with recipes from students, faculty, and staff.

Built and maintained by volunteers and a handful of student workers, the gardens are a gift to the school community and to its nearby neighborhood. In other words, the organic vegetables, flowers, and herbs are free.

"If you pick it, you can have it," Buddington says. "We don't want people in our community to be hungry because they need to pay for gas instead of food."

The garden's diverse selection of produce, especially at the peak of summer, is remarkable for a largely volunteer effort. There are plenty of Southern favorites: pole beans, tomatoes, sunflowers, okra, corn, basil, and a half-a-dozen different peppers. Mounds of perennial herbs such as thyme, rosemary, and mint tumble over cinder-block edging. Watermelon vines meander across plastic sheeting staked in place to hold back the weeds, and blackberry bushes hug a tiger statue, decorated with mirrored glass in the manner of a gazing ball.

The garden's growing season extends into winter with cold frames for vegetables such as beets, kale, and collards, and cover crops such as clover and winter wheat. "We even plant hops because they are so pretty to look at," Buddington says. "And who knows? Maybe someone will want to make beer."

The main garden is located on the University of Memphis campus behind the Elma Neal Roane Fieldhouse, 495 Zach Curline St., Memphis, TN 38152; (901) 682-7718.

Admittedly, students and neighbors sometimes pick vegetables too early or pull them up by their roots; increased PLEASE DON'T PICK ME signage helps. So does experience. "The garden is about learning for all of us," Buddington says. "Everyone makes mistakes."

For Buddington, the garden's most important lessons teach sustainability, healthy eating, and the value of slowing down. "Our lives are too busy," she says. "That's why we put tables and umbrellas in the garden. We want people to sit down, relax, and enjoy the day."

soups, churning out quarts of heart-warming goodness like matzo ball soup made with peas, celery, carrot chunks, shredded chicken, perfect (not greasy) chicken broth, and matzos the size of tennis balls. Shoaf's Loaf products are on the menu at **The Elegant Farmer** (p. 134) in East Memphis, at the downtown **Memphis Farmers Market** (p. 67) in the summer, and at the **Tsunami Winter Farmers Market** (p. 121) in Cooper-Young during the winter months. Check Facebook for the bakery's menu from week to week.

Memphis Suburbs

Germantown, Cordova, Collierville & Bartlett

Newcomers call the bedroom communities surrounding the city of Memphis the suburbs. Longtime residents simply say the County, lumping together the towns of Shelby County into a homogeneous reference that implies family-friendly neighborhoods, separate school districts, and no city taxes.

For the purposes of this book, Cordova is included, although the community is part of Memphis. Germantown, Collierville, and Bartlett, however, are governed independently with histories that stretch back to the early 1800s. Germantown was founded in 1825 and named Pea Ridge, but changed its name to Germantown in 1836 because of the town's growing German population. Collierville was incorporated in 1850, but was destroyed almost entirely during a battle in the Civil War. It was incorporated again in 1870, and its small-town appeal continues today, thanks to a historic town square with charming brick buildings from the turn of the century. Bartlett also dates back to about 1830 when the town was a way station on the stagecoach route from Nashville westward. It remained a small farming community for the next 100 years.

Similar demographics and growth tie these communities together in terms of retail businesses, residences, and restaurants. The towns stayed small and somewhat isolated for decades until developers started building homes to accommodate population shifts in the 1960s. For instance, from 1950 to 1999, Germantown's population grew from 400 to 40,000. Along with residential growth, came retail, but most businesses were national chains suited for malls and new strip centers.

The propensity in the suburbs for chain restaurants continues today. There are, of course, exceptions, and this chapter details some of the independently owned restaurants and markets that break the suburban mold. Some, like Germantown Commissary, have been serving family-friendly barbecue for more than 25 years. Others, like the sprawling international supermarkets, reflect burgeoning ethnic communities in suburbs once predominantly populated by white families. And, finally, there are longtime restaurateurs, like Ronnie Grisanti, who are trying something new. Grisanti, part of the city's best-known family of Italian chefs, is ready to open a cafe inside the Sheffield Antiques Mall in Collierville. Look for brunch on Sunday, lunch Monday through Saturday, and dinner on Friday and Saturday nights.

Bangkok Alley, 2150 W. Poplar Ave., Collierville, TN 38017; (901) 854-8748; bangkokalley.com; Thai/Sushi & Sashimi; $–$$. Roasted duck topped with bamboo shoots, pineapple, fresh basil, and rich red curry sauce is why Bangkok Alley now has three restaurants. Okay, that's an exaggeration, but the complex and complementary flavors in the dish illustrate why customers are so enthusiastic about this family-run restaurant. Thara and Dottie Burana opened their first restaurant in 2002, and since then their menu and reputation continue to grow. Bangkok Alley also serves nigiri, sashimi, and specialty rolls, but the dishes on the Thai side of the menu shine brightest. Choose chicken, tofu, shrimp, or beef in one of 5 different curries including a lovely spin on panang. Other dishes to try are *pad prik, larb* chicken on fresh lettuce, and seafood *keowhan,* a mix of shrimp, scallops, and fresh fish, squash, zucchini, and peppers in a green curry and basil sauce. The restaurant's Collierville location has a nice bar and an outdoor patio with privacy screens. Other locations are in Midtown (121 Union Ave., Memphis, TN 38103; 901-522-2010) and East Memphis (715 W. Brookhaven Circle, Memphis, TN 38117; 901-590-2585).

Elfo's Restaurant, 2285 S. Germantown Rd., Germantown, TN 38138; (901) 753-4017; elfosrestaurant.com; Italian; $–$$$. No name in Memphis is more associated with Italian food than the Grisanti family. At Elfo's Restaurant, Alex Grisanti continues cooking traditions started by his great-grandfather Rinaldo in the early 1900s, preparing northern Italian cuisine with fresh ingredients from long-standing family recipes. For instance, Grisanti still serves the Elfo Special, a pasta recipe developed by his grandfather with garlic, butter, mushrooms, and shrimp. The restaurant's house-made ravioli stuffed with chicken, beef, pork, eggs, spinach, and herbs is also excellent. So is the house-made manicotti baked in Tuscan meat gravy. Along with other traditional dishes like veal or eggplant parmigiana, Elfo's offers a delicious pan-seared sea bass in white wine, tomato, and artichoke sauce, and a bacon-wrapped beef filet stuffed with Gorgonzola and plated with wild mushrooms. For eating at home, consider family-size meals to go such as lasagna or fettuccini Alfredo or Grisanti's special sauces sold in individual quarts. Elfo's also has a spacious and sophisticated bar separated from the dining room for a nightcap or an appetizer after work.

Las Tortugas Deli Mexicana, 1215 S. Germantown Rd., Germantown, TN 38138; (901) 751-1200; delimexicana.com; Mexican; $–$$. Visit Las Tortugas just once, and you'll be friends with Pepe Magallanes and his lively storytelling from a stool behind the cash register. Pepe will tell you that Las Tortugas doesn't serve cheese dip, burritos, nachos, or sour cream because the restaurant is completely, unapologetically, Mexican. He'll explain how ingredients are purchased fresh and local every day, so tacos are a little more expensive than their Tex-Mex brethren. Don't worry. Order a sweet specialty tea from Mexico City made with freshly squeeze citrus and marvel at your plate of food before digging in:

grilled fish tacos plated with small warm corn tortillas, shredded lettuce, cilantro, sweet onion, slices of fresh avocado and lime, hand-cut tostada chips, and the restaurant's unbelievably wonderful green spicy salsa blended with avocados. Everyone leaves happy from Las Tortugas, which is unequivocally one of the best restaurants in 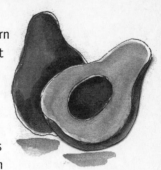 Memphis. Started by Pepe in 2003 and now owned and operated by his son Jonathan, the taqueria is unpretentious and authentic, offering tacos and tortas filled with such deliciousness as pork tenderloin rubbed with a dried house seasoning mix, wrapped in banana leaves, slow roasted, and finished with fresh chopped pineapple. Remember to check the daily chalkboard specials, which could include such choices as Rock Lobster Tortuga, shrimp seviche, ancho–black bean tostadas, chicken tortilla soup, or *carne asada* tacos made with prime dry-aged rib eye. See Chef Magallanes's recipe for **Braised Beef Brisket in Achiote** on p. 283.

Lavoro's, 5849 Summer Ave., Memphis, TN 38134; (901) 377-2141; lavorosmemphis.com; Italian; $$. The warm loaf of fresh bread with soft butter arrives to the table first. A side salad with house-made creamy Italian dressing comes next, followed by more bread and this entree: half a dozen large ravioli stuffed with portobello mushrooms in a rich broth studded with toasted walnuts and a sprinkle of herbs and chopped green onions. Sounds expensive, I know, but the cost of dinner so far is only $12.50, so go ahead and order another bottle of wine. What a pleasure it is to eat delicious food made from scratch without spending a day's wages. At Lavoro's, the menu is traditional but not heavy, offering standards such as lasagna Bolognese and chicken Marsala, along with chalkboard specials made with the fresh basil and rosemary that grow like hedges by the restaurant's front and back doors. Be forewarned: The penne is whole wheat at Lavoro's, so if that's a problem, don't order the baked ziti. There are many other wonderful options, including pizza; roasted stuffed peppers topped with cheese; and house-made pesto tortellini stuffed with chicken and kissed with cream. Lavoro is the Italian word for "working," which is also the last name of Mike Working who runs the restaurant with partner Melinda Gallimore. If you're lucky, Gallimore might also be your server. While the food is excellent at Lavoro's, the restaurant is a refurbished KFC. But the funky setting doesn't matter a bit, especially when you are floating in a fragrant cloud of mussels, garlic, and basil.

Mensi's Dairy Bar, 162 Washington St., Collierville, TN 38017; (901) 853-2161; Drive-in / Hot Dogs / Milk Shakes & Malts; $. Mensi's serves banana milk shakes, cheeseburgers, onion rings, and fries along with a large portion of nostalgia at their walk-up restaurant near Collierville's historic town square. Located a few blocks from what was Collierville High School (now it's the middle school), Mensi's is a no-frills setting for inexpensive and fast food

HOMEGROWN CHAIN: LENNY'S SUB SHOP

On my last visit to Lenny's, I was flabbergasted to see a couple of new sandwiches on the menu: black bean veggie, ultimate BBQ melt; and buffalo chicken Philly. For as long as I can remember, the menu at Lenny's Sub Shop had stayed the same: 9 cold subs, hot sandwiches including an authentic Philly cheesesteak, 5 deli sandwiches on freshly baked rolls, a couple of salads, 4 kid's meals, assorted bags of chips, and chocolate chip cookies. They also had great tea, and they still do. For years, I always ordered Lenny's homemade chicken salad, but at some point I switched to the shop's Italian sub, a heaping half pound of provolone, ham, prosciutto, capocollo, and Genoa salami. You can't go wrong with either sandwich because Lenny's prides itself on top-quality meats put together in a consistent way. Sheila and Len Moore started the chain in 1998 with the slogan "more food, more taste, more personality." It was a winning combination for Memphis, where few sub shops existed outside of the chains. Lenny's also is authentic thanks to Len Moore's background. He opened his first sub shop on the boardwalk in Wildwood, New Jersey, in 1979, and went on to work for corporate restaurants before opening Lenny's in Memphis. Today, more than 150 Lenny's are located in 19 states, including Michigan, Virginia, Florida, and Texas. To view complete menus and specific store addresses, click on the company's website at lennys.com.

such as shakes, malts, ice cream, hot wings, and hot dogs. Opinions on Mensi's food range from "okay" to "quite good" and probably have more to do with expectations than quality. One sure way to avoid disappointment is to order the dairy bar's hot-fudge cake. It's more like a chocolate cake sandwich with whipped cream, chocolate syrup, and ice cream in the middle. The butterscotch milk shake also is excellent. Service at Mensi's is take-out only, so there's nowhere to sit, but the shady town square with its pretty gazebo is only a short walk away.

Mulan Chinese Bistro, 2059 Houston Levee Rd., Collierville, TN 38017; (901) 850-5288; mulanbistro.net; Chinese/Sushi & Sashimi; $–$$. Click on the website for Mulan Chinese Bistro, and a parade of dishes marches by: Long Fong Wedding, honey shrimp, sizzling Singapore chicken, Mulan Basket, and Triple Delight. The ticker-tape treatment is a fun promise of what's ahead when you open up the restaurant's massive menu of more than 200 dishes. Some are excellent interpretations of Chinese-American classics like General Tso's chicken or crispy walnut shrimp in coconut milk dressing. Others are hot and spicy Szechuan dishes prepared in a myriad of ways. Mulan also serves dozens of appetizers, soups, chow mein, lo mein, and fried rice, along with nigiri, sashimi, sushi rolls, and hot pots prepared at the table. On my first visit for lunch, I was so overwhelmed with choices that I went with a Japanese bento box. Man, was that a mistake. Next time, I'll stick with Chinese and go with a house recommendation like golden sesame beef or shrimp rice noodles in curry sauce. In spring of 2012, Mulan opened a second restaurant in the Cooper-Young neighborhood with a full sushi bar: 2149 Young Ave., Memphis, TN 38104; (901) 347-3965.

Petra Cafe, 6641 Poplar Ave., Germantown, TN 38138; (901) 754-4440; petracafe.com; Middle Eastern; $. The menu at Petra Cafe describes the restaurant as "a taste of the Mediterranean," but a more apt explanation would be "Sandwich King." Yes, Petra makes falafels and classic Greek gyros, but the cafe also serves American deli-style sandwiches such as Philly cheesesteak and ham and cheese, along with a remarkable assortment of panini. Owner Lisa Bouba says Petra has more types of panini than any other restaurant in the Mid-South, and she's probably correct. Undoubtedly, the cafe wins for unique combinations, such as the East Meets West Panini, a hefty layering of roast beef, corned beef, pastrami, swiss, provolone, and mayo on grilled ciabatta. For more modest appetites, Petra has a nice selection of grilled chicken or lamb salads with house-made Greek dressing and an appetizer sampler with tabbouleh, eggplant dip, and hummus served with wedges of warm pita. The feta dip, described on the menu as "feisty," is exactly that, combining yogurt, lemon juice, red peppers, feta, and olive oil. The restaurant's delicious baklava also is house made. For years, Petra locations stayed in the suburbs, but the family finally opened a Midtown location in 2012. Here are the addresses for Petra's other locations: 9155 Poplar Ave., Germantown, TN 38138, (901) 755-5440; 1649 N. Germantown Pkwy., Cordova, TN 38138, (901) 754-6650; 1560 Union Ave., Memphis, TN 38104, (901) 722-4040.

The Presentation Room, 1245 N. Germantown Pkwy., Cordova, TN 38016; (901) 754-7115; lecole.edu/memphis; New American; $–$$. This contemporary American bistro is run by students of L'École Culinaire, a sister school to the culinary academy in St. Louis. Open since 2010, the school is a boon for students interested in culinary careers and for foodies who enjoy discovering young emerging chefs. Students cook, bake, and run the restaurant as their final coursework, so the menus change with each class. But no matter who is in the kitchen, the menu mixes classic American cooking and trendy ingredients, from a start for dinner of wild boar sliders with ginger-celeriac slaw to a lunchtime finish of braised pineapple with vanilla bean and pink-peppercorn ice cream topped with white truffle caramel. Hours are limited, but the restaurant's service, food, and prices merit some advance planning. Lunch is served Monday through Thursday from 11 a.m. to 2 p.m., and dinner is served Tuesday through Thursday from 6:30 to 8:30 p.m. Wednesday evening dinners are prix fixe at $15 for three courses and $25 for five. The menus are less complicated but still good, offering such fare as corn ravioli stuffed with truffles and pecorino and roasted leg of lamb with potatoes, haricots verts, and sauce bordelaise. Also check online for the restaurant's monthly themed dinners when local chefs lend a hand in the kitchen.

Jerry's Sno Cones, 1657 Wells Station Rd., Memphis, TN 38108; (901) 767-2659; Drive-in / Hot Dogs / Shaved Ice & Snow Cones; $. Perfectly shaved ice flavored with crimson-colored wedding cake syrup and a scoop of vanilla ice cream in a Styrofoam cup is a winning trio at Jerry's Sno Cones, a landmark drive-in located at the corner of Wells Station and Reed. The ice cream add-on may sound a bit odd, but mix it up a little as the ice melts down, and you'll understand why Jerry's is a treasured local gem. For more than 60 years, young and old alike have waited patiently in the summer heat to order a favorite snow cone flavor in one of three ways. A snow cone with ice cream is called a Supreme. A snow cone with soft-serve ice cream is called a Swish, and snow cone with a swirl of whipped cream on top is called a Cream. Selecting a snow cone flavor from dozens and dozens of choices can complicate decision making even more. There are simple flavors like cherry or raspberry plus combinations with names like Ninja Turtle and Hurricane Elvis. Jerry's also serves milk shakes and malts plus cheeseburgers, muffulettas and chili fries. Some people describe the area around Jerry's as sketchy, and the neighborhood called Nutbush can be tricky to find. Don't let either worry keep you from visiting. Just stick to Mapquest directions (they are accurate) and look for the line of customers circling a bright pink building with green and yellow trim.

Germantown Commissary, 2290 S. Germantown Rd., Germantown, TN 38318; (901) 754-5540; commissarybbq.com; Barbecue; $–$$. Ever wonder how many ribs you can eat in one meal? You can find out at Germantown Commissary, where every Monday night is all-you-can-eat ribs for $23. On other nights, $23 still goes pretty far, buying a slab of hickory smoked ribs for two plus beans, slaw, bread, and the commissary's touted deviled eggs. Since 1981, Walker Taylor's Germantown favorite has been a much-loved player on the barbecue circuit, turning out ribs, chopped or pulled shoulders, smoked sausage, barbecue shrimp, and great Brunswick stew topped, of course, with a mound of pulled pork. Expect waits on the weekends because this small roadhouse has a big reputation, attracting celebrities like Faith Hill, Jimmy Buffett, and Robert Duvall, and earning accolades from national media. In 2009 *Playboy* magazine named Germantown Commissary one of the country's top 10 barbecue restaurants. Along with good food, the commissary's rustic interior is saturated with history (it was a commissary, or small country store, for 90 years) and aromatic layers of spice and smoke.

Specialty Stores, Markets & Producers

Agricenter Farmer's Market, 7777 Walnut Grove Blvd., Memphis, TN 38120; (901) 757-7777; agricenter.org/farmersmarket.html. For more than 25 years, the Agricenter Farmer's Market has hosted vendors from throughout western Tennessee inside its big red barn. While outdoor markets typically operate one day a week, the Agricenter is open Mon through Sat from 7:30 a.m. until 5:30 p.m., selling meat, cheese, farm-fresh eggs, cut flowers, some crafts, and an impressive selection of fruit and vegetables. Conveniently located off Germantown Parkway, this market also attracts a number of vendors selling value-added farm products, especially pickles, jams, and specialty items like pimento cheese from Tom's Tiny Kitchen. During the summer season, you'll also find a smattering of food trucks and seasonal baked goods like blackberry pie. The market is open from May through Dec, when holiday vendors fill the barn with Christmas trees, garlands, and a gorgeous assortment of holiday wreaths.

Cordova International Farmer's Market, 1150 N. Germantown Pkwy., Cordova, TN 38016. When this large international market opened in a former Schnucks at the corner of Macon Road and Germantown Parkway, I wondered if it would appeal to nonethnic customers. My bad. On my first visit, people of all sorts were spilling into the sprawling produce department where fixtures are uniform,

Cocoa Van Cupcakes Bring
an Artist's Touch to the Cordova Suburbs

Truth be told, I was pretty much done with gourmet cupcakes until I walked into Cocoa Van Cupcake Bakery the Saturday before Father's Day and listened to Lauren Jackson describe the special weekend flavor for the dads of Memphis. "It's Bailey Irish Cream," Jackson said, lifting off the cover of the plate so I could get a closer look. "They are chocolate cake filled with Guinness ganache."

So much for my misplaced decisions about dessert. I ordered one Irish Cream for my husband, and then selected five more flavors more or less for me, including coconut (vanilla cake infused with coconut and capped with vanilla buttercream and toasted coconut flakes) and lemon berry (lemon cake made with blueberries and iced with a light glaze, lemon zest buttercream, and a fresh blueberry on top).

I ate the lemon berry cupcake as soon as I got home and was delighted by the berries baked throughout the cake. A few even stuck to the cupcake liner for a delicious surprise finish.

"All of Nicole's cupcake flavors include the cake," explains Brian Reed about wife Nicole Reed's extraordinary baking. "Nicole doesn't just take a flavor of icing and put it on a chocolate or vanilla cupcake. She layers in the flavors at every level."

Located in Trinity Place Shopping Center in Cordova, Cocoa Van is a rare artisan start-up in a suburban neighborhood dominated by big-box retailers and national chains. With Cocoa Van, the Reeds shake off predictability with a sophisticated shop and a changing cupcake menu of nuanced flavors.

Although the Reeds are new to retail, the couple's combined talents are a natural fit. Brian is a trained and experienced chef; Nicole is a classical pianist who brings her artistic nature to  the kitchen. "She thinks about every note of her cupcakes, stacking the flavors until they sing like a song," Brian explains.

Nicole started baking about eight years ago when Brian's mom talked her through an apple cake recipe on the telephone. "It was my favorite cake, and she wanted to bake it for my birthday," Brian says. Her baking continued to grow along with the couple's catering business. Soon, she was selling bundt cakes to **Gus's World Famous Fried Chicken** (p. 42) and supplying baked goods to downtown's **Trolley Stop Market** (p. 50).

These days, the couple stays focused on cupcakes made with premium ingredients such as European chocolates, sweet cream butter, and fresh fruits and zests. Nicole crowns all the bakery's cupcakes with a picturesque swirl of buttercream for a pleasing ratio of cake and topping. Her icing doesn't overshadow her cake, except for the Campfire, a whimsical nod to s'mores made with Valrhona chocolate, chocolate buttercream, graham cracker crumbs, and a single roasted marshmallow.

Cocoa Van Cupcake Bakery, 7990 Trinity Rd., Cordova, TN 38018; (901) 308-1536; cocoavancupcake.com; $.

bright, and much like their big-box competitors. Produce selection on the other hand is emphatically global, mixing in exotics like dragon fruit, plantain, and yucca with regional favorites like peaches and tomatoes. The market also offers aisle after aisle of international groceries and housewares, 50-pound bags of rice, and a meat and seafood counter that stretches across the back of the entire store. In addition to traditional beef, pork, and chicken, the market sells rabbit, goat, and quail. Seafood selections also are extensive, including fresh-fish standards like tilapia along with large tanks for lobsters and crabs. The owners of Cordova Farmer's Market operate a similar store in southeast Memphis called Winchester Farmer's Market, 6616 Winchester Rd., Memphis, TN 38115; (901) 795-1525.

John's Pantry, 8046 Willow Tree Lane, Cordova, TN 38018; (901) 308-2404; johnspantry.com. Ask John Moberly why he opened a gourmet specialty market in a Cordova strip mall, and he will say, "I got tired of not being able to buy Dutch processed cocoa and pink peppercorns." His decision also followed a few beers with friend Patrick Garety, who is now Moberly's partner at the market that sells "eclectic ingredients for good cooks." Eclectic indeed. In addition to those pink peppercorns, John's Pantry sells items such as Pappardelle's pastas (try the dark chocolate linguine), locally sourced coffee, homemade croutons seasoned with garlic, and an endless assortment of spices, salts, and rubs. Moberly roasts and mixes many of the combinations, so the flavors are unique, espe-cially his chile and curry rubs and his salts seasoned with smoked hickory and apple wood. About six months after opening, the store added pastries, cookies, brownies, and freshly baked breads. The selection of bread changes from day to day, but typically includes a wonderful cinnamon raisin and a sourdough made from a 35-year-old starter given to Moberly by a chef who teaches down the street at L'École Culinaire. While the inventory is good, the personal atten-tion from store owners is even better. Moberly worked as a chef in Cincinnati for 20 years, and he is happy to explain unfamiliar products and how to cook with them.

Paradise Seafood, 7777 Walnut Grove Blvd., Cordova, TN 38120; (251) 401-9193. It takes a little courage to buy fresh seafood from a roadside vendor, but folks on US Hwy 51 near Atoka have been doing it for years. With coolers and an umbrella to block the sun, Don Willadsen built a loyal following for his fresh seafood, purchased wholesale from boats in Gulf Shores, Alabama, and hauled back home. For landlocked Memphians, Paradise Seafood is the next best thing to a coastal seafood market, especially when the prices are competitive and the quality is top-notch. These days, Ted Perkins works the coastal end of the business, while Willadsen coordinates expansion in Memphis and Jackson, Tennessee. The company still sells roadside in Atoka but has added other locations to its roster, including summer markets in downtown's **Memphis Farmers Market** (p. 67) and in Collierville, and the year-round **Cooper-Young Community Farmers Market** (p. 113). Paradise also

has a permanent truck at the **Agricenter Farmer's Market** (p. 189) in Cordova, a market with an indoor site. Seafood selections at all markets are seasonal, and the options are plentiful. On opening day at the downtown market in early April, Paradise sold out of crabmeat and sea bass quickly, but they still had oysters, trigger fish, grouper, and two-pound bags of Royal Reds, a ballyhooed shrimp from deep water in the Gulf of Mexico favored for its color and salty taste.

Square Beans, 103 N. Center St., Collierville, TN 38017; (901) 854-8855; squarebeans.com. Proprietors Walt and Kelli Geminn bring a lively shot of hip caffeine to the historic town square in Collierville with a complete menu of frappes blended with ice, espresso, milk, and flavored syrup and espresso creations like caramel macchiato and flavored lattes. The coffee shop also serves a simple cup of drip coffee or french press, along with noncoffee drinks such as fruit smoothies, Mexican hot chocolate, and chai tea latte. The shop's storefront dates back about 100 years, so the place couldn't be any cuter with its comfy sofas, historic photos, and exposed brick walls. The owners also embrace local products, a nice change of pace from corporate retail. There is a sizable display of local honey and a freezer with responsibly raised meat from Top of the World Farm in middle Tennessee. To satisfy a midmorning snack attack, look for homemade muffins such as cranberry orange and chocolate chip. At lunch, rotating specials offer choices like tomatoes stuffed with chicken salad, and prosciutto and brie on a fresh baguette. During Collierville's summer Thursday night concert series, Square Beans also puts together a nice box dinner with sandwich, side salad, and cookie for about $10.

Beer, Cocktails & Pub Grub

If you don't know the term *liquor by the drink,* then you probably aren't from the Mid-South, where religious and social norms confined drinking to homes and private clubs until the 1960s. In Memphis, city leaders approved liquor by the drink in 1969, and the new ordinance amped up everybody's dance card, especially entrepreneurs and developers who revitalized tired commercial neighborhoods with new restaurants and entertainment.

There is no better example of the impact of liquor by the drink than Midtown's Overton Square, a large block of historic storefronts near Madison Avenue and Cooper Street. In 1970, a group of young businessmen started Overton Square's heyday by opening the first T.G.I. Friday's outside of New York. The restaurant and bar were hits from the start, with long waits for dinner and revelry at the bar stretching late into the night.

For the next 10 years or so, Overton Square remained the heartbeat of Memphis entertainment with bars and restaurants that ranged from Chicago-gangster theme to romantic and French. Music venues opened, too, bringing nationally known acts to such places as the much-loved Lafayette's Music Room. But gradually, demographic and economic shifts changed perceptions of Overton Square from hip-and-happening to down-and-out. Businesses headed to Midtown's nearby Cooper-Young neighborhood or downtown to Beale Street and the city's revitalized core.

These days, bars and pubs in Cooper-Young, East Memphis, and Downtown continue to thrive, and more are on the way. Bardog's Aldo Dean just opened Aldo's Pizza Pies to bring beer and New York–style pizza to downtown's Barboro Flats building, and the city's second microbrewery, High Cotton Brewing Company, is planning to open in a historic building at 598 Monroe Ave.

The future also looks bright for an extensive redevelopment of Overton Square as an entertainment and theater district with updated amenities and more parking. Already, downtown's popular Local Gastropub is renovating a building at Cooper and Madison for a second location, and developers have announced plans for a new hotel across the street.

Beale Street Favorites

Alfred's on Beale, 197 Beale St., Memphis, TN 38103; (901) 525-3711; alfredsonbeale.com. Alfred's has been holding down the southeast corner of 3rd and Beale since 1986 with a large 2nd-story patio where (I swear) there is a tiki bar. Inside Alfred's stages a mix of solo artists, rock, acoustic bands, karaoke, and the largest collection of gold records in the US. Every Sunday evening from 6:30 to 10 p.m., the bar also showcases swing with a 17-piece big band called the Memphis Jazz Orchestra. As expected, plenty of bar food comes along with the entertainment. During the week Alfred's serves meat-and-threes with fresh veggies in addition to its standard menu of burgers, po' boys, catfish baskets, and a few pastas. House specialties include Chicken Alfred's, a marinated chicken breast grilled with barbecue sauce and smothered in mushrooms, bacon, and swiss cheese. It's a little heavy-handed, but the chicken dish is good fuel for an evening of drinking. In the 2009 **World Championship Barbecue Cooking Contest** (p. 16), the restaurant's cooking team placed third in the Grand Champion category. That's a big prize, which is why the best bets on the menu revolve around barbecue. Try a half rack of ribs served with beans, slaw, and garlic bread for $15.

B. B. King's Blues Club, 143 Beale St., Memphis, TN 38103; (901) 524-5464; bbkingclubs.com. B. B. King moved to Memphis in the late 1940s, and the city is justifiably proud of its longtime connection to the King of the Blues. Yes, there are B. B. King's Blues Clubs in Las Vegas, Orlando, Nashville, and West Palm Beach, but the B. B.'s on Beale Street is the original location. Since opening in 1991, B. B.'s has anchored Beale with a classy club where B. B.

himself periodically joins the All Stars, a rocking house lineup of guitar, bass, drums, keyboards, vocals, and horns. Guitar prodigy Will Tucker and his band also play on weekends when the club gets crowded and big-name musicians show up for spontaneous jams. The club also serves lunch and dinner, and the food is a step up from typical club grub. Try B. B.'s signature beer chili simmered in brew, fried pickles with horseradish dipping sauce, hickory burgers topped with fried onions, or grilled pork chops served with cinnamon apples, green beans, and garlic mashed potatoes. For a more upscale and romantic meal, head upstairs to **Itta Bena** (p. 44) restaurant where local favorite Susan Marshall performs on Friday and Saturday nights.

Blues City Cafe, 138 Beale St., Memphis, TN 38103; (901) 526-3637; bluescitycafe.com. Hickory-smoked pork ribs basted in maple barbecue sauce from Blues City Cafe were featured on an episode of the Food Network's *Bobby Flay Show,* so you can find the recipe and cooking technique online. But in Memphis, why bother when the real deal is made at the corner of Beale and 2nd? Originally called Doe's Eat Place when it opened in 1991, the restaurant changed its name and owners two years later. Since then, Blues City Cafe has stayed true to its charming neon sign that proclaims BAR-MUSIC-KITCHEN OPEN LATE. In addition to ribs with steak fries and Texas toast, the cafe also serves hand-cut steaks (try the cowboy-cut rib eye), catfish dinners, skillet shrimp, and tamales. After dinner, slip next door to the restaurant's music venue called the Band Box. You'll join a list of luminaries like the Reverend Al Green, Robert De Niro, and

Tastin' 'Round Town: Culinary Tours Plate Good Eating with Memphis History

Carol and Lance Silkes are both experienced chefs, and when they transferred to Memphis from the Midwest, they explored opening their own restaurant. They ate out a lot and discovered a vibrant restaurant scene. "We realized pretty quickly that restaurants in Memphis are alive and well," Carol Silkes explains. "We asked ourselves, do we really want to compete?"

So instead of starting a restaurant, the couple embraced culinary tourism with a series of restaurant tours called Tastin' 'Round Town. For now, they conduct two tours: a walking tour of downtown eateries and a tour specifically on barbecue. Tours typically last about 3 hours.

Carol, who is also an assistant professor at the Kemmons Wilson School of Hospitality at the University of Memphis, is an expert on destination branding through food. And Memphis, she says, is a culinary hotbed because the city blends chef-driven cuisine with food traditions and history. "When you talk about food in relation to the history of Memphis, visitors start to understand why this city is so special," Carol says.

A tireless cheerleader for her adopted home, Silkes is an informed and entertaining Memphis foodie. Here are a few of her comments from an interview in June:

What restaurants are on the tour?
Carol: Usually we go to **Bleu** (p. 35) at the Westin hotel to eat shrimp and grits. The secret is the greens in the dish. They are hot and spicy, cooked with apple juice, and they still have a little crunch. We like the pulled pork at Pig on Beale (167 Beale St., Memphis, TN 38103;

901-529-1544; www.pigonbeale.com; Barbecue; $) because it's a textbook example of good Memphis-style barbecue. It has bark, a smoke ring, and great flavor. We usually go to **Automatic Slim's** (p. 34). They have an excellent four-cheese macaroni and $5 martinis every day from 11 a.m. to 7 p.m. You can choose from 25 different varieties. And we go to the **Majestic Grille** (p. 47) and get their dessert sampler. We eat it round robin, so everybody gets a taste.

What are some of your barbecue favorites?
Carol: The barbecue spaghetti at the **Bar-B-Q Shop** (p. 109) tastes great. Even my husband thinks the barbecue spaghetti is somewhat of an art form, and he's Italian. We also like that **Cozy Corner** (p. 57) has a Chicago-style glass smoker, and the ribs at **Corky's** (p. 158) are unique. Both Cozy Corner and Corky's use family recipes, but they are very different.

Many people think Memphis is an up-and-coming foodie town. Do you agree?
Carol: Absolutely. Memphis is a hidden secret, and I'll be sad when the rest of the world realizes how many great chefs are here. In Memphis, it's not where to eat, it's what to eat.

Southern food is a hot trend nationally right now. Why do you think that is?
Carol: I'm not entirely sure, but Southern cooking is great-tasting comfort food. It has so many flavors, and I don't mean just heat. Most Southern cooking takes old-family recipes and elevates them to a higher culinary level. Maybe Southern cooking is popular because people are looking for the story behind their food.

Tastin' 'Round Town; $45 and $65 plus tax; (901) 870-1824; sites .google.com/site/tastinroundtowncom.

President Bill Clinton who have boogied to the band or jumped on stage to play along. The venue's regular performers are top-notch, including Gary Hardy and the Memphis 2 who play a Sun Studios review and a tribute to Johnny Cash several times a week.

Blue's Hall Juke Joint, 174 Beale St., Memphis, TN 38103; (901) 528-0150. Even during the day, it's almost impossible to walk by the Blue's Hall Juke Joint when the house band is cranked up and the music pours into the street. So why try? Friday afternoons are a good time to settle into this small narrow bar, which fills up quickly at night. While many places on Beale Street cater to tourists, Blue's Hall is the real deal: an authentic juke joint that feels like it should be on a back road in Mississippi. A long wooden bar stretches down one side of the place and there's room for a few tables, but the action takes place on the rear stage where the harmonica of Dr. Feel Good James Potts turns his blues band into a feel-good jam of American music.

Dancin' Jimmy's, 310 Beale St., Memphis, TN 38103; (901) 521-4308. The building at 310 Beale is a cavernous 2-story space on the east end of the street that has had trouble making it all work. Most recently, it was New Orleans–based Pat O'Brien's. Now Dancin'

Jimmy's is the building's newest reincarnation, and things are looking up. The new owners, Bud Chittom and Preston Lamm, are club veterans, operating six kitchens between the two of them. At 310 Beale, they plan to operate three separate banquet rooms along with Dancin' Jimmy's, a bar named after Dancin' Jimmy Grantam, a ballyhooed party starter from Overton Square's heyday in the 1970s and '80s. The nicest feature of the bar is a bright and airy courtyard with wrought-iron tables and a large central fountain. The courtyard feels like New Orleans, at least until the blues music from Handy Park floats over the courtyard wall. The food at Jimmy's is streamlined and hardy: Texas chili, barbecue bologna sandwiches, sausage dogs with onions and peppers, and gator strips, breaded, seasoned spicy, and fried.

Rum Boogie Cafe, 182 Beale St., Memphis, TN 38103; (901) 528-0150; rumboogie.com. Located at the corner of Beale Street and Highway 61—one of the great musical crossroads in America—this cranked-up club is serious about the blues. Even in the mid-1980s when Beale Street's revival looked doubtful, Rum Boogie staged music seven nights a week. It still does. James Govan and the Boogie Blues Band play regularly along with local and nationally renowned musicians who like to slip on stage and join the jam. Many musicians autograph guitars before leaving, a tradition started by Billy Gibbons of ZZ Top. Today, Rum Boogie has more than 350 autographed guitars, and many hang from the rafters in a 3-D garland of local favorites like Larry Raspberry and big-name icons such as Alice Cooper and Sting. Visit midday for a good look at the guitars and to order lunch. The cafe now serves meat-and-threes, but stick with their signature dishes: red beans and rice with kielbasa sausage, and the Beale Street Barbecue Special, a rack of Memphis dry ribs, pulled pork shoulder, slaw, baked beans, and fruit cobbler.

Silky O'Sullivan's, 183 Beale St., Memphis, TN 38103; (901) 522-9596; silkyosullivans.com/entertainment.html. Silky O'Sullivan's feels more New Orleans than Irish, except for the shamrocks and the piece of Blarney Stone that is supposedly imbedded in the south wall of the bar. But hey, who's going to quibble with an Irishman, especially on a gorgeous afternoon when patio favorites Lanier and Buddy are riffing through a great rendition of "The Thrill Is Gone." A favorite stop for Beale Street tourists, Silky O'Sullivan's has a lot to offer besides its resident goats. Scaffolds out front hold up the historic Gallina Building, whose 100 years of saloon history include poker and betting on the horses. Today, bar entertainment revolves around dueling baby grand pianos, where Barbara Blue belts out Beale Street's storied music genre. Silky's special libations include the Diver, a secret blend of liquor served in a gallon bucket. Strong players on the menu include chili, oysters, dry barbecue ribs, and Silky's pulled pork plate. The house-made gumbo is also unique because it's made with seafood stock instead of more traditional flour-and-butter roux.

Ghost River Brewery, 827 S. Main St., Memphis, TN 38106; (901) 278-0140; ghostriverbrewing.com. The Ghost River in nearby Fayette County is a section of the Wolf River that meanders through hardwood forests, open marshes, and cypress swamps. This fragile wetland feeds the Memphis Sands Aquifer, which produces some of the best drinking water in America. Ghost River Brewery understands that great beer starts with great water, so the brewery contributes a portion of its sales to the Wolf River Conservancy, a nonprofit watchdog of the river's watershed. Widely available at Memphis bars and restaurants, Ghost River's handcrafted beers continue to ride a wave of popularity thanks to the local food movement and brewmaster Chuck Skypeck's excellent taste. The brewery's Copperhead Red recently won a silver medal at the Great American Beer Festival, the largest national beer competition in the country. The brewery also expanded its downtown production facility in order to bottle its signature Golden Ale into six-packs for local groceries. While the bottles are convenient, it's more fun to stop by the microbrewery's rear dock for a fresh growler and a look inside at the casks. Try one of the brewery's seasonal picks like Ghost River Witbier for spring and summer, a Belgian-style wheat beer flavored with orange peel and coriander.

Old Millington Vineyard and Winery, 6748 Old Millington Rd., Millington, TN 38053; (901) 873-4114; oldmillingtonwinery.com. Perry and Carrie Welch grow Chambourcin grapes, a hybrid from the early 1960s with a full aromatic flavor that pairs beautifully with dark chocolate desserts. Their small country winery is located about 15 miles from downtown Memphis and well worth a visit, especially on a Sunday afternoon in spring or fall when the Welchs throw an outdoor party. From April through October (except for July and August when it's just too damn hot) the winery has wine tastings and live local music for visitors who provide their own blankets and food. The winery shop is open with chilled bottles of dry whites, along with dry reds, semidry blushes, ports, and fruit wines. At about $10 a bottle, the wines are tasty and affordable. The Big Red is especially nice to cook with and to drink. Old Millington is the only winery in the Memphis area, so it merits support from both tourists and locals. The music on Sunday afternoon runs from 3 to 6 p.m. The winery is open Wed through Sat from 10 a.m. to 6 p.m., and on Sun from 1 to 6 p.m.

Bars & Gastropubs

Bardog Tavern, 73 Monroe, Memphis, TN 38103; (901) 275-8742; bardogtavern.com. After tending bar for 18 years in New York City and in Memphis restaurants, Aldo Dean struck out on his own, renovating a former barbecue joint into a neighborhood pub that is comfortable and sophisticated. Bardog is a moniker for bartenders in the old American West, and the pub's massive red-oak bar can accommodate plenty of drinking. Located down the street from the University of Memphis law school, Bardog is a popular stop off for both students and professionals who like the pub's bartenders and neighborhood kinship. Even a downtown running club begins and ends a weekly run at Bardog on Monday evening. The kitchen's long hours also pull in customers. Breakfast begins at 8 a.m. Monday through Friday, serving pancakes, breakfast burritos, and a delicious fried-egg slider with bacon and spicy mayo. Brunch on the weekends runs from noon to 3 p.m. with expanded choices and $4 Bloody Marys. Menus for lunch and dinner offer bar snacks, sliders, supper, and meals to go until 2 a.m. Think gourmet picnic food with an Italian twist. Family recipes also lend a hand to the menu. In fact, Dean's grandmother traveled to Memphis from New Jersey to teach her spaghetti and meatball recipe to the kitchen staff.

Belmont Grill, 4970 Poplar Ave., Memphis, TN 38117; (901) 767-0305. For years, I've heard people rave about the Belmont burger, a fistful of ground beef served on a french roll. Still, I'd never tried it until a delayed plane from New York City pushed my Memphis arrival to 11 p.m. I was starving when my husband picked me up, but I didn't want fast food. "Let's go to the Belmont for a burger," he suggested. When we arrived, a few regulars sat at the bar, and the place smelled like smoke. It is, after all, a bit of a dive. But it was easy to overlook the negatives when the juicy 6-ounce burger arrived. I ordered my burger with cheddar cheese, but the Belmont offers a long list of add-on toppings, including ham, chili, mushroom gravy, and smothered onions. The grill's appetizers are predictable except for the deep-fried cheese sticks: They are made with Monterey Jack instead of mozzarella and served with a tasty honey-mustard sauce for dipping. Be forewarned: Parking is tight at the Belmont. Only seven or eight parking spots are located behind the bar, so most people park in a nearby shopping center and walk over. There also is a second Belmont Grill in Germantown that is no longer affiliated with this original location, but they still serve a Belmont-style burger on a baguette.

Blue Monkey, 513 S. Front St., Memphis, TN 38104; (901) 527-6665; bluemonkeymemphis.com. Downtowners quickly embraced the Blue Monkey when it opened in the South Main arts district because they needed a bar in the neighborhood. But a fire in 2005 destroyed the Monkey's historic building, and almost three years elapsed before a new bar resurfaced next door. Some of the delay stemmed from a meticulous renovation that used recycled materials. For instance, Memphis restaurants contributed more than 10,000 bottle corks that were used to build the Monkey's trolley-shaped bar. The pub's menu stayed about the same, offering a mix of American standards such as prime rib and catfish platters. The bar's plate lunches served during the week from 11 a.m. to 2 p.m. are immensely popular, and lunch can get crowded. A type of crispy quesadilla called Trolley Car Crisps are the bar's signature dish. Try the California, a mix of feta, cheddar, Monterey Jack, and bacon topped with tomatoes, green onions, and picante sauce. The original Blue Monkey is located in Midtown and also serves Sunday brunch: 2012 Madison Ave., Memphis, TN 38104; (901) 272-2583.

The Brass Door, 152 Madison Ave., Memphis, TN 38104; (901) 572-1813; thebrassdoor.com. Most pubs don't win kudos for their architecture, at least in Memphis. Not so with the Brass Door, where the building's original details shine even with an extensive renovation. Built as a bank in 1918, the building is beautiful both inside and out, starting with its polished-brass front door, large windows, and ornamented frieze. The building's deco tile flooring is intact, along with the worn wooden stairs leading to the 2nd floor mezzanine. The mezzanine is a nice private escape if the bar gets a little rowdy, which can happen when fan club members of the Memphis Gooners show up for a soccer game. Beer choices are plentiful, including domestic bottles, premium bottles like Strongbow and Kronenberg 1664, and a half-dozen drafts such as Smithwick's, Stella, and Guinness, of course. Managing partner Seamus Loftus is an Irishman who ensures the authenticity of traditional dishes such as shepherd's pie topped with cheddar-whipped potatoes and Irish breakfasts served all day. (Yes, they include bangers and rashers.) The pub's other food skews New American with changing specials for sandwiches (grilled eggplant with roasted peppers) and sliders (cod cake with Sriracha tartar sauce). In

HOMEGROWN CHAIN:
BOSCOS RESTAURANT &
BREWING COMPANY

In 1992 Boscos opened Tennessee's original brewpub in Germantown to much fanfare. Customers loved the idea of beer brewed in-house, especially the light-bodied Golden Ale called Famous Flaming Stone. The beer is a Steinbier, or stone beer. Brewmasters heat pieces of pink Colorado granite to 700 degrees in Boscos' wood-fired oven and then lower the stones into the wort, or unfermented beer, while it is brewing. The steam from the stones caramelizes the sugars in the wort, giving the beer a sweet, slightly caramel taste. Boscos also brews about two dozen other beers every year, including seasonal varieties and its award-winning Cask Conditioned Ale. Boscos' Germantown location is now closed, but Boscos Squared in Midtown is a popular pub for drinking, dinner, and Sunday jazz brunch. The restaurant's wood-fired ovens used to heat the granite for brewing also turn out 8 different pizzas, including the Chesapeake, a combination of pesto, shrimp, scallops, mozzarella, and Vermont white cheddar. Along with pizzas, the restaurant serves pastas, sandwiches, salads, soups, steaks, chops, and a seasonal catch of the day. In addition to its Memphis location, Boscos operates restaurants in Nashville near Vanderbilt University, in downtown Little Rock, Arkansas, and in historic Franklin, Tennessee. For hours and addresses, click on the company website at boscosbeer.com.

keeping with the pub's ambience, there's no smoking, so feel free to bring the kids.

Celtic Crossing, 903 S. Cooper, Memphis, TN 38104; (901) 274-5151; celticcrossingmemphis.com. Try walking past Celtic Crossing on a summer evening and see if you start smiling. Bet you do. It's almost impossible to ignore the party banter that spills over the pub's large sidewalk patio, wrapping passersby in a friendly, feel-good moment. Head inside D. J. Naylor's traditional Irish bar and the party keeps up with a dozen draft beers and almost two dozen varieties of Irish and Scotch whiskeys. Since 2005 the Celtic has tweaked its pub package with improved food and some interior renovations. Otherwise, it carries on with a winning formula: Guinness pints, live soccer broadcasts, weekly trivia nights, and happy hours from 2 to 7 p.m. The menu is broader than most pubs. During the week, a $6 lunch special offers dishes like shepherd's pie and Paddy Melts, along with sandwiches and fish-and-chips. For dinner, try a goat cheese burger, mixed grill, or corned beef boxty, a traditional potato pancake. The pub also serves Sunday brunch starting at 10:30 a.m. with live Celtic music and $4 Bloody Marys. Look for American favorites plus Irish standouts like sausage-wrapped hard-boiled eggs served with potatoes and Guinness-Dijon dipping sauce.

Double J Smokehouse and Saloon, 124 G. E. Patterson, Memphis, TN 38103; (901) 347-2648; doublejsmokehouse.com.

The large smoker and stacks of hickory logs behind the Double J Smokehouse make you feel good about this downtown roadhouse from the start. So do the burly police officers who like to eat at the Double J, named after pitmasters John Harris and Jeff Stamm. Cops must know good ribs, right? Meat rules at the Double J, where the only seafood on the menu is the surf and turf. Even the twice-baked potatoes are stuffed with cheddar, green onions, and pulled pork. And the egg rolls? Yep, they are also stuffed with pulled pork along with a little slaw. Sausages at Double J are house-made and a variety of steaks join the smokehouse lineup of baby back ribs and chopped pork plates. The ribs are flavorful and crusty and served with a tangy sweet sauce. The ambience of Double J benefits from an extensive renovation several years ago by landlord Norma Crow. The building, built in 1946 as the Tri-State Bank, has good bones with a cozy mezzanine that looks down on a center stage where country and blues musicians play weekend nights. Visitors to the National Civil Rights Museum who are looking for lunch should remember that the Double J is a nearby neighbor on Mulberry Street.

The Green Beetle, 325 S. Main St., Memphis, TN 38103; (901) 527-7337; greenbeetleblog.blogspot.com. A sidewalk sandwich board in front of the Green Beetle says HEALING BROKEN HEARTS SINCE 1939. The slogan has been part of the tavern's persona since owner Josh

Huckaby's grandfather Frank Liberto opened the Green Beetle that year. "We have no idea how he came up with it," Huckaby says. Ditto for the pub's name. "My grandfather just always said that one day he would have a tavern and name it the Green Beetle." Liberto also owned Frank's Liquors next door—now **Frank's Main Street Market and Deli** (p. 66)—and both businesses are rich in downtown lore. Locals remember it as a speakeasy with a pass-through window to Frank's and rooms for rent upstairs. These days, the tavern is comfortable for all ages (there's even a kid's menu) since Huckaby brought the tavern back into the family in 2011. With a brick wainscot, green plank walls, and front doors that open to sidewalk seating, the small tavern feels a little like a Swiss chalet. Not so for the tavern's beer selection, one of the best downtown. It's all here: local drafts like Lazy Magnolia, high gravity beers like Napa Smith Bonfire, and dozens of other imports, domestics, crafts, and specialty beers. The food at the Green Beetle is also good, especially the Big Frank Burger (two 8-ounce hand-formed patties with bacon and all the trimmings) and Grandmama's Lasagna (12 layers of tomatoes, ricotta, and meat sauce).

Half Shell Restaurant, 688 S. Mendenhall, Memphis, TN 38117; (901) 682-3966; halfshell-memphis.com. Since 1973 the Half Shell has been tucked near the train tracks at Mendenhall and Poplar, so the persistent freight engine whistles add to its sense of place. Before 1973 this mainstay pub held down the intersection's northwest corner, and when it moved, its customers came right along. Today, customers are as loyal as ever, packing the Half Shell's central bar for craft beers like Sea Dog Wild Blueberry and grilled oysters topped with spicy butter that's so good you'll drink it right out of the shell. Maybe it's the strands of Christmas lights strung about or the shingled porch overhangs that shelter tables, but the Half Shell on a busy weekend feels like a mini vacation. The food adds to that feeling. There are burgers and hand-carved steaks, but most of the menu skews coastal, offering Cajun fish tacos, pan-blackened amberjack, wild Alaskan Dungeness crab, and Southern-style crab cakes with house-made remoulade. During the week, the pub serves blue plate specials that mix up traditional dishes like salmon cakes with more fancy choices such as smoked jalapeño chicken on linguine. In 2003 the Half Shell opened a second location in Southwind with an oyster bar and patio dining: 7825 Winchester Rd., Memphis, TN 38125; (901) 737-6755.

Hog & Hominy, 707 W. Brookhaven Circle, Memphis, TN 38117; (901) 207-7396; hogandhominy.com. In a refurbished rambler across the street from **Andrew Michael Italian Kitchen** (p. 128), Chefs Andrew Ticer and Michael Hudman hit another home run in summer 2012 with the opening of Hog & Hominy, an upbeat gastropub with a seasonal and pig-centric menu. The name Hog & Hominy references an early nickname for the state of Tennessee and the chefs' wizardry in the kitchen with heritage breed pork. The food is simple but contemporary. There are eight types of Naples-style pizza cooked in the bar's wood-burning oven, including the Boom-Bada, a mix of prosciutto, fennel, taleggio, fresh figs, and lardo, a type of Italian charcuterie made with spices and fatback. (When I first tasted this pizza, it sent me over the moon!) The Red Eye is another delight and a great way to deal with a hangover. The pizza is topped with a soft fried egg and *sugo,* a traditional Italian pasta sauce made with dried pork jowl, cheese, and tomato. Hog & Hominy also serves half-a-dozen seasonal veggie sides, along with appetizers like arancini (fried risotto balls garnished with Parmesan) and small plates like the house Mortadella hot dog with caraway beer mustard. The bar is lively and fun with an outdoor bocce court and a nice menu of beer, wine, and classic cocktails.

Jack Magoo's Sports Bar & Grill, 2583 Broad Ave., Memphis, TN 38112; (901) 746-9612; jackmagoos.com. Driving west on Broad Avenue, the pink Cadillac cutout edging the rooftop says this about the neighborhood's newcomer: Jack Magoo's is no ordinary sports bar. Sheltered in a 2-story brick building from 1930, Jack Magoo's is a charming synthesis of flat-screen televisions and burnished oak flooring mellowed by time. Located in the historic Broad Avenue arts district, the bar's 2nd floor takes full advantage of the neighborhood's elevated setting with oversize windows and 14 beers on tap including Magic Hat #9, a "not quite pale ale." Downstairs manager Mike Turner mixes up beer cocktails such as his off-menu Barbecue Beer, a mix of PPR draft, Whiskey Willie's Bloody Mary Mix, a shot of Cattleman's BBQ sauce, and a house mix of salt and celery seed on the glass rim. Turner also serves 6 more beers on tap and is happy to talk about his new favorite: Wheach Peach Wheat. When the weather is nice, remember that Jack Magoo's also has the largest patio in Memphis with umbrellas to block the sun and a DJ on the weekends. Plus, the bar is open late and serves food that is a step up from expected pub grub: 6 different salads, appetizers like deep-fried jalapeño cheese balls, and a full component of quesadillas, wraps, burgers, and a house-made Guinness chili pie.

Local Gastropub, 95 S. Main St., Memphis, TN 38103; (901) 473-9573; localgastropub.com. I've found the food at Local Gastropub to be erratic, but plenty of people disagree. "I think I might have eaten Gastropub's Thai noodle salad four times in the last four days," tweeted a local food blogger. One thing is certain. The pub's green chile and bacon mac 'n' cheese is a head turner, and the pub's menu has a depth not typically seen in Memphis bars. Wild boar sausage is served with red-cabbage kraut, cranberry relish, and crumbled blue cheese, and crispy Spanish shrimp comes with sweet-paprika mayo for dipping. For drinking, Gastropub offers lots of nice choices. There are 6 high gravity beers and domestic and imports on tap. Bartenders also mix excellent specialty cocktails made with spirits, fresh fruits, herbs, and muddled syrups. Try the Velvet Elvis, a mix of Justin Timberlake's 901 Silver Tequila, Champagne, fresh orange slices, and lavender syrup. If the bar gets too noisy, head outdoors to a covered patio or downstairs to the basement. The cellar is a particularly nice respite, and its brick walls and white tablecloths make it easy to ignore the party upstairs.

Max's Sports Bar, 115 G. E. Patterson Ave., Memphis, TN 38103; (901) 528-8367; maxssportbar.com. It's beer and ball at Max's, and if you don't like the combination you might as well leave. Since 2007, this friendly neighborhood bar has kept its recipe simple: PPR for $2.50; pitchers of Yuengling Lager for $12; and plenty of flat-screen TVs for watching the University of Memphis Tigers duke it out with Louisville. Even if basketball isn't your favorite sport, stop by Max's when both the Memphis Grizzlies and the Memphis Tigers are heading for play-off games. The excitement is contagious, and you'll probably leave the bar with new friends and another team to follow. During warm weather, some of the bar action moves to a small outdoor deck equipped with more televisions so customers don't miss a winning point. The menu at Max's also is streamlined with drinking essentials: barbecue nachos, grilled cheese, chicken wings, pulled pork sandwiches, pizza by the slice, and fried mozzarella cheese sticks.

Neil's Bar, 5727 Quince Rd., Memphis, TN 38119; (901) 628-9094; neilsbar.com. The night before an early-morning fire destroyed Midtown mainstay Neil's Bar, dozens of performers staged a benefit for a local musician's daughter who was injured in a car accident. The benefit and the many musicians who participated explain why owner Neil Heins is such an appreciated fixture in the Memphis music community. Heins resurfaced about six months after the fire with a new location in East Memphis not far from his home. While not as large as its predecessor, the new Neil's Bar is keeping up a format that works: local music three or four nights a week and a bar that stays open late. "We're here 365 days a year from 11 to 3 a.m.," says longtime bartender Jerry Deron. "We never close because our customers are our family." In addition to live music, Neil's has flat-screens, pool, local brew **Ghost River** (p. 205) on tap, and a pretty good menu with plenty of barbecue, including pork ribs, pulled pork, beef brisket, nachos, chicken, and smoked bologna. House specialties include chicken breast and artichokes baked in a wine and cream sauce with Greek seasonings and what Neil's calls Fat Man Food: hearty meat-and-threes with side dish daily specials.

R. P. Tracks, 3547 Walker Ave., Memphis, TN 38111; (901) 327-1471; rptracks.com. Located on the edge of the University of Memphis campus, R. P. Tracks is a favorite hang for college students and for faculty members who like to throw back a few. Vegetarians are also happy because the bar's signature dish is barbecue tofu nachos, a gooey melted mess of cheddar, jalapeños, corn chips, black bean chili, sour cream, and squares of spicy barbecue tofu. The tofu also shows up in sandwiches, quesadillas, burritos, and buffalo fingers. In fact, it is so popular that the bar buys as much tofu as it does ground beef. In addition, there are other veggie options including an excellent chipotle hummus and a sandwich melt made with spinach, artichoke hearts, and provolone cheese. Since meat eaters are probably pouting a little by now, don't worry. The R. P. Burger is half a pound of Angus beef loaded with toppings and choice of cheese. For a bit of nostalgia, try a Homewrecker Hot Dog (open-faced and smothered with homemade chili, cheese, and yellow peppers) or Pigs in a Blanket (sausage wrapped in pancakes) for brunch. Saturday and Sunday brunch, served from 11 a.m. to 3 p.m., also includes basics like french toast, breakfast sandwiches, and build-you-own omelets served with home fries, chipotle sour cream, and fresh fruit.

The Slider Inn, 2117 Peabody Ave., Memphis, TN 38104; (901) 725-1155. Two years after opening his smash hit **Bardog Tavern** (p. 206) in downtown Memphis, Aldo Dean put his Midas touch on Midtown's Slider Inn. From the street, the place looks like some sort of cross between a biker bar and a seafood shack at the beach. Inside, Slider's feels more pub-like with a long center table and wall-mounted flat screens. Inside or out, the service is top-notch. Ask the waitress to describe the homemade potato salad, and she's likely to answer like this: "It's better on some days than others. Go with the fries." That's excellent advice because Slider's fries (some with skins on) are perfect, and they make a mountain on your plate. Think gourmet McDonald's made with a 50/50 mix of sugar and salt and served with bourbon mayo for dipping. The fries, along with the bar's menu of sliders, are fresh and cooked to order. Sample three different sliders with the mix-and-match option until you settle into a favorite. (For me, it's jerk pork tenderloin with Jamaican slaw.) Two more crowd-pleasers are lobster rolls and chunky chili. Both are excellent along with a craft ale or Slider's specialty drink: a mix of vodka and house-made lemonade.

South of Beale, 361 S. Main St., Memphis, TN 38103; (901) 526-0388; southofbeale.com. The first gastropub in Memphis, South of Beale opened in 2009 in a lovely refurbished brick storefront with a pretty menu to match. Owners Brittany Whisenant and Ed Cabigao know the restaurant business, but they leave the cooking to Chef Brian McDaniel, who elevates the menu with a gourmet touch. McDaniel updates menus seasonally, so dishes stay fresh and interesting. He also rotates in weekly blackboard specials like blackened shisto peppers or grilled marlin with candied lemon, corn relish, and turnip greens. Even the pub's desserts step up the game. How about a slice of grilled peach shortbread with mint whipped cream or Jack Daniels ice cream with Coca-Cola bread pudding? Despite its upscale swing, the menu is hearty enough to attract Food Network celeb Guy Fieri. The host of *Diners, Drive-ins and Dives* made two of the pub's signature dishes: duck fried rice and sweet-and-spicy popcorn. The popcorn seasoning is a secret, but the taste hints of brown sugar, cumin, and cayenne. It's an addictive combination, especially when paired with the pub's seasonal sangria. Enjoy the duo outside at sidewalk tables or on a spacious deck, especially on the last Friday in May when zombies of all ages parade by in the annual Zombie March down South Main Street.

Sweet Grass Next Door, 937 S. Cooper St., Memphis TN 38104; (901) 278-0278; sweetgrassmemphis.com. Sweet Grass Next Door is the best neighborhood bar in Memphis. Admittedly, that's a

HOMEGROWN CHAIN:
DAN MCGUINNESS PUB

Dan McGuinness's interpretation of the Irish pub theme is so successful that it's grown from a single Memphis location to six franchises in Tennessee, Mississippi, and Oklahoma. The pubs appeal to young people and middle-age types because they add special events, trendy beers on tap, and home cooking into the Irish-food mix. The pub's specialties are good, especially the Highland Chicken crusted with buttered panko and served with Chardonnay beurre blanc, sautéed spinach, feta cheese, and tomatoes. In addition to pub classics like fish-and-chips and beer cheese soup, Dan McGuinness pleases early birds and late risers with daily lunch specials almost the entire day. They serve popular lunch plates like turkey and dressing and country-fried steak from 10:30 a.m. to 4 p.m. every day. Some vegetable sides are fresh and seasonal, while others are Southern classics like greens, purple hull peas, and fried okra. Breakfast shows up on the midday menu on weekends with omelets, breakfast sandwiches, and french toast with cinnamon and apples. Along with affordable food, Dan McGuinness has $2.50 Monday-night pint nights and a nice line of beers, including popular brews on tap such as Blue Moon and Stella. Special events add to the pub's frivolity, including karaoke, trivia, and live music. Locally, find Dan McGuinness at 4698 Spottswood Ave. in East Memphis or in nearby Southaven, Mississippi. For details and other locations, check the company's website at danmcguinnesspub.com.

big statement, but this bar stands out thanks to a stellar family pedigree, customers who are hip and lively, and a signature Bloody Mary garnished with olives, a lime slice, and pickled string beans. Made with house-infused vodka, the bar's signature cocktail has enough buzz to carry through lunch, served Friday through Sunday. Monday through Thursday, the bar opens at 3 p.m., when the same chef-driven plates are available. Chef Ryan Trimm owns both the bar and its big sister restaurant next door (p. 98), so the food is top-notch. Beef carpaccio is thinly sliced eye of round served raw and dressed with Dijonnaise, red-wine vinaigrette, pecorino, and pickled okra. Grilled slices of sourdough come with the plate so you can make tasty 2-bite sandwiches. Other sure-bet choices are the Sweet Grass take on chicken and waffles (deep-fried chicken breast with pecan waffles and bourbon-made syrup) and the fried-egg, cheddar cheese, and avocado sandwich on sourdough. The bar is full service and specializes in updated traditional cocktails, like the old-fashioned made with muddled oranges and cherries. Sweet Grass also has plenty of specialty brews including high gravity beers on tap, a favorite when locals stay glued to the bar's flat screens to cheer on the University of Memphis Tigers. See Chef Trimm's recipe for **Frogmore Stew** on p. 278.

Young Avenue Deli, 2119 Young Ave., Memphis, TN 38104; (901) 278-0034; youngavenuedeli.com. The Young Avenue Deli serves fast (usually) and cheap food in a trendy neighborhood of more expensive restaurants. A favorite with young people who spend time playing pool, the deli stages shows on weekends with local performers and an occasional out-of-town band that is trending up. Pint night on Wednesday is another favorite because the deli's three dozen draft beers are $3. The bar also serves dozens of domestics and imports in bottles plus half a dozen cans if your favorite is Schlitz. The menu kicks off with more than a dozen munchies, including house-made french fries voted the best in the city. There are also artichoke hearts, mushrooms, and dill pickles beer battered and fried. Daily specials like a BLT with fresh basil aioli fill out a menu of subs and sandwiches. Try the 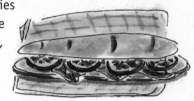 muffuletta with salami, ham, and house-made olive spread or the Death Row Pimento Cheese. You can also build-your-own pizzas and quesadillas with dozens of cheeses, veggies, meats, hummus, and fried tofu. All in all, Young Avenue Deli has some nice vegetarian choices, especially the vegetarian chili that is loaded with peppers, corn, green beans, and okra.

Cocktails & Lounges

Alchemy, 940 S. Cooper St., Memphis, TN 38104; (901) 726-4444; alchemymemphis.com. A newcomer to the clutch of restaurants hugging the corner of Cooper and Young, Alchemy keeps rocking with small plates and big cocktails in a cavernous space that manages to still feel personal. A favorite stopover for professionals, Alchemy brings a much needed metropolitan bar scene to Midtown, serving handcrafted cocktails to fashionable folks of all ages. On weekends, the place is packed and loud, but the energy adds to Alchemy's magic. Plus there are the drinks, such as the A. Schwab's Voodoo Martini, stirred and sexy with a long curl of orange peel, and the Zippin' Pippin, an elixir of Bulleit Bourbon, apple cider, lemon, and maple syrup. Alchemy's wine, beer, and liquor menus are equally impressive: 60-plus wines (half are served by the glass), a dozen boutique beers on draft, and almost 50 varieties of bourbon and scotch. Vegetarians and meat eaters will appreciate the selection of small plates, ranging in price from $6 to $12 and including these favorites: wild mushroom pancakes with wilted spinach and chèvre, rock shrimp and chorizo mac and cheese, chile-roasted fish tacos, and deconstructed ravioli with Italian sausage in roasted red-pepper cream. Many of the plates match the best New American menus in Memphis, thanks to Chef Karen Roth's prodigious skill.

Blind Bear Speakeasy, 119 S. Main St., Memphis, TN 38103; (901) 417-8435; blindbearmemphis.com. The Blind Bear's Facebook page says you'll need the password on Thursday, Friday, or Saturday nights to get inside Downtown's newest (and only) speakeasy. That's not really true, but the ploy fits right in with the bar's Prohibition theme devised by the trio of bartenders who own and operate the lounge. Here are a few more examples: draft beer served in mason jars, a signature mango vodka martini called the Flapper, and menu descriptions such as Crush salads, Bee's Knees sandwiches, Hotsy-Totsy soups, and Cat's Meow sides. Pretty cute, don't you think? The bar also serves traditional plate lunches on Wednesday and Friday, but the schedule may change so call ahead to check. Sunday "Hung Over Like a Bear" brunch is guaranteed from 3 to 6 p.m., along with a lineup of weekly events including reduced wine prices on Monday, poker on Tuesday, trivia on Wednesday, and live entertainment on Thursday.

East Tapas & Drinks, 6069 Park Ave., Memphis, TN 38119; (901) 767-6002; east-tapas.com. This cocktail and tapas bar is the next-door neighborhood to **Wang's Mandarin House** (p. 154), one of the oldest and most popular Chinese restaurants in Memphis. Shelly Ansley owns and operates Wang's, while her daughter Lisa Ansley steers East Tapas. It's a great one-two punch because the cocktail and tapas bar appeals to younger adults who prefer regional craft beers and drinks infused with lovely flavors like elderflower. The cocktails at East Tapas taste expensive but are priced under $10. Try a lychee gimlet (gin, orange liqueur, lychee juice, and freshly squeezed lime juice) or a Dark 'n Stormy (Gosling's Black Seal Rum, Gosling's Ginger Beer, and lime). The menu offers cold small plates, hot small plates, personal size pizzas, and desserts. The Asian guacamole is a good and spicy spin on the Mexican standard, and the truffle mac 'n' cheese is a more sophisticated version of a Southern favorite. Other good choices include sliders stuffed with blue cheese and topped with minced mushrooms and shallots, and Chinese eggplant dipped in tempura batter and filled with vegetables and minced shrimp.

Mollie Fontaine Lounge, 679 Adams Ave., Memphis, TN 38105; (901) 524-1886; molliefontainelounge.com. Mollie Fontaine is both eclectic and elegant, much like Karen Carrier who owns and operates the lounge, located in Victorian Village at the edge of downtown Memphis. The historic house was built in 1886 by Noland Fontaine as a wedding gift to his daughter Mollie. Carrier moved into the home when she returned to Memphis from New York and started her catering company called Another Roadside Attraction. The business is still located on the property, but customers to the lounge may never know. They will be too taken with settling into a drawing room settee and listening to Di Anne Price at the baby grand piano. Open Wed through Sat starting at 5 p.m., the 2-story house accommodates both smokers (upstairs) and nonsmokers (downstairs). The food served in small plates is global and very good. Crispy duck rice-paper rolls are filled with pickled plum, candied lemon zest, shiitakes, and arugula, and the calamari tastes like Thai basil and smoked paprika. Meat eaters should try the lounge sliders, grilled chicken wings, or sliced serrano ham served on crostini with arugula, fennel, Asian pear, and olives. While the plates fuse culinary traditions, the combinations aren't overly complicated. In fact, two of my favorite plates are tempura green beans served with ponzu dipping sauce and steamed mussels in a fragrant sea of coconut curry. See Carrier's recipe for **Thai-Style Beef Salad with Chipotle Honey Vinaigrette** on p. 268.

Silly Goose Lounge, 100 Peabody Place, Memphis, TN 38103; (901) 435-6915; sillygoosememphis.com. The casual motto at the Silly Goose is "all the drinks you can handle." An accurate add-on could be all the different drinks you can handle because the list of spirits at this uptown lounge is impressive to say the least. Go ahead and order a Stohli martini if you must, but consider branching out and trying something different. The lounge has more than 100 vodkas, along with 30 varieties of tequila, 40 liqueurs, and a decent list of Champagnes. Add in the beer and wine and it's easy to understand why Silly Goose is so popular with just about everybody. Bartenders also understand the nuances of a perfectly mixed cocktail. Try one of bartender Jeff Barber's signature drinks like the Kim Jong-Chill made with Godiva chocolate, Rumple Minze, and a splash of Frangelico. The setting at Silly Goose is New York urban with couches, tables, and an elevated patio for nice weather. The lounge food is simple but adequate: a few salads, munchies like baked pretzels with *queso,* and 12-inch pizza pies including a grilled chicken Alfredo and a 4-cheese with mozzarella, Parmesan, goat, and cheddar. Silly Goose also has brunch, where $8 buys fruit, muffin, and an excellent omelet (there are 9 combinations). From noon to 3 p.m. on Sunday, the lounge also offers bottomless mimosas for $15.

The Cove, 2559 Broad Ave., Memphis, TN 38112; (901) 730-0719; thecovememphis.com. Fresh oysters shipped in daily, classically prepared cocktails, and purse hooks. So goes my top three accolades for The Cove, a hip dive bar on historic Broad Avenue. However, there are more reasons to visit The Cove, starting with the vintage pirate ship bar rescued from Anderton's East, a former midcentury landmark restaurant located in Midtown. Other Anderton's fixtures add to The Cove's ambience, so be sure to look around. The bar's cocktails, however, are their own, especially the signature Sazerac, a New Orleans classic lovingly re-created with rye whiskey, and absinthe. If you prefer gin, try the Parisian Fog, a mix of absinthe, Hendrick's, orgeat syrup, and dry vermouth. Dozens of classic and artisan cocktails spiff up the menu at The Cove, a 21-and-up venue where people can smoke and not feel bad about it. The food is also good, especially oysters on the half shell that are shucked as ordered and served with traditional trimmings. The Cove also has oysters Rockefeller and oysters casino, along with a wonderful house-made hummus and iceberg wedge. The bar has panini, pizzas, and blonde butter brownies for dessert, but The Cove's signature dish is a tamale casserole with cream cheese Rotel called the Stoner Pie. On Wednesday, the Cove offers 6 free oysters with the purchase of a dozen, and on Saturday, the place can get very loud when the bands start playing at 10 p.m.

Earnestine & Hazel's, 531 S. Main, Memphis, TN 38103; (901) 523-9754. One Saturday night, I wandered into this downtown dive. Two or three dozen hipster types were gussied up and remnants of a buffet were on the pool table. "Is this a private party or a regular Saturday night?" I asked the bartender. "It's both," he said. "What are you drinking?" His response still makes me smile, especially when I think about how many people have melted or broken hearts at Earnestine & Hazel's, a treasured landmark in Memphis located across the street from the city's historic train station. Much of the bar's soul derives from its colorful past when a sundry store downstairs diverted attention from (and to) its upstairs brothel. Visitors can still wander around the upstairs, which many believe is haunted by the ghosts of the girls who worked there. There is a visceral feel to the rooms, especially on hot humid nights when the windows are open. Downstairs, the vibe is more upbeat from spontaneous dancing to a jukebox playing Memphis music. The bar opens for lunch, but the party doesn't typically rev up until midnight. Either way, order Earnestine and Hazel's signature Soul Burger, cooked on a hot grill that sizzles with every squirt of the bar's secret sauce. For a more romantic meal, steal around the corner to the bar's Five Spot, a tiny hole-in-the-wall restaurant that serves some very nice food, including tuna steak with lemon dill, white wine, and caper sauce.

Kudzu's Bar & Grill, 603 Monroe, Memphis, TN 38103; (901) 525-4924. For several years, a co-worker at the *Memphis Flyer* insisted that the only Friday lunch option was fried catfish at

Kudzu's. We obliged, not so much for the food, but because we liked the bones of the place and the large endless refills of crushed ice and tea. Built in the early 20th century, the blue-green brick building is down the street from a Wonder Bread bakery (be sure to check out the original WONDER BREAD sign), and the sweet smell of Hostess cakes adds to the bar's appeal. There is nothing sophisticated about Kudzu's, but it is funky and very cool because it's been some sort of bar since the late 1920s. Kelly and Jerry King took over Kudzu's in 2010 from longtime owners. They cleaned up the place a bit and added more draft beers, but otherwise Kudzu's carries on its neighborhood role with trivia nights, Wiffle ball on Sunday, and lots of local music. Regular entertainment includes a blues jam on Tuesday, and a Thursday night Pickin' Party with Nancy Apple, the Queen of Country in Memphis. Occasionally, punk bands show up on the roster. The new owners have made some changes to the menu. Sorry, Cheryl, but they replaced catfish with beer-battered cod and added a deep-fried pork tenderloin sandwich called the Hoosier.

Wine & Liquor Stores

Arthur's Wine & Liquor, 5475 Poplar Ave., Memphis, TN 38119; (901) 767-9463; arthurswineandliquor.com. Spend any time driving in Memphis, and you'll likely spot a billboard that says ARTHUR'S BACK. The billboard campaign trumpets the return of Arthur Kahn, who spent two years in legal disputes after a buyer reneged on a deal to purchase his East Memphis liquor store, located on Poplar Avenue near I-240. Customers are relieved Kahn is back in the saddle, because they like the store's great deals promoted in weekly newspaper inserts and the staff's excellent taste in wines. Kahn got into the liquor business after a career as

a federal prosecutor. He traveled to Europe, where he studied wines and learned to cook. He opened Arthur's in 1985, using his acquired European tastes to add new and interesting winemakers to the typical commodity producers sold at most stores. He moved Arthur's a few years ago to a larger 4,000-square-foot store, where he and his staff continue to build on their winning competition of inventory and customer service.

Buster's Liquors and Wines, 191 Highland St., Memphis, TN 38111; (901) 458-0929; bustersliquors.com. The Hammond family has operated Buster's for three generations, first in a location near Graceland and now in a shopping center about a block from the University of Memphis. A perennial winner for best wine store in the city, Buster's also sells everything else: 100 single-malt scotches; 100 cognacs, 100 bourbons, and more than 200 cordials and liqueurs. During the year-end holidays, the store seems like a Toys R Us for adults, a feeling pretty much duplicated on any Friday or Saturday night. Inventory fills up 10,000 square feet of space, but the wines are still organized in a sensible way with shelf labels

HOMEGROWN CHAIN: HUEY'S

Thomas Boggs joined Huey's a few years after it opened in 1970, and his unexpected death at age 63 hurt the city's soul. Many people, regardless of age or income, had a connection to Huey's, and most still do. Now a chain of 7 pub-grub restaurants, Huey's started as a single bar for blues and burgers. Huey's still has live music on weekends, along with weekday trivia nights, but it's the burgers that customers cherish. *Memphis* magazine readers have handed Huey's the best-burger title every year since 1984. They love the burger's secret mix of beef and spices blended fresh every day at **Charlie's Meat Market** (p. 161) on Summer Avenue. Customers also can't stop using their straws to blow toothpicks into the restaurants' ceilings, a pastime that is very 1970s, but fun nonetheless. The toothpick frills also serve a philanthropic purpose. Every so often, Huey's knocks them all down and holds a toothpick-counting contest. Proceeds, more than $30,000 so far, benefit the Memphis Zoo, Boggs's favorite nonprofit. These days, Huey's caters to families and late-night drinking buddies with a menu that includes hand-breaded onion rings, a surprising good grilled tuna burger, and homemade desserts like brownie a la mode and lemon icebox pie. There are also lots of twists on the original World Famous Huey Burger, such as a Texas toast burger with Pepper Jack cheese, grilled onions, and jalapeños, and the West Coast burger with guacamole and Monterey Jack cheese on a buttered and toasted whole wheat bun. Menus are the same at all seven locations, but entertainment varies. Check Huey's website, hueyburger.com, for locations and schedules.

for national ratings and staff picks. Personal attention at Buster's can be erratic, but it's a fun store to wander in until a staffer shows up to help.

Corkscrew Wine and Spirits, 511 S. Front St., Memphis, TN 38103; (901) 523-9389; corkscrewmemphis.com. A neighborhood wine store in the truest sense, the Corkscrew brings wine and spirits to this growing residential area in downtown's historic arts district. Located on the north side of a building facing Front Street, Corkscrew is a little hidden, so look for the more visible sign of its neighbor, a popular pub called the **Blue Monkey** (p. 208). Managed by Scott Vincent since its opening in 2008, the Corkscrew is one of the smallest liquor stores in the city, which limits its specials but ensures top-notch attention for regular customers. About 450 liquors and 1,800 wines from around the world squeeze into this corner store which is open Mon through Thurs until 9 p.m., and Fri and Sat until 10 p.m.

Joe's Wine & Liquors, 1681 Poplar Ave., Memphis, TN 38104; (901) 725-4252. Joe's opened at the corner of Poplar Avenue and Belvedere in 1962, and the store's remarkable ROTO-SPHERE sign was featured in its newspaper ads. The neon beauty had rotating 8-foot spikes, earning the sign its nickname of Sputnik. By the mid-70s, the sign had stopped working, but the store's owners left it intact until 1999 when a $12,000 restoration launched it back into orbit.

One of the most recognizable landmarks in Memphis, Joe's retro sign is a promising hint of what's inside the store: a thoughtful and complete inventory with knowledgeable and friendly employees to explain all the choices. In June 2011, state legislators finally approved wine and liquor sampling at restaurants, bars, and liquor stores. General manager Michael Hughes embraced the change right away, offering regular tastings of wine, high gravity beers, and cocktails like margaritas. After years in its packed small space, the store also expanded into an adjoining minimart, allowing the store to buff up its merchandising and to expand its inventory even more.

Liquor and Wine Depot, 756 Mount Moriah Rd., Memphis, TN 38117; (901) 685-3080. Since 2007, the Liquor and Wine Depot has been filling an important niche: popular wines and liquors at low prices. Comparisons are tricky, but the store is certainly in the running for the best prices in town. Granted, the store's bright red-and-yellow signage is a little lowbrow, but inside employees are knowledgeable and accommodating, making it comfortable to ask for help finding a decent $10 bottle. Great prices don't mean limited selections. Liquor and Wine Depot stocks more than 1,000 different wines and 500 liquors and offers case discounts, monthly specials, and 10 percent off for ladies every Tuesday. Employees also are service oriented, reminding customers about new selections and pointing out discounts for popular favorites.

Wine Market, 4700 Spottswood Ave., Memphis, TN 38117; (901) 761-1666; winemarketmemphis.com. Located in a busy East Memphis shopping center near a Target, Superlo grocery store, and Williams-Sonoma outlet, the Wine Market easily piggybacks on customers' weekly errands. While convenience and plenty of parking figure into the Wine Market's success, service and selection are more important draws. An informed staff works with customers one-on-one, giving equal attention to both novice and oenophile. They tour West Coast wineries regularly and work hard to bring in new wines at different price points. The store also features a full component of wines from Europe and South America, as well as spirits, beer, and an excellent selection of scotch whiskies. A frequent participant in wine pairings with local chefs, the Wine Market also features a monthly wine club and holds regular in-store tastings on Saturday afternoons.

Worth the Drive

Memphis is the population center of the Mid-South, a designation used by residents and local media to define the area where western Tennessee meets up with Arkansas and Mississippi. Stand on the bluff top in downtown Memphis to watch the barges drift by, and you see the low-lying riverbanks of Arkansas. Drive 10 minutes south on I-55 and you come to the bedroom community of Horn Lake, Mississippi, where world championship barbecue chefs Melissa Cookston and John Wheeler own the Memphis Barbecue Company. Be sure to stop for a rack of baby back ribs.

Head in almost any direction from downtown Memphis, and you're likely to stumble across local pitmasters loading smokers with hickory logs or roadside produce stands with jars of homemade jam and chow chow. Do-it-yourselfers also should visit Millington, not far from where music icon Justin Timberlake was born, to see Jones Orchard, a family-run farm for more than 60 years. Have lunch at the country cafe and then head outdoors to pick seasonal fruit such as apples, peaches, and blackberries.

While a good plate lunch is commonplace in the Mid-South, a few communities mix history and food into more updated packages that are well worth the extra travel. Oxford has William Faulkner's lovely Rowan Oaks and the University of Mississippi. The university also is home base for the Southern Foodways Alliance, a respected nonprofit that studies Southern food culture through documentaries, anthologies, and oral histories. And then there are the town's chefs, a talented and sophisticated group that includes John Currence, named James Beard Best Southern Chef in 2009.

The town of Hernando, Mississippi, the DeSoto County seat, is a little closer to Memphis but still mixes old charm with new energy. Founded in 1836, the town centers around a historic town square with a lively Saturday morning farmers' market, a European-style bakery, and an up-and-coming eatery featured on *Diners, Drive-ins and Dives*. A block away is Velvet Cream, a drive-up burger stand from 1947 with milk shakes and malts in 180 different flavors.

Foodie Faves

Blue Daze Bistro, 221 E. Commerce St., Hernando, MS 38632; (662) 469-9304; bluedazebistro.com; American; $$. A filet mignon cooked to order and topped with whiskey-mushroom sauce is quintessential American cooking at this cozy small-town restaurant where dinner is served on Thursday, Friday, and Saturday nights. American standards done right round out the rest of the dinner menu: chicken

Florentine, pan-seared salmon, shrimp and grits, and meatballs with marinara, house-made or course. At lunch, served Monday through Friday, 8 entree salads move from hearty to sublime. Try the Black & Blue Salad (greens topped with blackened flank steak, blue cheese crumbles, and the restaurant's signature blue cheese dressing) or a three-scoop sampler of old-fashioned pimento cheese, tuna, and chicken salad on a bed of lettuce. The restaurant also serves daily soup specials and yummy sides like broccoli-bacon salad. Sunday brunch, served from 10 a.m. to 2 p.m., rolls out the weekday salads plus loaded omelets, buttery biscuits in Southern gravy, and french toast casserole topped with cinnamon and cream.

Buon Cibo, 2631 McIngvale Rd., Hernando, MS 38632; (662) 469-9481; buonciborestaurant.com; Cafe/Pizza; $. Buon Cibo is Italian for "good food," and that's exactly what you get at this cafe operated by husband-and-wife team Katie and Josh Belenchia. Josh is the chef, but Katie makes the pies including chocolate chess, lemon chess, and french coconut. From its shopping center parking lot, Buon Cibo seems at first like a chain restaurant. But walk inside and the feeling dissipates. A cooler sells farm-fresh eggs and healthy foods to go. A huge chalkboard menu announces pizzas, sandwiches, soups, and salads made from scratch with locally sourced products like sausage, grits, and goat cheese. Clearly this place is no Panera Bread. Instead, it's like an easy hipster cafe in Brooklyn. Try the cobb salad with house-made green goddess dressing or a grown-up grilled cheese made with sharp cheddar and mozzarella on brioche. Pick your own pizza toppings if you must. Otherwise, leave it to the house unless you can beat The Oxford topped with kalamata olive marinara, pepperoni, roasted chicken, pepperoncini, mozzarella, feta, and fried capers. Weekend dinners add an entree or two to the standard menu such as shrimp and grits or a grilled rib eye with twice-baked potato, sautéed spinach, and Creole hollandaise sauce.

Marlo's Down Under, 102 E. Court Sq., Covington, TN 38019; (901) 475-1124; marlosdu.com; American; $$. Folks in Covington don't have many choices for fine dining. Fortunately, Marlo's Down Under is a pleasing respite from chain restaurants and fast food. Chef-Owner Nick Scott mixes French and Southern influences into his dinner menu of appetizers (ahi tuna nachos), prime-cut steaks (strip, rib eye, and filet), fresh seafood (mahimahi with roasted yellow pepper pesto), and pasta dishes (Creole shrimp and tasso ham in cream sauce over linguine). Margaritas are the house specialty and make a nice companion drink to half a dozen grilled pizzas like barbecue duck confit and Moon Pie, a combination of grilled chicken, basil pesto, black olives, artichoke hearts, and Asiago cheese. Scott serves a more abbreviated menu at lunch with similar types of entrees along with burgers, classic clubs, and shrimp po' boys. Check the restaurant's Facebook page for daily lunch specials priced under $10. Here's an example of an affordable but tasty lunch: spicy chicken wraps with chipotle aioli, jalapeños, slaw, and Pepper Jack cheese served with house-made chips.

Memphis Street Cafe, 2476 Memphis St., Hernando, MS 38632; (662) 429-9299; American; $–$$. Food Network celeb Guy Fieri sampled the Rueben and chicken salad during his recent visit to the Memphis Street Cafe, but he filmed the cafe's outstanding take on Bananas Foster for the *Diners, Drive-ins and Dives* episode. Chef Chris Lee uses banana nut bread and homemade vanilla ice cream for the scrumptious dessert, one of many sweet standouts that rotate through the restaurant's updated American menu. The former chef of Fitzgerald's casino in nearby Tunica, Lee and his wife Natalia reopened their popular cafe in June of 2011 after a late-night fire shuttered the business for three months. The renovated basement eatery located off Hernando's historic town square duplicates its former charm: pale yellow walls, polished cement floors, framed local art, and a simple but appealing menu with dishes like blackened chicken and grits, European-style stuffed cabbage rolls, and catfish po' boys with house-made remoulade. The cafe's side dishes are also quite good because they are updated but still familiar. Try sweet potato fries, chipotle cheddar grits, or a generous serving of russian potato salad.

Ravine, 553 Pea Ridge Rd., Oxford, MS 38655; (662) 234-4555; oxfordravine.com; New American; $–$$. Smoked quail with prosciutto, spring vegetable salad, and rosemary crème fraîche is the sort of dish at Ravine that shows off Chef Joel Miller's blended influences. Miller started his restaurant training with Karen

Carrier's restaurants in Memphis, moving on to kitchens in New Orleans, San Francisco, and Puerto Rico. His menus showcase the local produce he and his wife, Cori, grow at their restaurant and bed-and-breakfast in the outskirts of Oxford. Local purveyors for poultry, meat, eggs, cheese, and bread dominate Ravine's menu, which is organized in about 15 small, middle, and large plates. Even the restaurant's duck and quail come from Mississippi and Tennessee, building on a menu where ingredients shine in simple but sophisticated combinations. Try house-made fettuccine with roast peppers, mushrooms, and herb pesto; duck breast on wild rice pancakes with sweet-and-sour cherry sauce; or savory crepes filled with ratatouille and ricotta, also house made. Ravine serves dinner Tuesday through Saturday and Sunday brunch beginning at 10:30 a.m. Also look for special-event dinners about once a month, such as a pork and Pinot tasting or tapas on Wednesday. Consider a stay at the couple's charming cabin, where you can swim in the pool and have time for another meal.

Waltz on the Square, 1110 Van Buren Ave., Oxford, MS 38655; (662) 236-2760; waltzonthesquare.com; New American; $$–$$$. Ordering a steak is usually a simple decision between a filet, a strip, and a rib eye. Not so at Waltz on the Square, where four different toppings offer almost impossible choices between the New Orleans (crawfish and étouffée sauce), the Coleman (blue cheese and shallot compound butter), and the Festival (golden Madeira mushroom sauce). Don't ponder too long because all the toppings are a flavorful tribute to Chef Erica Lipe, who can trill American classics in

Even Memphis Heat Can't Tucker Out Prolific and Delicious Tifblue Berries

In Memphis, strawberries don't amount to much. The season is short lived, and unpredictable spring rains can wipe out entire crops. Blueberries, on the other hand, thrive in the thick, humid heat of summer, especially Tifblue, a prolific native treasured for its sweet taste and beautiful pale-blue color.

Part of the rabbiteye family, Tifblue is the best match for Memphis because the berries are pest free and tolerate drought, says farmer Alvin Harris. He should know. Harris has been growing blueberries for more than three decades at his farm in Millington, and his bushes are tall and wide enough to make a little shade.

If you want to pick blueberries at Harris Farms, they are typically ready from mid-June through early August. Stop by the couple's roadside produce stand, get a bucket, and then head up the rise to the blueberry bushes. "The ripest berries have an opaque color to them, and when you pick them, they roll into your hand," Alvin Harris explains. "If they are real shiny, they're not ready to eat."

Here's some additional advice: Tifblues are initially light green. As they ripen, they turn red and then blue. If berries are for eating, don't pick them until they are blue with a blush. (Blush, in berry parlance, is the touch of whitewash on the fruit.) For cooking, mix some red berries into the bucket because they add a little tartness to pie fillings and jams.

While berry picking is popular with many Memphis families, restaurant chefs also embrace seasonal berry dishes. At **Erling Jensen** (p. 135), chefs top fresh field greens with crispy Camembert and a blueberry and blackberry compote. At **The Elegant Farmer** (p. 134), Leslee Pascal smothers a rich, buttery pound cake with blueberries, yogurt, honey, and confectioners' sugar. (To make Pascal's pound cake, see her recipe on p. 287) For something less ambitious, follow these simple instructions for Shirley Harris's excellent blueberry syrup. "Take two cups berries, one cup water, no pectin," she says. "Then cook it down with about half a cup of sugar."

In addition to Harris Farm, a handful of other growers also operate pick-your-own farms, including Nesbit Blueberry Plantation, where George Traicoff grows row after row of blueberry bushes on 22 acres. A listing of blueberry farms follows, but be sure to call ahead to check on availability or follow Traicoff on twitter @nesbitberry.

Harris Farms, 7521 Sledge Rd., Millington, TN 38053; (901) 872-0696

Hudspeth Blueberry Farm, 400 Pioneer Way, Senatobia, MS 38668; (662) 562-4192

Jones Orchard, 6824 Big Creek Church, Millington, TN 38053; (901) 872-2923

Nesbit Blueberry Plantation, 690 Bankston Rd., Nesbit, MS 38651; (662) 429-3778

Pontotoc Blueberry Ridge, 240 Carter Ln., Pontotoc, MS 38863; (662) 489-8481

simple but distinctive ways. Her salad wedge, for instance, adds almonds to the bacon/blue cheese combo, and her grits are made with smoked Gouda instead of the more typical cheddar. In her mid-20s, Lipe brings a youthful energy to Waltz, open since 2007 and located just off Oxford's historic town square. Try to sit at a cozy table in one of the restaurant's window bays so you can watch the interesting parade of passersby while the courses keep coming: fried green tomato napoleon, she-crab soup made with sherry and fresh cream, or lemon-brined chicken breast with wild rice, collard chiffonade, and chorizo vinaigrette. Desserts change day to day, but order this if you dare: a warm brownie topped with Oreo cookie crumbles, vanilla ice cream, pecan fudge icing, and a garnish of mint leaves.

Landmarks

Blue & White Restaurant, 1355 Highway 61 North, Tunica, MS 38676; (662) 363-1371; blueandwhiterestaurant.com; Cafe/Diner; $–$$. To figure out what kind of food comes out of the kitchen of this longtime favorite, look at the Blue & White breakfast for $6 (two eggs with sausage, ham or bacon, grits or hash browns, and biscuits or toast) or the appetizers (fried dill pickle chips, Delta fried green tomatoes, and fried green beans). The description of the cafe's $12 Imperial Salad is another giveaway: fresh iceberg lettuce, tomato, boiled eggs, pickles, olives, bacon, roast beef, turkey, and ham. Makes you want to jump in the car and drive immediately to the Blue & White, established in 1924 on US 61 in downtown Tunica decades before the casinos showed up. For many years, Pure Oil Company operated the restaurant, along with a full-service gas station, newsstand, and Greyhound bus stop. These days, just the diner remains, but that's plenty because the food is Southern style and made from scratch. In addition to diner standards such as homemade chili and vegetable soup, Blue & White serves country-fried steak sandwiches, flat iron steaks, grilled baby beef livers, and hand-battered and deep-fried jumbo frog legs. For the squeamish, they also have cheeseburgers.

City Grocery, 152 Courthouse Sq., Oxford, MS 38655; (662) 232-8080; citygroceryonline.com; Creole/New American; $$–$$$. The cucumber and onion salad with charred pecans and New Orleans remoulade hints at the Creole twist to City Grocery, the celebrated first restaurant of Chef John Currence. But then the menu turns seasonal and modern with dishes like this: grilled red snapper with sun-dried tomato and root vegetable hash, lemon sautéed kale, and basil vinaigrette. Unpredictability is one of many culinary imprints from Currence, voted best Southern chef in 2009 by the James Beard Foundation. City Grocery, which celebrated its 20th anniversary in 2012, is the most trumpeted of Currence's restaurants. Located in a Reconstruction-era livery stable, City Grocery's exposed brick walls and excellent service bring a casual elegance to restaurant's exciting menus. The location also attracts other well-known chefs who sometimes come to Oxford for cookbook signings at the town's celebrated independent bookstore up the street, Town Square Books. Adam Perry Lang of Barbecoa in London, for instance, hosted a multicourse dinner at City Grocery in June for the release of his book *Charred and Scruffed*. Since starting City Grocery, Currence has opened two more restaurants in Oxford. Boure, also located on Courthouse Square, is a Creole casual eatery popular with students, and Big Bad Breakfast is exactly that: hearty fare for lunch and dinner that includes house-made biscuits and house-cured Tabasco brown-sugar bacon.

Barbecue & Blue Plates

Ajax Diner, 118 Courthouse Sq., Oxford, MS 38655; (662) 232-8880; ajaxdiner.net; Diner/Plate Lunches; $. The meat loaf is stuffed with Jack cheese, and the sweet potato casserole tastes like pie without a crust at Ajax Diner, a throwback to Southern home cooking at its best. Open since 1997, the diner feels much older because of its checkered linoleum floors and permanent strands of Christmas lights. Bring a big appetite to Ajax and get there early. Lunch lines can start forming at 10:30 a.m., especially on game days at the nearby University of Mississippi. Happily, you'll forget about the wait when you bite into a fried oyster po' boy dressed with cabbage, mayo, and pickles. Plate lunches served with jalapeño corn bread and 2 sides also rock, especially the chicken and dumplings swimming in white Southern gravy. Expanded but similar home cooking shows up at dinner, served until 10 p.m. Try the Hot Jerk Pork Steak marinated in scotch bonnet pepper and blackberry sauce or the hot tamale pie, a full-bodied undertaking of spicy cheese grits, corn, tomatoes, smoked pork, and green chiles. Homemade lemonade is another specialty of the house, and it's served alone with ice and in cocktails like the Jon Daly, a mind-altering mix of lemonade, sweet tea, and vodka.

Johnnie's Drive In, 908 E. Main St., Tupelo, MS 38804; (662) 842-6748; Burgers/Barbecue; $. If you're old enough to know what a dough burger is, you are probably an Elvis fan. Dough burgers, a combination of dough and ground beef, spun out of America's Great Depression, and they are a signature dish at Johnnie's Drive In. (Go ahead and try one!) The Dixie diner has been operating since 1945, when Elvis attended 5th grade down the street at Lawhon Elementary. Elvis was born in Tupelo, about 100 miles from Memphis, and according to the historic marker out front, he used to stop by Johnnie's for his favorite combo: a cheeseburger and RC Cola. These days, the menu is pretty much the same, just like everything else at Johnnie's: hot dogs, pimento cheese sandwiches, chicken salad, and barbecue. You can get car-hop service at the drive-in, but unless you are feeling very lazy, go inside and sit at the Elvis booth. You'll love the kitschy memorabilia and the friendly waitresses who are happy to talk about Tupelo's most famous son. After lunch, visit Tupelo Hardware Co. It's where a young Elvis bought his first guitar.

Jones Orchard Country Cafe, 7170 Highway 51 North, Millington, TN 38053; (901) 873-3150; jonesorchard.com; Home Cooking; $. Juanita Jones has spent a lifetime cooking, first for family and then in the kitchen of **Jones Orchard** (p. 258), where her pies, jams, jellies, and relishes were sold at the roadside market along with seasonal produce. Next she added a limited to-go menu of soup and sandwiches and a few tables where customers could sit down to eat. A full-service country cafe came next and continues today, serving Jones's renowned home cooking made with fresh ingredients from her family farm. Her white beans and corn bread are robust and filling. So are her salad, yeast rolls, and lunch-plate specials served Monday through Saturday from 11:30 a.m. to 2:30 p.m. Check the Jones Orchard Facebook page for daily updates, but expect dishes like meat loaf, catfish, beef potpie, purple hull beans, fried green tomatoes, buttered summer squash, corn cheese pudding, strawberry shortcake, and homemade fruit pies.

Memphis Barbecue Company, 709 Desoto Cove, Horn Lake, MS 38637; (662) 536-3762; memphisbbqco.com; Barbecue; $–$$. A Grand Champion platter at Memphis Barbecue Company includes this mind-blowing assortment of food: half a slab of spare ribs, half a slab of loin ribs, smoked legs and thighs, sausage, pulled pork, corn bread, and 3 large sides. Now that's some serious eating pulled together by award-winning barbecue chefs Melissa Cookston and John Wheeler. No other barbecue restaurant in the country can claim the kudos of these to pitmasters, both members of championship cooking teams at the Memphis in May **Barbecue Cooking Contest** (p. 16). In fact, they are both multiple winners, and their trophies are prominently displayed at their restaurant, even in the gift shop. The restaurant's menu does include a few items unrelated to barbecue, like orange-chipotle-grilled salmon and strawberry chicken salad. But why mess with a sure thing? The ribs are perfectly prepared so the meat falls off the bone with just a tiny tug. Sides are also hearty, especially the Big Honkin' Baker, a 1-pound Idaho potato stuffed with pulled pork, cheese, green onions, sour cream, and barbecue sauce. Oh, Lord. Help me.

10 Bones BBQ, 5960 Getwell, Ste. 126, Southhaven, MS 38672; (662) 890-4472; eatdrinkboogie.com/10bonesbbq; Barbecue; $–$$. A newcomer to the restaurant scene, pitmaster Mark West is a competition veteran with more than 200 first-place trophies for shoulders, whole hogs, and ribs. At 10 Bones BBQ, he uses fresh dry rubs, marinades, and hickory wood to smoke baby back ribs, pulled pork, and chicken for a menu of sandwiches, slab dinners, and salads like the smoked chicken Caesar. Sides are fairly predictable (slaw, fried okra, green beans, baked beans, and corn on the cob), but the appetizers do score a perfect 10 with barbecue fried ribs. The ribs cost $2 each, but consider this process: First, ribs are cooked and then they are frozen. When customers order the appetizer, they are flashed fried and tossed with buffalo or barbecue sauce. Who in the world could even think to do this? It's just one more reason to try 10 Bones BBQ. Plus, they have dessert. Some barbecue joints wisely skip a final course, but at 10 Bones, things just get sweeter. Try cleansing your palate with one of these: brownie a la mode or a slice of peanut butter pie.

Specialty Stores, Markets & Producers

Bonnie Blue Farm Goat Cheese, Dry Creek Road, Waynesboro, TN 38485; (931) 722-4628; bonniebluefarm.com. **Jim Tanner of Bonnie Blue Farm might be the friendliest guy at the local farmers' markets. When his cheese stock starts to dwindle, he's happy to cut a deal so he can keep talking about his goats (100 head, and 42 are for milking), his cheese (the Camembert has a rich mushroom flavor), and his wife, Gayle (master cheesemaker, trained**

chef, and world-record holder in swimming). In 2006, the Tanner's farm in Waynesboro became the only licensed grade-A goat dairy in Tennessee. Fortunately for Memphis, Bonnie Blue Farm is close enough to accommodate farmers' markets and the dozen or so chefs who use the farm's chèvre in a variety of different dishes. The chèvre is rolled in delicious mixes of herbs and seasonings, such as rosemary and garlic or a Southwest blend with chipotle. In addition to Camembert, Bonnie Blue sells cheddar, which is wrapped in cheesecloth, coated in lard, and aged about a year. The farm is also open for small group tours and rents a cozy log cabin, where visitors can stay and relax in the country or help out with the work.

Bottletree Bakery, 923 Van Buren Ave., Oxford, MS 38655; (662) 236-5000; waltzonthesquare.com. The rustic bread rack, colorful mismatched chairs, and BE NICE OR LEAVE sign on the front window give Bottletree Bakery a hippie-yippie vibe, but the baked goods at this poplar place are quite contemporary. Black pepper and salt bagels, apple and raspberry brioche, black-bottom cupcakes, banana-walnut whole wheat muffins, and white-chocolate cherry cookies are a sampling of the wonderful ways to begin your day. A very busy gathering spot for locals of all types, Bottletree has been serving baked goods, breakfast, and lunch since 1995. The mochas and lattes are also excellent thanks to the Bottletree Blend, a medium-bodied and spicy house coffee. Be sure to get a pound of the house blend to go, especially since staffers are happy to grind a bag to order. In addition to the bakery's scrumptious baked goods, they serve granola, fruit cups and juices for breakfast. For lunch, try the soup of the day, such as roasted pepper and smoked Gouda, or one of half a dozen sandwiches like the Van Buren Bestseller: smoked turkey, provolone, red onion, lettuce, tomato, and raspberry mustard. Get to Bottletree early (they open at 7 a.m.) because lines can form, especially on weekends.

Boulangerie Olivier, 2485 Memphis St., Hernando, MS 38632; (662) 469-9450. Baker Holly Loomis says it's the egg wash that makes her macaroons crispy on edges, turning each chewy bite into a perfect burst of toasty coconut. At a dollar each, the macaroons piled artfully on a bone china cake stand are an affordable and delicious introduction to Loomis's repertoire. Don't even try to stop with the cookies. Her European-style breads and baguettes will make you pity anyone who must eat gluten-free. Dense with texture and flavor, the baker's grain breads include red wheat, spelt, and dark German rye. The french country white bread is the perfect breakfast toast, unless you wake up with a sweet tooth. Then head straight for a toasted slice of dark chocolate so a smear of creamy butter can melt along with the bread's chocolate chips. Trained at the French Pastry School in Chicago, Loomis started baking as a youngster thanks to homeschooling and her encouraging mom, Vonda

Loomis, who helps out at the basement bakery located behind the Hernando town square. While the bakery's kitchen is state of the art, the bakery's retail space feels a little Old World, like a cozy courtyard cafe in Tuscany.

City Hall Cheesecake, 2465 Highway 51, South Hernando, MS 38632; (662) 469-9117; cityhallcheesecake.com. Good luck picking a favorite flavor of cheesecake at this charming artisan bakery run by Melissa and Kyle Mansell and Diane and Ron Bishop, who are Melissa's folks. It's much more sensible simply to try a new flavor every time. But where do you start? Kyle suggests white chocolate raspberry, while Melissa has two favorites: caramel white chocolate with macadamia nut and chocolate peanut butter. Either way, the cheesecake will be rich and creamy and made with a master's touch. The bakery offers more than a dozen flavors of cheesecake regularly, including triple chocolate, strawberry, and turtle, and more exotic flavors rotate in and out each week. Cakes can be ordered online, but try to visit one of the bakeries' two locations. Both are charming because they are located on historic town squares in lovely old buildings. Hernando's original City Hall is home (and namesake) to the bakery's first store. A vintage bank vault is still part of the second bakery in Collierville, adding a bit of local history to the location's old-brick ambience at 114 N. Main St., Collierville, TN 38017; (901) 457-7149.

Delta Grind, 353 Panola St., Water Valley, MS 38965; deltagrind .com. Grits originated with southern Native Americans, who used

Newman Farm Pork:
It's Local, Flavorful & Raised Right

In Memphis, where pork is both a food staple and a cherished food tradition, Mark and Rita Newman are locavore royalty. Chef-driven menus across the city feature pork from the couple's Berkshire hogs, which they raise on a sprawling farm in the southern Ozarks of Missouri.

Competitive grill masters also are discovering the tasty advantages of the heritage breed. In fact, Yazoo Delta Q used Newman Farm pork in 2012 to win top honors at the Memphis in May **World Championship Barbecue Cooking Contest** (p. 16), the world's premier barbecue competition.

Mark, who spent years working in the commercial pork industry, embraced responsible farming and heritage breeds in the late 1990s, riding the cusp of the pork-belly craze with Momofuku's celebrated New York City chef David Chang. Since then, the couple has supplied pork to renowned chefs from California to Louisiana, including Kevin Nashan of Sidney Street Cafe who served Newman Farm pork to Michelle and Barack Obama at a $25,000-a-plate fund-raiser in St. Louis.

Chefs like the Berkshire breed because the meat has more fat and flavor than commercially raised pork. "We like to say, fat is back," Mark Newman says. "The chefs are not so concerned with the health-conscious customer. They want flavor instead."

Typically, Mark handles restaurant deliveries (he drives hundreds of miles every week), while Rita coordinates orders for the farm's extensive range of products including chops, jowls, Boston butts, ground pork, and sugar-cured smoked-pepper bacon, a customer favorite. Both are personable advocates for their great-tasting meat, which is available at local farmers' market along with plenty of customer service. Ask Rita how to cook pork roast and her advice stays pretty simple: "All the meat needs is salt, pepper, and an oven," she says. "It couldn't be any easier."

Every spring, the Newmans also host a farm-to-table celebration to introduce friends and customers to the farm's operation. There are tours, a potluck lunch, butchering demonstration, tastings from local wineries, and an evening of pig-centric cooking orchestrated by local chefs. "It's a nice low-key day, but nobody's going home hungry, that's for sure," Rita Newman says. "We do this as a way to say thank you to our customers."

Back in Memphis, chefs continue to serve Newman Farm pork (and the farm's recently added Dorper lambs) in delicious and inventive dishes. At **Acre** (p. 127), tenderloin is smoked and served with braised ham, Brussels sprouts, and miso-maple jus. At **Andrew Michael Italian Kitchen** (p. 128), pork is plated with hominy, potatoes, lentil *sugo,* and turnip greens. And at **Las Tortugas Deli Mexicana** (p. 180), warm and soft house-made tortillas are filled with chopped pork, shredded lettuce, avocado slices, and fresh lime for a wonderful combination of texture and taste.

Newman Farm, Rt. 1, Box 141, Myrtle, MO 65778; (417) 938-4391; newmanfarm.com stones to grind corn into small particles for a type of cooked cereal, much like Southerners make grits today. Delta Grind uses a similar technique to make 4 versions of the same thing: grits, cornmeal, polenta, and masa. Many commercially made grits are white, but the grits at Delta Grind are yellow because owner Becky Tatum prefers the stronger flavor. She contracts with local farmers, who grow and dry her corn in the field. Then she uses a mill with granite stones (one is stationary, the other turns) to grind the corn in different ways. So cornmeal, for instance, is coarsely ground corn, while masa is corn flour. Stones also don't heat up like steel grinders, so Delta Grind products taste fresh and retain more natural nutrients. Delta Grind's mill is located in Water Valley, Mississippi, about 20 miles south of Oxford, but the products are prominently featured at Memphis restaurants, sold at local farmers' markets, and stocked at specialty grocery stores like **Miss Cordelia's** (p. 68), **Urban Farms** (p. 121), and **Trolley Stop** (p. 50).

Earth Sprung Grain, PO Box 732, Pocahontas, AR 72476; (901) 494-3364. Arkansas, which is a neighbor state for western Tennessee, grows 40 percent of the country's rice, or more than any other state. Despite the proximity, finding locally sourced rice in Memphis is difficult because most farmers sell their crops to commercial wholesalers. Earth Sprung Grain is trying to change all that with white and brown jasmine rice grown and hulled in Walnut Ridge, Arkansas. Business partners Jennifer Wells and Lance Schmidt are veterans of the rice industry (Wells in seed, Schmidt in machinery). They wanted a seed adapted for the growing conditions of Arkansas with the taste and nutty aroma typical of jasmine rice imported from Thailand. Open a bag of jasmine rice from Earth Sprung Grain, and the heady aromatics verify the company's success. The rice is soft milled, so tiny pieces of hull remain even in the white variety, making it naturally more nutritious. The vendors are newcomers to the **Memphis Farmers Market** (p. 67) and are also marketing their products in Jonesboro, Arkansas.

Hernando Farmers' Market, Hernando Courthouse Square, 2535 Highway 51 South, Hernando, MS 38632; localharvest.org/ hernando-farmers-market-M27791. Vendors at the Hernando Farmers' Market only pay $10 a week to participate, so the group that circles the courthouse square includes small local truck farmers and start-up entrepreneurs like Kevin Doran, who makes his own laundry soap. Doran's natural stain-buster combines, among other ingredients, baking soda and Fels Naptha, a soap as old as your grandmother's scrub board. "I have a mechanic who buys my soap because he says it's the only detergent that gets the smell of diesel out of his clothes," Doran says. This kind of friendly conversation is typical at the Hernando market, because vendors aren't too busy to exchange trade secrets or to explain the best way to cook purple hull peas. The market runs from May through October on Saturday, starting at 8 a.m. In addition to produce and handmade goods, vendors sell local milk and butter, European-style bread, meat, herbs, cut flowers, jams, and jellies.

Jones Orchard, 7170 US 51 North, Millington, TN 38053; (901) 873-3150; jonesorchard.com. For seven decades, the Jones family has been growing fruits and vegetables for area markets and for their own roadside stands. But most folks associate the orchard with their pick-your-own properties and their line of country-style jams and jellies. Today, the Jones family farms 600 acres, with more than 100 acres devoted to their juicy and flavorful peaches. They grow two dozen varieties of peaches, including heirlooms seldom seen in commercial groceries. This vast selection spreads ripening dates across several months, so customers can pick peaches from June through early September. Since harvest dates change from season to season, the orchard maintains a calendar on its website for all its pick-your-own produce, which in spring and summer also includes strawberries, blackberries, plums, pears, and nectarines. In the fall, look for turnip greens, Arkansas Black apples, and a field of ripe pumpkins ready for Halloween. In addition to the facility on US 51, Jones also operates two other pick-your-own properties: 6880 Singleton Pkwy., Millington, TN 38053; and 6824 Big Creek Church Rd., Millington, TN 38053.

LadyBugg Bakery, 205 E. Commerce, Hernando, MS 38632; (662) 449-7000; ladybuggbakery.com. Most people in Memphis discovered LadyBugg Bakery when Chelsea Bugg started baking at **YoLo Frozen Yogurt**'s Midtown store (p. 130). But in October of 2011, she moved to her own shop in Hernando, where Chelsea's husband,

David, makes the bread and daughters Valerie Hawkes and Heather Ries bake a treasure trove of cupcakes, cookies, brownies, and scones. The bakery's special-order cakes are certainly gorgeous, but the cupcake case is where the family's finesse turns into a garden tableaux of taste and color. Who can resist cupcakes with names like pistachio rosewater, Italian cream cake, or green tea and honey? The bakery also makes half a dozen varieties of brownies, including salted caramel, black forest, and rocky road, along with Texas-size muffins, petits fours, and vegan cupcakes. LadyBugg's scones are exceptional, especially maple pecan and the savory bacon, green onion, and cheddar. Bakery hours are 6:30 a.m. to 6 p.m. Tues through Fri and at 8 a.m. to 6 p.m. on Sat. In the Memphis area, look for baked goods at the **Cooper-Young Community Farmers Market** (p. 113) on Saturday and the seasonal West Memphis Farmers Market on the first and third Thursday of the month (900 block of N. Missouri St.; www.broadwaywestmemphis .com/projects_003.html).

McCarter Coffee, 5995 US 51 North, Millington, TN 38053; (901) 626-4924; mccartercoffee.com. The strip of US 51 into Millington seems an unlikely location for a small-batch coffee roaster, but there it is in a small former restaurant, hugging the edge of the highway. After traveling in Italy where they were spoiled by local coffee roasters, Debra and Jim McCarter opened their own company in 2008. They offer 17 single-origin selections such as organic fair-traded beans from Mexico, Nicaragua, and Ethiopia, along with organically flavored beans from Costa Rica. Coffees from decaf to full-bodied roasts include signature blends such as African espresso and a Louisiana-style french roast with chicory. McCarter sells its coffees online, in local retail stores, and at local farmers' markets. The retail store is open when the McCarter's roast beans on Tues through Thurs from 9 a.m. to noon and Sun from noon to 5 p.m. "On roasting days, people follow the smoke and come in to sample whatever we are brewing," Jim McCarter says. "When we do the dark roasts, people say you can smell the smoke half a mile down the highway."

Millington Farmers' Market, 5152 Easley, Millington, TN 38053; (901) 873-5770; millingtonparks.com. The Millington Farmers' Market started in 2010, bringing local fruit, vegetables, farm-fresh eggs, and plant swaps to a cute Old West shelter with a roof. The market operates from early May through Oct on Sat from 8 a.m. to 1 p.m. Experts typically hold gardening seminars on the second Saturday of each month. Vendors for arts and crafts join in the last Saturday of every month. Look for special events throughout the season, including a pumpkin patch in the fall.

Velvet Cream, 2290 US 51, Hernando, MS 38632; (662) 429-6540. On a summer afternoon, the town of Hernando gets a little sleepy, except at the Velvet Cream where a couple dozen customers mill around the drive-up window trying to decide what to order. The decision isn't easy. This burger and milk shake shop, built in 1947, has so many choices that the large mounted menu is color-coded by category and shape. Select from 180 flavors served in shakes, sundaes, slushes, malts, snow, and flakes. (A flake, BTW, is ice cream blended with a flavor and topped with more ice cream like a float.) The flavors are a mind-blowing list of spices, fruit, nuts, pies, sodas, chocolates, cobblers, cakes, candies, cookies, and candy bars. Feel like a pineapple upside-down cake shake? Check. What about a hot fudge and strawberry combo called Yo Mama? No problem. How about a Nutter Butter malt? Got that, too. If flavor combinations aren't your thing, no worry. Velvet Cream has soft-serve ice cream in vanilla and chocolate, but you'll still have to decide between 3 cones: regular, sugar, and waffle dipped in chocolate. Called the Dip by locals, the Velvet Cream also dishes up a remarkable assortment of burgers (21 kinds); hot dogs, sandwiches, and wraps. They have veggies, too, including cream-style corn fritters and green beans that are battered and deep fried.

Wolf River Honey, PO Box 224, Moscow, TN 38057; (901) 877-7763; wolfriverhoney.com. In Memphis, where people like to drizzle honey on homemade biscuits, creamed honey is quite a grand idea. It doesn't run off the bread. At Wolf River Honey, the honey is whipped, so it crystalizes into a spread. Even better, the gourmet spread comes in different flavors, including cinnamon, pumpkin pie spice, and amaretto pecan. Of course, the local beekeepers also sell honey the old-fashioned way: pure, unpasteurized, and unfiltered. In addition, they have beeswax candles in 10-inch tapers, lip and lotion bars made with beeswax, shea butter, and essential oils. Wolf River Honey has been part of Memphis for so long that it's easy to take the company for granted. Don't. Look for their products at seasonal farmers' markets and at independently owned retail stores such as **Square Beans** (p. 194) in Collierville and Germantown Hardware.

Recipes

Tomato Tartare with Chickpea Panisse, Chèvre & Baby Arugula

Andrew Adams started working with Wally Joe as a teenager at the family restaurant of Joe's father in Cleveland, Mississippi. When Joe headed for Memphis to start his own restaurant, Adams came, too. These days, the chefs continue to collaborate in the kitchen, most recently with the opening in 2011 of their celebrated restaurant Acre in East Memphis. This tomato tartar has been on Acre's menu from the start, and for good reason. It is pleasing and picturesque, fusing international flavors into a Lincoln Log stack of warm panisse, (a fried chickpea flour cake from France) goat cheese, and preserved lemon. Adams uses chickpea flour from a local grocery for the panisse. If it's not readily available, he suggests purchasing it at nutsonline.com.

Serves 4

Berbere Butter

1 stick (½ cup) butter, melted	½ teaspoon ground cardamom
2 teaspoons fenugreek seeds	1 teaspoon ground coriander
1 teaspoon minced ginger	1 clove garlic, minced
Pinch of ground cumin	½ teaspoon paprika
Pinch of ground black pepper	½ teaspoon chili powder

Heat butter to about 160°F (just until hot to the touch). Pull off the heat and add all remaining ingredients. Steep (like tea) for 2 hours or overnight at room temperature. Strain.

Tomato Concassé

1 gallon water	2 medium-size tomatoes
½ cup salt	Bowl of ice water

Boil water and salt. Slice the skin of the tomatoes with an X. Place tomatoes in water for 20 seconds. Remove and place in the ice-water bath until they cool down. Peel off the skin and remove the seeds. Dice tomatoes into small pieces. Toss with steeped, strained berbere butter, reserving ¼ cup for garnish. Drain and keep warm.

Chickpea Panisse

4 cups vegetable stock or water	1 teaspoon ground coriander
2 cups chickpea flour	1 tablespoon salt
1 teaspoon cumin	2 cups olive oil for crisping

Boil vegetable stock. Whisk in chickpea flour. Add cumin, coriander, and salt. Pour mixture into a lightly greased casserole dish. While hot, cover with parchment paper, waxed paper, or plastic wrap. Press lightly with a small pot to flatten. Refrigerate until cool.

Cut into rectangles. Heat olive oil over medium heat. Gently add the panisse and cook until golden. Pull panisse out of oil with a spatula and drain on paper towel.

To assemble:

Chèvre	Fresh baby arugula
Preserved lemon slices	

To assemble, stack the panisse like Lincoln Logs and add the warm tomato concassé layered with chèvre and lemon. Garnish with arugula and a little of the berbere butter.

Courtesy of Executive Chef Andrew Adams of Acre (p. 127)

Bacon, Lettuce & Fried Green-Tomato Salad

In 2012, Felicia Willett celebrated the 10-year anniversary of her restaurant Felicia Suzanne's, a culinary star of downtown Memphis. Her bacon, lettuce, and fried green tomato salad is a customer favorite because the recipe is a fresh and updated version of a classic Southern dish. It's like a BLT sandwich (only better) without the bread. I like to make this salad with pepper-smoked bacon from Newman Farm (p. 254), as the pepper gives a nice finish to the crunchy bacon. Either way, don't skip the salt on the tomatoes and don't be disappointed if your fried tomatoes aren't as perfect as Willett's. She's had a lot of practice.

Serves 4

2 large green tomatoes
Salt
Freshly ground black pepper
1 cup all-purpose flour
2 eggs beaten with 2 tablespoons water
1 cup fine bread crumbs
2 cups vegetable oil
4 cups mixed baby greens

4 tablespoons remoulade dressing (or your favorite salad dressing), plus additional for plating
4 slices fresh mozzarella, ½-inch thick
8 slices crispy apple wood–smoked bacon
Toothpicks
Fresh parsley for garnish

Slice each tomato into 1-inch slices. Season both sides of the tomatoes with salt and pepper. Let the tomatoes sit for 15 minutes. Season flour, egg wash, and bread crumbs separately with salt and pepper. Dredge tomatoes in flour, coating completely. Dip each tomato in egg wash, letting the excess drip off. Dredge tomatoes in bread crumbs, coating completely.

Heat oil in a large frying pan. Fry the tomatoes in batches until golden brown, about 2 minutes on each side. Remove from pan and drain on a paper-lined plate. Season tomatoes with salt.

In a mixing bowl, toss mixed greens with 4 tablespoons dressing. Season greens with salt and pepper. Mix well.

To assemble, spoon some additional dressing in the center of four plates. Place a tomato on top of the dressing. Layer each salad with a slice of the cheese, criss-cross with 2 slices of the bacon, and top with one-eighth of the mixed greens. Top each salad with the remaining tomatoes and mixed greens. Secure each salad by placing a toothpick through the center of the salad. Garnish with parsley.

Courtesy of Felicia Willett, Chef/Owner of Felicia Suzanne's (p. 39)

Thai-Style Beef Salad
with Chipotle Honey Vinaigrette

When Karen Carrier, who grew up in Memphis, started cooking in 1980 in the kitchens of New York City, she discovered the flavors of the foods her co-workers brought to the table. The bold flavors of Thailand, Belize, Mexico, Vietnam, Puerto Rico, Texas, and Louisiana were permeating through every street corner and kitchen, she recalls: "We were constantly exchanging ideas and cooking staff meals based on our childhood traditions." When Carrier returned to Memphis in 1987 and opened the first of several restaurants, she duplicated those experiences, hiring women from Bangkok, Vietnam, and Mexico to cook. Today the menus at Carrier's three restaurants—Dō, the Beauty Shop, and Mollie Fontaine Lounge—still celebrate the flavors of the sun-drenched countries she loves.

Serves 4

½ pound beef tenderloin, rinsed and patted dry, wrapped in plastic wrap, and partially frozen

4 tablespoons extra-virgin olive oil, divided

Kosher salt and pepper to taste

1 package wonton wrappers

½ cup canola oil

Chipotle-Honey Vinaigrette

½ cup chipotle in adobo sauce (available at Asian or Latin grocery)

⅓ cup plus 3 tablespoons honey

⅓ cup plus 3 tablespoons sugar cane vinegar (available at Asian grocery)

½ tablespoon chopped garlic

4 cups salad oil

Kosher salt to taste

Salad

Herb salad greens

3 oranges (peeled and
    segmented with pith
    removed)

6 tablespoons coconut flakes

3 Hass avocados, peeled, pitted,
    and cut into small cubes

4 lime wedges

Rub beef tenderloin with 2 tablespoons extra-virgin olive oil. Dust with kosher salt and black pepper. In a small skillet over medium to high heat, add ½ tablespoon oil. Sear beef tenderloin, constantly turning until all sides are charred and beef is rare to medium rare. Remove from skillet. Set aside and let rest for 10 minutes.

Wrap tenderloin in plastic wrap and place in freezer for 1 hour. This will make it easier to slice.

While beef is in the freezer, deep fry the wonton wrappers in ½ cup canola oil in a small pot over medium-high heat. Set crispy wonton wrappers aside on paper towels to drain.

Remove beef tenderloin from freezer. Slice beef into ½-inch rounds and place between two pieces of plastic wrap. With a rolling pin or wine bottle, roll the tenderloin into ⅛-inch-thick slices.

Combine all ingredients for the chipotle-honey vinaigrette but oil and salt in a blender. While blender is running, slowly add oil until emulsified. Remove vinaigrette and season with salt to taste.

In a small bowl, mix greens, orange segments, coconut, and avocado. Lightly drizzle salad with chipotle-honey vinaigrette.

To assemble, in the middle of four dinner plates, place 4 or 5 slices of tenderloin, overlapping slightly. Drizzle with 1 tablespoon extra-virgin olive oil and season with salt and pepper.

Place a handful of tossed salad mix in the middle of each plate over the beef tenderloin. Crumble the crispy wonton wrappers over each plate. Serve with a wedge of lime.

Courtesy of Karen Carrier, Owner of Dō (p. 82), the Beauty Shop (p. 74), Mollie Fontaine Lounge (p. 226), and Another Roadside Attraction (p. 34)

Shrimp Mole with Apple Kohlrabi Slaw & Johnny Cakes

In 2012, Rodelio Aglibot, popularly known as the Food Buddha, redesigned the concept for Eighty3, the sister restaurant for downtown's Madison Hotel. He brought in Connor O'Neill to take over the restaurant, a young energetic chef who likes flavors, textures, and temperatures to collide into inventive dishes. "This is a collision of sweet and spicy, soft and crunchy, hot and cold, and it all comes together perfectly," he says about his shrimp mole, a sentimental favorite because he prepared it as a contestant on The Next Food Network Star *and served it to the general manager of the Madison Hotel when he first started working. There are several steps, but much of the recipe can be prepared ahead of time.*

Serves 4

Slaw Base

¼ cup **Thai chile sauce**
¼ cup **cider vinegar**
¼ cup **apple juice**
⅛ cup **red wine vinegar**
½ tablespoon **garlic**

½ tablespoon **salt**
½ teaspoon **black pepper**
½ cup **mayo**
1 tablespoon **brown sugar**

Combine all ingredients and whisk until smooth.

Apple Kohlrabi Slaw

½ red bell pepper, julienned
½ green bell pepper, julienned
½ red onion, julienned
2 cups cabbage or slaw mix

½ Granny Smith apple, run across mandolin
½ cup kohlrabi, run across mandolin
½ tablespoon salt

Combine all ingredients and add 2 cups slaw base (recipe p. 271). Mix well. Store in refrigerator.

Southern Mole Sauce

½ tablespoon oil
1 cup diced white onion
½ tablespoon minced garlic
½ tablespoon chili powder
½ teaspoon cumin
½ (12-ounce) can adobo peppers

1 cup Thai chile sauce
½ cup orange juice
⅛ cup fresh lime juice
¼ cup oil
1 tablespoon cocoa powder
½ bunch cilantro, bottom trimmed by 1 inch

In a heavy bottom sauce pot over medium heat, combine oil, onions, and garlic. Sweat until onions are transparent.

Add remaining ingredients, except cilantro, to sauce pot and bring to a simmer. Allow to simmer for 10–15 minutes. Add cilantro and simmered sauce to a blender and puree. Store in refrigerator.

Johnny Cakes (makes 12)

½ cup flour, plus 1 cup for rolling

1 cup cornmeal

1–2 teaspoons sugar

1 teaspoon salt

1 tablespoon baking soda

1 tablespoon baking powder

1 egg, lightly beaten

1 cup hot milk

1 tablespoon shortening

Mix ½ cup flour plus the other dry ingredients together, then stir in the remaining ingredients. Place 1 cup flour on cutting board and pour batter out into flour. Knead dough on board until it has a consistency like pie crust. Cover lightly and chill in refrigerator for 1 hour.

Roll dough out on cutting board to ½-inch thickness and cut with biscuit cutter. Place on wax paper–lined sheet pan and place in fridge until ready to use.

For advance preparation, freeze johnny cakes for 4 hours. Individually wrap and date once they are firm. Defrost 30 minutes in the refrigerator before preparing.

Shrimp

20 shrimp, peeled and deveined

1 tablespoon butter

1 tablespoon oil

Fresh cilantro for garnish

Place Southern mole sauce in a small pot on the grill to warm. Grill shrimp until pink basting with sauce.

In a small skillet, heat butter and oil on medium-high heat and cook johnny cakes until lightly browned on both sides.

To assemble, layer 3 johnny cakes with 3 pinches of slaw to create a napoleon-style stack on each plate. Place 5 shrimp around each stack. Garnish with cilantro.

Courtesy of Executive Chef Connor O'Neill of Eighty3 (p. 38)

Crispy Ahi Tuna with English Pea–Wasabi Puree & Orzo Pilaf

"I don't want food to just be good," says José Gutierrez, Chef and Owner of River Oaks Restaurant in East Memphis. "I want it to be great." Gutierrez, who updates classic French cooking with New American flare, is true to his word with this recipe for ahi tuna wrapped in brik *pastry dough. The crispy brik dough, available at international markets, is the recipe's first surprise. The second is the pea and wasabi puree. "I like to put special touches on all of my food," Gutierrez explains. "It's the unexpected puree that takes this dish from good to great."*

Serves 2

- 1 small onion, diced
- 2 tablespoons butter
- ¾ cup orzo
- 1½ cups vegetable stock or water
- ⅓ cup heavy cream
- Salt and pepper to taste
- ¼ cup halved cherry tomatoes
- ¼ cup green peas, blanched if fresh or thawed and drained if frozen
- ⅓ cup shredded mozzarella cheese
- 1 Idaho baking potato
- 1 quart soy oil
- 1 garlic clove, sliced
- ¾ cup dry white wine

- Sprig of fresh thyme
- 1 shallot, chopped
- 2 teaspoons prepared horseradish
- 1 tablespoon cream
- 3 ounces (¾ stick) butter, softened and cubed
- 1 cup fresh green peas or frozen peas, thawed and drained
- 1 teaspoon salt
- 2 teaspoons wasabi
- 2 tablespoons soybean oil
- 2 pieces tuna, each 5 inches long x 1½ inches thick
- 2 sheets brik dough

Sauté diced onion in 2 tablespoons butter; add orzo and stock. Bring to a boil and simmer until orzo is tender. Drain if necessary. Add ⅓ cup cream, salt, pepper, tomatoes, peas, and cheese. Stir.

Peel and slice potato on a mandolin using the gaufrette or ridged blade. Heat oil to 280°F and cook until crisp.

In sauté pan, add garlic, wine, thyme, shallot, and horseradish. Reduce by half and add 1 tablespoon cream. Reduce again by half and whisk in butter. Do not allow to boil. Test the temperature of the sauce by touching with your finger. If you have to remove your finger immediately, it is too hot; if it is cold to the touch, increase the heat. Add salt and pepper. Strain the sauce and set aside.

Puree peas with salt and wasabi.

Heat 2 tablespoons soybean oil in sauté pan until hot, and sear tuna on all sides. Remove. Spread pea-wasabi puree on brik dough. Place tuna in center and fold dough in half. Heat sauté pan and sear on all sides until lightly golden. Add more oil if necessary.

To assemble, cut each tuna packet into 2 pieces. Spoon orzo on two long plates. Place tuna slices on top, equally spaced. Place potatoes in front of each piece of tuna. Spoon sauce around orzo pilaf and serve immediately.

Courtesy of José Gutierrez, Chef/Owner of River Oaks Restaurant (p. 147)

Amandine of Gulf Flasher & Cauliflower Puree

Chef Kelly English is a native of Louisiana, and he specializes in French/Creole cuisine at his award-winning restaurant in Midtown called Restaurant Iris. This recipe is his interpretation of amandine, a traditional fine-dining dish in New Orleans. As with most of his dishes, this recipe reflects traditions that are both familial and culinary. "When we went out to eat to celebrate a good report card or a winning season, someone in my family always ordered trout amandine," he explains. "So to me, trout amandine represents family and celebration."

Serves 4

- 1 head cauliflower, florets removed from body
- Salt to taste
- 1 cup heavy cream
- 8 tablespoons unsalted butter, divided
- 4 (7-ounce) portions of flasher or speckled trout
- Creole seasoning to taste
- 1 quart buttermilk
- 2 cups flour seasoned to taste with salt and your favorite Creole seasoning
- Canola oil for frying
- ½ cup toasted sliced almonds
- 4 tablespoons chopped parsley
- 8 lemons, juiced

Blanch the cauliflower florets in slightly salted water at a rolling boil while heating the heavy cream and 2 tablespoons butter in a separate pot. When the cauliflower is tender, strain and dry slightly in a 300°F oven.

Put the dried florets in a blender with the cream and butter mixture and puree till smooth. Season puree with salt. Reserve.

Season the fish with salt and Creole seasoning, dip in buttermilk, and then in seasoned flour. Heat a cast-iron pan to medium heat, add enough oil to coat the pan, and fry the fish on both sides till done. Remove the fish and pour off the oil. Put the pan back on the heat and add the remaining 6 tablespoons butter and cook till brown. Add the almonds and toss until the nuts brown a little more. Add chopped parsley and lemon juice. Season the sauce with salt.

Place a spoonful of cauliflower puree in the center of a plate, top with the fish, and spoon on the sauce.

Courtesy of Chef/Owner Kelly English of Restaurant Iris (p. 92)

Frogmore Stew

Since opening his low-country restaurant called Sweet Grass in 2010, Chef Ryan Trimm has continued to charm customers with his trademark cooking style: combining coastal flavors of South Carolina with locally sourced ingredients. This dish originated in a small fishing community in South Carolina and is a family staple along the coast. "It is actually a traditional shrimp boil," Trimm explains, "but we added and changed it slightly."

Serves 4

- 2 tablespoons oil
- ½ cup diced Yukon Gold potatoes, blanched
- ¼ cup julienned Vidalia onions
- ½ cup (about 4 ounces) sweet fennel sausage (a smoked sausage also works)
- 16–20 Gulf white shrimp, peeled and deveined
- 1 tablespoon butter

- 2 ounces (¼ cup) white wine
- 4 ounces claw crabmeat
- 2 cups chicken stock
- ¼ cup diced tomatoes
- ½ cup yellow corn cut off the cob
- Fresh parsley and fresh thyme to taste
- Salt, pepper, and Tabasco to taste

Heat sauté pan to high heat, add oil. Sauté potatoes and onions, turn heat to medium-high, and add sausage. Once sausage is slightly brown, add shrimp, butter, and sauté until just barely pink.

Deglaze the pan with white wine. Add crab, chicken stock, tomatoes, corn, and herbs. Reduce by half. Season with salt, pepper, and Tabasco to taste.

Courtesy of Ryan Trimm, Chef/Owner of
Sweet Grass (p. 98) and Sweet Grass Next Door (p. 220)

Shrimp & Grits

Chef Ryan Trimm was nice enough to offer up an additional recipe for this guide, this one for the Southern staple shrimp and grits. Both recipes are customer favorites—and for good reason. They are delicious and not difficult to make. His take on this popular Southern favorite updates the classic version with scallops, Benton County ham, and white shrimp from the Gulf of Mexico.

Serves 4

16–20 Gulf white shrimp
10–20 fresh scallops
Salt, pepper, and Cajun spice
    to taste
2 ounces Benton Country ham,
    chopped
1 tablespoon vegetable/olive oil
    blend
4 ounces sweet fennel sausage
2 ounces (¼ cup) dry white
    wine

1 cup chicken stock
1 tablespoon butter
2 cups yellow stone-ground
    grits, cooked
Fresh parsley, chopped
½ cup seeded and coarsely
    chopped tomatoes
    (concassé)

Season shrimp and scallops with salt, pepper, and Cajun spice. Render ham and set aside. In a separate sauté pan over high heat, heat the oil and sear scallops. Once scallops are golden, flip them over.

Add shrimp and sausage to the pan. Once they are seared to golden brown, add wine and stock. Remove scallops to a paper towel.

Allow liquids in the pan to come to a boil, add butter and reduce liquids by half. Serve over hot grits in a bowl. Garnish with fresh parsley and concassé.

Courtesy of Ryan Trimm, Chef/Owner
of Sweet Grass (p. 98) and Sweet Grass Next Door (p. 220)

White Bean Chicken Chili

Cookbook author Jennifer Chandler runs a popular restaurant near the Greenline bike trail called Cheffie's Cafe, serving sandwiches and salads that are fresh and healthy. Chandler also has written several cookbooks that revolve around her mantra that busy families need to find the time to cook. To that end, the recipes in her books are simple and come together quickly. Plus they taste great, like this White Bean Chicken Chili from her cookbook Simply Suppers. "This hearty soup was a favorite at my restaurant Cheffie's Market and More," says Chandler, referring to her first cafe in Memphis. "Serve it on its own or garnish it with your favorite Tex-Mex toppings." For more family recipes you can prepare in hurry, check out Chandler's other two books called Simply Salads *and* Simply Grilling, *a new edition to the series published in 2012.*

Serves 6

- 1 tablespoon olive oil
- ½ cup finely diced yellow onion (1 small onion)
- ⅓ cup seeded and finely diced poblano pepper (½ pepper)
- 1 (4.5-ounce) can diced green chiles
- 4 cups chicken stock
- 2 cups shredded cooked chicken
- 4 (15-ounce) cans cannellini beans (do not drain or rinse)
- 1 tablespoon dried thyme
- ½ teaspoon ground cumin
- Kosher salt and freshly ground black pepper
- 6 tablespoons sour cream (optional)
- ¼ cup sliced fresh or pickled jalapeños (optional)
- ¼ cup fresh cilantro leaves (optional)

In a large stockpot over medium-high heat, warm the oil until a few droplets of water sizzle when carefully sprinkled in the pot. Add the onion and poblano pepper and sauté until soft, about 10 minutes. Add the green chiles and sauté until combined, about 1 minute.

Add the chicken stock, chicken, beans, thyme, and cumin. Season with salt and pepper to taste. Over high heat, bring to a boil. Reduce the heat to medium-low and simmer uncovered, stirring occasionally, until thickened, about 35 to 40 minutes. Adjust seasonings as needed.

Serve hot. Garnish with a dollop of sour cream, sliced jalapeños, and/or fresh cilantro, if desired. Leftovers freeze well.

Cooking tip: A flavorful staple of Mexican cuisine, poblano peppers are chile peppers that are spicy but not extremely fiery. They look similar to bell peppers in shape but they are a much darker green. Most markets now carry fresh poblanos, but if you cannot find them at your neighborhood store, substitute bell peppers for a milder chili or jalapeños for more heat.

Courtesy of Jennifer Chandler, Cookbook Author and Consulting Partner
for Cheffie's Cafe (p. 132)

Braised Beef Brisket in Achiote

Jonathan Magallanes brings authentic food from Mexico City to Las Tortugas Deli Mexicana, his restaurant located in the suburbs of Germantown. This recipe is a classic slow-cooked brisket, and it is one of the restaurant's bestsellers. It shows off the wonderfully fragrant aroma and flavors of real achiote paste and Mexican oregano, which can be purchased online or at international grocery stores. "Achiote is a staple seasoning in Mexican cooking and features the crushed annatto seed married with spices for an amazingly savory and pungent kick," Magallanes explains. "For the chicken stock, I use Thomas Keller's recipe from Ad Hoc at Home."

Serves 5–6

- **10–12 pounds whole, untrimmed beef brisket**
- **5 cloves garlic**
- **4 tablespoons kosher salt**
- **6 tablespoons Mexican oregano**
- **12 ounces (1½ cups) water**
- **Olive oil for searing the brisket**

Poke 10 holes on each side of brisket with a small knife.

Place garlic, salt, oregano, and water in a food processor and chop into a rough paste. Smear garlic-herb paste all over brisket, especially in holes. Place in container, seal, and let marinate overnight in refrigerator.

Remove brisket from refrigerator and sear all sides in a heavy cast-iron pan or heavy skillet until well browned.

Achiote Mixture

24 ounces (3 cups) fresh-squeezed orange juice

8 ounces (1 cup) fresh-squeezed lime juice

6 ounces (¾ cup) apple cider vinegar

50 grams (a little over 3 tablespoons) achiote paste

4 tablespoons orange zest

2 tablespoons lime zest

Chicken stock

Fresh cilantro, sliced radishes, and fresh lime wedges for garnish

Steamed corn tortillas

Combine all achiote mixture ingredients in food processor and blend well. Place browned brisket in a large pot. Pour achiote mixture over the brisket. Add chicken stock to cover the brisket.

Cook brisket on medium-low heat, covered, 4–5 hours or until brisket is tender and easily pulls apart.

Garnish with sprigs of fresh cilantro, sliced radish, and fresh lime wedges.

Serve with steamed corn tortillas for tacos.

Courtesy of Jonathan Magallanes, Chef/Owner of Las Tortugas Deli Mexicana (p. 180)

Braised Pork Cheeks
with Sweet Potato Puree

Rick Saviori recently took over the kitchen of Napa Cafe after operating his own restaurant called Thyme Bistro. He likes to take classic flavor combinations and give them a twist, which is what he's done with this recipe for braised pork cheeks. For instance, most people are familiar with sweet potatoes and pork, but Saviori uses a new cut of meat to make his recipe stand out. "Using cheeks instead of loin or tenderloin, which most people would do, is my way of making a classic combination better," he says. Texture also matters to Saviori, which is why he added walnuts to the dish for some extra crunch.

Serves 2

1 pound pork cheeks
Flour for dusting
Olive oil
2 cups red wine
About 1 cup chicken stock
1 sweet potato
1 teaspoon dried thyme
2 ounces (4 tablespoons) butter, melted
5 ounces (½ cup plus 1 tablespoon) milk, more if necessary

9 stalks broccoli rabe
½ to 1 teaspoon salt
Oil for sautéing broccoli rabe
1 clove garlic, minced
Salt to taste
4 ounces walnuts
6 ounces blue cheese, crumbled

Clean pork cheeks of any silver skin or fat. Dust with flour and sear in a little olive oil on each side. Place in a braising pan.

Add red wine and enough stock to cover cheeks. Braise for 4 hours at 300°F.

Peel sweet potato and boil until tender. Drain and then transfer to food processor. Puree with thyme, melted butter, and milk (enough to make potatoes smooth in texture).

Blanch broccoli rabe in boiling water with ½ to 1 teaspoon salt for 4 minutes, shock in cold water, and drain. When ready to plate, sauté rabe in oil with a little salt and garlic until tender but still crunchy.

Toast walnuts in 350°F oven for 8 minutes to release some of the oils.

To assemble, put half of the warm sweet potatoes on each plate in a straight line. Add sautéed rabe on top of the puree. Place cheeks on top of the rabe and pour a little braising jus over them. Crumble walnuts over the cheeks and finish with blue cheese on top.

Courtesy of Executive Chef Rick Saviori of Napa Cafe (p. 146)

Butter Pound Cake

Four days a week, Leslee Pascal manages the front of the house at The Elegant Farmer, while Chef Mac Edwards handles the kitchen. But on Monday and Thursday, Pascal stays home to bake the restaurant's desserts, including key lime pie and rich, buttery pound cake. Pascal says she grew up baking with her family. "When we opened the restaurant," she says, "the baking just fell to me." At The Elegant Farmer, where ingredients are locally sourced, the pound cake marches through the seasons with whatever fruit is most plentiful. My favorite topping is made with blueberries, yogurt, and honey.

Serves 12–16

1 cup (2 sticks) unsalted butter, softened	½ teaspoon salt
	3 cups flour
2½ cups sugar	1 cup heavy cream
6 large eggs	1 teaspoon vanilla extract
½ teaspoon baking powder	1 teaspoon almond extract

Preheat oven to 325°F. Grease and flour a 10-inch bundt pan.

Cream butter and sugar thoroughly using a mixer. Add the eggs one at a time and beat well. Add baking powder and salt and mix well. Add the flour and cream alternately, beginning and ending with flour. Mix in flavorings.

Pour batter into pan. Bake for 1 hour. Cake should be a medium golden brown. Remove from the oven and allow the cake to cool for 20–30 minutes. Invert cake onto a rack let cool.

Serve the cake plain, with a blueberry glaze, or topped with strawberries or other fresh fruit in season and a dollop of freshly whipped cream.

Courtesy of Leslee Pascal, Manager at The Elegant Farmer (p. 134)

Strawberry Rhubarb Pie

Here's what Kat Gordon of Muddy's Bake Shop has to say about her recipe for strawberry rhubarb pie: "This will win friends and influence people." I'd have to agree, but Gordon's personal objectives for baking this scrumptious pie are much more reflective. "The process of making a pie, from forming and rolling out the dough to slicing the berries to spooning the filling into the shell, enchants me," she says. "This pie particularly is a joy to make because it turns out so pretty. The pale red of the filling always looks nice against the pastry crust, regardless of how much it bubbles over or how messy it gets."

Serves 6–8

- **2 (9- or 10-inch) unbaked pie crusts**
- **2 cups chopped rhubarb**
- **3 cups sliced strawberries**
- **½ cup sugar, plus additional for sprinkling**
- **½ cup light brown sugar**
- **¼ cup flour**
- **2 tablespoons cornstarch**
- **1 teaspoon cinnamon**
- **1 teaspoon lemon juice**
- **1 teaspoon vanilla**
- **1 egg yolk mixed with 2 tablespoons heavy cream or whole milk**

Roll out one pie crust and fit it into a pie pan. (If you want to cheat and use a premade one, I won't tell anyone.) Refrigerate while making the filling.

Dump strawberries and rhubarb into a large bowl and gently toss with sugars, flour, cornstarch, cinnamon, and lemon juice. Allow to sit for 15–30 minutes. Using a slotted spoon, transfer the fruit filling into the chilled pie shell. Discard the leftover juice.

Return pie to the refrigerator while making the other crust.

For the top crust, make a lattice or use a cookie cutter to cut shapes into the second dough. When you have your topper ready to go, take the pie out of the refrigerator and place the shapes or lattice on top. Brush the top crusts with egg wash and sprinkle with sugar.

Preheat oven to 400°F.

Freeze for 20 minutes. (*See below for optional step.)

Place pie on parchment-lined baking sheet and bake 20 minutes. Reduce heat to 350°F and bake for another 30–40 minutes or until crust is golden and juices are bubbling.

Cool thoroughly before serving, at least 2 hours.

*At this point, you can freeze the pie and bake it later. After the pie's initial 20-minute cooloff, remove it from the refrigerator and wrap it tightly in several layers of plastic wrap and then place it inside a large ziplock freezer bag. When you're ready to bake it, just put it directly in the oven and bake as instructed. This approach is perfect if you are serving a crowd and want to do the bulk of the preparation ahead of time.

Courtesy of Kat Gordon, Owner of Muddy's Bake Shop (p. 171)

Appendices

Appendix A: Eateries by Cuisine

American
Automatic Slim's, 34
Blue Daze Bistro, 237
Cafe Eclectic, 78
Jim's Place Restaurant and
   Bar, 151
Kooky Canuck, 45
Majestic Grille, The, 47
Marlo's Down Under, 239
Memphis Street Cafe, 240
Mortimer's, 153
Paulette's, 55
River Oaks, 147
Rizzos Diner, 49
Three Angels Diner, 99

Asian Fusion
East Tapas & Drinks, 225

Mosa Asian Bistro, 146

Barbecue
A&R Bar-B-Cue, 56
Alfred's on Beale, 197
Bar-B-Q Shop, The, 109
Blues City Cafe, 199
Central BBQ, 110
Charlie Vergos' Rendezvous, 52
Corky's Ribs & BBQ, 158
Cozy Corner, 57
Double J Smokehouse and
   Saloon, 211
Germantown Commissary, 188
Johnnie's Drive In, 247
Marlowe's Restaurant and Ribs, 61
Memphis Barbecue Company, 249
Neely's Bar-B-Que, 159

Bistro
Cafe 1912, 79

Brewery
Ghost River Brewery, 205

Cafe
Blue & White Restaurant, 244
Bluff City Coffee, 63
Booksellers Bistro, 129
Buon Cibo, 238
Cafe Eclectic, 78
Cheffie's Cafe, 132
Cordelia's Table, 68
Fratelli's Cafe, 136
Fresh Slices Sidewalk Cafe
  & Deli, 83
Grawemeyer's, 42
Kay Kafe, 45
La Baguette, 90
Lunchbox Eats, 46
Soul Fish Cafe, 94
Stone Soup Cafe &
  Market, 95
Trolley Stop Market, 50
20/20 Diner, 101

Chinese
Mulan Chinese Bistro, 184
Saigon Le, 93
Wang's Mandarin House, 154

Cocktail Lounges
Alchemy, 223
Blind Bear Speakeasy, 224
East Tapas & Drinks, 225
Mollie Fontaine Lounge, 226
Silly Goose Lounge, 227

Cocktails
Acre, 127
Andrew Michael Italian Kitchen, 128
Automatic Slim's, 34
Bari, 73
Beauty Shop, 74
Bleu Restaurant and Lounge, 35
Cafe Society, 80
Circa, 133
Eighty3, 38
Erling Jenson, 135
Felicia Suzanne's, 39
Grove Grill, The, 137
Interim, 138
Napa Cafe, 146

Restaurant Iris, 92
River Oaks, 147
Silly Goose Lounge, 227
Sweet Grass, 98

Continental
Cafe Society, 80
Erling Jenson, 135

Creole
City Grocery, 245
Dejavu, 58
Restaurant Iris, 92

Cuban
Los Compadres, 142

Deli
Bogie's Delicatessen, 102
Fresh Slices Sidewalk Cafe
    & Deli, 83
Front Street Deli, 67
Kwik Chek, 89

Diner
Ajax Diner, 246
Arcade, The, 51

Blue & White Restaurant, 244
Chrome Grille, 60
CK's Coffee Shop, 111
Three Angels Diner, 99
20/20 Diner, 101

Drive-in
Jerry's Sno Cones, 187
Mensi's Dairy Bar, 182
Velvet Cream, 260

Ethiopian
Abyssinia Restaurant, 73

Farm-to-Table
Elegant Farmer, The, 134
Trolley Stop Market, 50

Food Blogs
Best Memphis Burger, 6
Chubby Vegetarian, 6
Dining with Monkeys, 8
Eat Local Memphis, 8
From the Southern Table, 9
Fuzzy Brew, 10
Hungry Memphis, 11
Memphis Stew, 10

Saigon Le, 93

Upscale Southern
Felicia Suzanne's, 39
Itta Bena, 44
Revival: Southern Food
    Company, 26

Vegan
Cosmic Coconut, 162
Dejavu, 58
Fuel Cafe, 84
Imagine Vegan Cafe, 86
Muddy's Bake Shop, 171
Pho Hoa Binh, 91
R. P. Track's, 218
Three Angels Diner, 99

Vegetarian
Evelyn & Olive Restaurant, 38
Fuel Cafe, 84

Jasmine Thai and Vegetarian
    Restaurant, 88
R. P. Tracks, 218
Three Angels Diner, 99

Vietnamese
Lotus, 152
Pho Hoa Binh, 91
Saigon Le, 93

Winery
Old Millington Vineyard and
    Winery, 206

Wine & Liquor Stores
Arthur's Wine & Liquor, 230
Buster's Liquors and Wines, 231
Cockscrew Wine and Spirits, 233
Joe's Wines and Liquors, 233
Liquor and Wine Depot, 234
Wine Market, 235

Appendix B: Dishes, Specialties & Specialty Food

Bakery
Big Ono Bake Shop, 63
Bluff City Coffee, 63
Bottletree Bakery, 251
Boulangerie Olivier, 252
Cafe Eclectic, 78
La Baguette, 90
LadyBugg Bakery, 258
Muddy's Bake Shop, 171
Shoaf's Loaf Organic Bakery, 173
Urban Treats, 69

Baking Supplies
Mary Carter's Decorating
   Center, 116

Beef Jerky
Wayne's Candy Company, 70

Bread
Bluff City Coffee, 63
Boulangerie Olivier, 252
Cucina Breads, 65
La Baguette, 90
Mary's Gluten-Free Goods, 117
Ricki's Cookie Corner, 172
Sharon's Chocolates & Bread
   Cafe, 120
Urban Treats, 69

Breakfast
Arcade, The, 51

Blue Plate Cafe, 155
Bob's Barksdale Restaurant, 109
Brother Juniper's, 156
CK's Coffee Shop, 111
Front Street Deli, 67
Holiday Deli & Ham Co., 166
Poplar Perk 'N, 172
Trolley Stop Market, 50

Brunch
Automatic Slim's, 34
Beauty Shop, The, 74
Blind Bear Speakeasy, 224
Brass Door, The, 209
Brushmark, The, 77
Celtic Crossing, 211
Grove Grill, The, 137
Jack Magoo's Sports Bar & Grill, 215
Local Gastropub, 216
Majestic Grille, The, 47
Rizzo's Diner, 49
R. P. Tracks, 218
Sharky's Gulf Grill, 149
South of Beale, 220
Sweet Grass, 98
Three Angels Diner, 99

Burgers
Belmont Grill, 207
CK's Coffee Shop, 111
Dyer's Burgers, 37
Earnestine & Hazel's, 229
Huey's, 232
Johnnie's Drive In, 247
Kooky Canuck, 45
Rockabilly's Burger Shop, 60
Velvet Cream, 260

Butchers
Charlie's Meat Market, 161
Folk's Folly Original Prime Steak House, 150
Mediterranean International Grocery, 169
Miss Cordelia's, 68
Viet Hoa, 122

Cakes, Cookies & Cupcakes
Cocoa Van Cupcake Bakery, 190
Cosmic Coconut, 162
LadyBugg Bakery, 258
Makeda's Homemade Butter Cookies, 115
Mary's Gluten-Free Goods, 117

Stone Soup Cafe & Market, 95
Trolley Stop Market, 50

Sushi & Sashimi
Bangkok Alley, 179
Bluefin Sushi Lounge, 35
Dō, 82
Mulan Chinese Bistro, 184
Sekisui, 76
Sekisui Pacific Rim, 148
Sharky's Gulf Grill, 149

Tacos & Tamales
Fuel Food Truck, 24
Lunchbox Eats, 46
Mark's Grill Food Truck, 25
Tacos Los Jarochos Food Truck, 28
Tamale Trolley, 29

Tapas
Alchemy, 223
East Tapas & Drinks, 225
Mollie Fontaine Lounge, 226
Wang's Mandarin House, 154

Index

Curb Side Casseroles, 163